Thinking in Literature

Thinking in Literature
Joyce, Woolf, Nabokov

Anthony Uhlmann

continuum

Continuum International Publishing Group
80 Maiden Lane, New York, NY 10038
The Tower Building, 11 York Road, London SE1 7NX

www.continuumbooks.com

© 2011 Anthony Uhlmann

All rights reserved. No part of this book may be reproduced, stored in a retrieval system, or transmitted, in any form or by any means, electronic, mechanical, photocopying, recording, or otherwise, without the permission of the publishers.

Library of Congress Cataloging-in-Publication Data

ISBN-13: 978-1-44114-7-820 (hardcover)
ISBN-13: 978-1-4411-4056-2 (paperback)

Typeset by Pindar NZ, Auckland, New Zealand

Australian Government
Australian Research Council

For Nicola, Alistair, Andrea, Liam and Xavier

Contents

Acknowledgments	ix
Introduction	1
Part I: Literature and Thinking	
1 Spinoza, Relation, and Ratiocination	9
2 Leibniz's "Perception": the Incompossible, the Viewpoint, and the Composition of Sensation	20
3 Composition as the Externalized Expression of Sensation	34
Part II: Thinking in Modernist Fiction	
4 James Joyce: the Art of Relation	51
5 Virginia Woolf: the Art of Sensation	83
6 Vladimir Nabokov: the Art of Composition	114
Conclusion	147
Bibliography	150
Index	160

Acknowledgments

I would like to acknowledge the support of the Australian Research Council, as this research was supported under the Australian Research Council's *Discovery Projects* funding scheme (project number DP0559731). I also wish to acknowledge the Research Office, the School of Humanities and Languages, the College of Arts, and the Writing and Society Research Group at the University of Western Sydney for their generous support of this project.

I would also like to thank a number of people who helped, in various ways, to direct my thinking. At the University of Western Sydney: Ivor Indyk, Gail Jones, Dimitris Vardoulakis, Chris Fleming, Roger Dean, Wayne McKenna, Jane Goodall, Sara Knox, Lindsay Barrett, Chris Conti, and Judith Snodgrass. At the University of New South Wales: Helen Groth; at Macquarie University: Paul Sheehan; and Brian Boyd at Auckland University. I would also like to thank a number of research students at the University of Western Sydney with whom I fruitfully discussed most of the ideas developed here: Jay Johnston, Ben Denham, Jason Tuckwell, James Gourley, Stephen McLaren, and Gavin Smith. I was also fortunate to be able to discuss elements of this research internationally, and am particularly grateful to Bruno Clément in Paris.

I would like to thank my wife Andrea Curr for her terrific support (both moral and technical) and our children Liam, Xavier, Nicola, and Alistair for their love.

I would also particularly like to thank the team at Continuum, and particularly Haaris Naqvi, whose enthusiasm for the project made me see the benefits of approaching Continuum.

Versions of material that appear in this book have appeared in different forms, with different points of emphasis in various collections of essays: *Literature and Sensation*, edited by Anthony Uhlmann, Helen Groth, Paul Sheehan, and Stephen McLaren (Cambridge Scholars Publishing, 2009), *The Edinburgh Companion to Virginia Woolf and the Arts*, edited by Maggie Humm (Edinburgh: Edinburgh University Press, 2010), *Beckett's Proust/Deleuze's Proust*, edited by Mary Bryden and Margaret Topping (London: Palgrave, 2009), *Deleuze and Performance*, edited by Laura Cull (Edinburgh: Edinburgh University Press), and *Spinoza Now*, edited by Dimitris Vardoulakis (University of Minnesota Press, 2011). The publishers of these works are gratefully acknowledged.

I wish to thank my brother, Paul Uhlmann, for permission to use his photograph as cover for this book, and my sister Amanda who spoke with me about mathematics and patterns.

Finally, I want to thank my mother Mary, with whom I discussed Spinoza one quiet morning, and who made me understand that all of this had meaning.

Introduction

The term "aesthetic" has been criticized in recent years, and not without reason (see, for example, Eagleton 1991; Connor 1999). The substance of the critique rests, first, on the view that the term has taken on so many, often incompatible, meanings that it has itself become meaningless, and second, that the term has been used largely for social and political purposes: to buttress certain kinds of artistic practice and generate cultural capital.

While the force of this critique needs to be acknowledged, I do not agree with the contention that the term itself needs to be abandoned. The term "aesthetic" is not alone in being a site of contestation; it is not alone in being used in many ways; it is not alone in being made use of for social and political agendas. In short, rather than having to be abandoned, it needs to be used with care.

In this study, the term "aesthetic" will be used in line with its original meaning, as it was developed by Alexander Baumgarten in his 1735 study, *Reflections on Poetry*: that is, related to the kind of perceptual cognition, or thought, developed through sensations and perceptions. The kind of thought, that is, which Baumgarten felt had been excluded by the discussions of thought developed by the seventeenth-century rationalists (in particular Descartes and Leibniz). While much of Baumgarten's system has dated and he clearly considers the perceptions of the senses simply inferior to the faculty of logic, his distinction remains useful. He offers the following definition:

> The Greek philosophers and the Church fathers have already carefully distinguished between *things perceived* [αἰσθητά] and *things known* [νοητά]. It is entirely evident that they did not equate *things known* with things of sense, since they honored with this name things also removed from sense (therefore, images). Therefore, *things known* are to be known by the superior faculty as the object of logic; *things perceived* [are to be known by the inferior faculty, as the object] of the science of perception, or aesthetic.[1] (Baumgarten 1954: p. 78)

---

1 The editors and translators of Baumgarten (1954), Aschenbrenner and Holther, offer a footnote (n. 122), which indicates the source of Baumgarten's distinction between

2 Thinking in Literature

One might argue with Baumgarten in suggesting that the dichotomy is too stringently defined here; in suggesting, with Deleuze, Nussbaum, Damasio, and others, that logic is implicated *within* sensory perception. Yet, the distinction remains useful because it allows us a space in which to claim an importance for creative expression in literature and the other arts: while they too might well make use of certain kinds of logic, the logic they develop is, properly speaking, a logic of sensations, a logic of perception.

In short, then, I will understand "aesthetic" to refer to understandings of perception, and "aesthetic method"[2] to refer to the manner in which writers (here, more specifically, Modernist novelists, though I also touch upon dramatic and critical writings by these authors) make use of these understandings and of sensations and perceptions in developing their works as meaningful expressions. To put this another way, I am interested in how writers develop works which can be used to think through sensation and perception, and which, further, shed light on the nature of perceptual thought itself.

Understood in this way a consideration of aesthetic method involves the examination of what a work of literature (especially the novel) can do. Here the question will be narrowed further, to consider specific works within a specific period: the Modernist era, here confined to a period from about 1910 to the mid-1930s. This was a period of great achievement and exploration in the form of the novel, and it has been chosen in part because of this, and because the question of the nature of thought itself was an overt concern for the major writers I have chosen to consider in this study: James Joyce, Virginia Woolf, and Vladimir Nabokov.

Early and extremely influential receptions of the Modernist fiction developed by Joyce, Woolf, and others such as William Faulkner, linked these works to the representation of cognitive perception, through the concept of the "stream of consciousness." This term was adapted from the American philosopher William James (see James 2001: pp. 18–43),

---

things known and *things perceived* in Plotinus, *Enneads*, IV, 8, 7: "This nature has two aspects, the one intelligible, the other sensible ..." (Baumgarten 1954: p. 88).

2 I avoid the word "poetics" because my focus here is not on language or the literary use of language per se (on this point see Bakhtin 1994: p. 271), but the manner in which works develop and require thought. So too, as I will discuss in more detail below, my own approach is developed through my readings of Gilles Deleuze, whose understanding of thought and thinking in literature provides my point of departure. I approach the question of aesthetic or artistic practice from a particular side, then, and in doing so leave aside the aesthetic philosophies developed by many other important philosophers and theorists (such as Kant, or Lyotard). While I make use of the term "aesthetic" and "aesthetic method," then, in emphasizing the relation between this term and perception, my principle point of focus is not Aesthetic Philosophy and the relation of this discipline to literature but the expression of thought, and thinking in literature.

and particularly emphasized the strong interest in interior monologue apparent in certain of the works of Joyce and Woolf in particular (see, for example, Humphrey 1954; Kumar 1963; Freidman 1955). The term has atrophied over the years, and it is fair to claim that the concept of the "stream of consciousness" has born little fruit recently, or for many years. This is in large part because the concept itself is reductive: it simply does not adequately account for the various elements brought to bear in these novels, which, for the most part, do not exclusively limit themselves to the mode of interior monologue.

It is apparent, however, that the critics who developed these readings were responding to a genuine tendency, which announced itself in the works of this period: that is, these works were aesthetic in the sense outlined above; they were concerned with questions of perception, and the nature of perception. I feel it is time to reassess the manner in which these works function as ways of understanding perception. In order to do this, however, it is necessary to shift the focus of analysis away from the narrowly subjective mode of interior monologue to a fuller understanding of thought and thinking: one which takes into account not only "internal" modes of thought, but "external" modes, as well as the interactions between them. Thought is tied to perception, but perception is not simply understood as being subjective or "internal" in the manner of consciousness; rather, as I will set out in detail in the first part, it is "external," or more properly it offers a surface that is folded so that the internal and external become complex, or inter-involved.

This study, then, sets out to examine how the Modernist novel might be understood to be a machine for thinking, and further how it might offer a means of coming to terms with what it means to think. Indeed, I will challenge Baumgerten's assumption that the aesthetic is only concerned with the sensible, arguing that it can, in effect, become concerned with thought itself, in all its manifestations, and that in doing so it is able to draw into dialogue logic and sensation (or, to make use of the terminology from Spinoza I develop below, the three kinds of knowledge: imagination, rational logic, and intuition).

I begin the study with a theoretical analysis of the concept of thought and thinking in literature. I make use of the work of the major contemporary philosopher Gilles Deleuze as a point of departure, as he has explicitly concerned himself with the question of the interrelation between thought and the arts and with the question of what it means to think more generally. Some of Deleuze's work involves a highly compressed style, and so I have developed two strategies here in developing my readings. First, in making use of Deleuze I draw out the line of argument most relevant to my own project and set this out as clearly as possible, rather than attempting a full exposition of Deleuze's position. Second, I return directly to the work of two philosophers who were among the

4   Thinking in Literature

most important to Deleuze in the development of his understanding of the nature of thought, and thinking in literature: Spinoza and Leibniz. That is, I develop my own readings of these philosophers with regard to the question of thought, and bring these readings back into dialogue with Deleuze, in order to develop my own understanding of the central question of the nature of thinking in literature.

If Deleuze is chosen in part because his system remains current and highly influential, Spinoza and Leibniz are also important to this study because of the associations they bring with them. Spinoza is a philosopher who has exerted extraordinary influence on the arts since the Romantic period. He was adopted and read avidly by both German and English Romantics, nineteenth-century novelists, and Modernists (including Joyce, as I will outline in Chapter 4). He continues to be a major figure in both political and aesthetic philosophy today, but in the Modernist era he influenced not only artists but also scientists such as Einstein who famously affirmed that he believed in "Spinoza's God" (Feuer 1982: p. 79). So too, both analytical and continental philosophers[3] took a strong interest in aspects of his system. So too, Leibniz was extremely influential at the beginning of the twentieth century, with numerous thinkers drawn to his logic: that is, his understanding of the thinking process.[4]

In developing these arguments I will set out three principal elements which continually announce themselves as crucial to the process of developing an aesthetic expression: relation, sensation, and composition. These three elements, which are considered in the first part, are all interlinked or, to be more precise, implicated with one another.

Having outlined a theoretical understanding of what it means to think in literature, and how literature understands thought, I move to a second related methodological approach. If one is to take seriously the idea that literature can develop a kind of thinking of its own, one particular to itself, it is necessary to move from a purely theoretical exposition to specific readings of artistic practice, tracing processes through which artists develop and articulate their particular aesthetic methods. In Chapters 4, 5, and 6, I examine elements of the aesthetic practice or aesthetic methods developed by three major Modernist writers: James Joyce, Virginia Woolf, and the young Vladimir Nabokov. Each of these writers can be understood as working with relation, sensation, and composition, yet each emphasize the interrelations between them in differing ways. I have

---

3   For example, Wittgenstein's (1995) *Tractatus Logico-Philosophicus* takes its title from Spinoza's *Tractatus Theologico-Politicus*, and Bergson saw himself in part as inverting, or directly responding to aspects of Spinoza.
4   For example, Bertrand Russell, Louis Courturat, Willard Quine, Kurt Gödel. In his notes to Pushkin's *Eugene Onegin*, Nabokov calls Leibniz a "philosopher and mathematician of genius" (Pushkin 1975: p. 30).

underlined this process of emphasis in the particular studies of Joyce (relation), Woolf (sensation) and Nabokov (composition) I offer in Part II. Yet rather than seeking to directly apply the ideas outlined in Part I to readings of the works of Joyce, Woolf, and Nabokov, I turn to their own writing and internal and contextual evidence related to their various writing practices in mapping important elements of their aesthetic ideas, specifically as they relate to thinking in literature, to better exemplify the processes of literary thinking.

In doing this I am conscious of avoiding repeating material that is already well known. Here, then, I offer new insights into the aesthetic methods of each writer. I offer the first sustained reading of Joyce's use of Spinoza and the importance of ideas he outlines in notes he wrote while working on his only play *Exiles* to aspects of the aesthetic practice he develops in *Ulysses*. I argue that his aesthetic method continues to develop after *A Portrait of the Artist as a Young Man* and *Stephen Hero* and that the dialogue with Spinoza he enters into is crucial to this process.

I offer the most sustained reading to date of Virgina Woolf's interaction with the ideas of Paul Cézanne (via Roger Fry and through Cézanne directly),[5] drawing out her understanding of "sensation" and processes of translation between the visual arts and literature. Finally, I draw on the work of Boyd, Appel, and others in developing an overview to Nabokov's compositional method before offering a detailed reading of *Despair*, arguing both that Nabokov had developed the greater part of his aesthetic method by the early 1930s, and that the "method of composition" he develops in *Despair* offers important insights into that method. From these specific readings I derive a number of elements which open themselves to general application: the ideas of relation, sensation, and composition mentioned above, but also a new idea: "the analogue real," which I examine in detail in relation to Nabokov, but, as I touch upon in that chapter and in the conclusion to this study, is more generally applicable to a certain kind of artistic practice.

---

5 While, as I set out in Chapter 5, others (such as Banfield 2000; Goldman 1998; McLaurin 1973) have looked at Fry and Woolf, they have not moved back from Fry to Cézanne as fully as I do here.

Part I Literature and Thinking

This part will consider, first, the manner in which literature might be understood to *be* thought, and, second, set out why such an understanding might be productive or useful. This will be done by working with philosophical understandings of "thought" that shed light on the nature of literary production and the effects of literature and its connection to thought. The method that will be adopted here involves an interrogation of some of the central concepts developed by the French philosopher Gilles Deleuze to better understand the nature of literature. In doing this I will return to those texts, principally by the seventeenth-century philosophers, Spinoza and Leibniz, which Deleuze draws heavily upon in developing his system. In the reading of Spinoza, however, I will draw out ideas that are not developed in detail by Deleuze, in offering my own reading of Spinoza's "relation." The part has three chapters: the first develops a reading of Spinoza's understanding of "relation" or "ratio," indicating how these terms are intimately connected with the idea of thought itself. The second chapter considers Deleuze's claim that ideas developed in Leibniz are "a source of all modern literature." The third chapter develops a reading of the concept of "expression" which Deleuze finds in Spinoza and Leibniz and relates to an understanding of literary expression. Each of these chapters touch upon the three themes or elements of thought that organize this book: relation, sensation (here with regard to the ideas of perception, viewpoint and possibility), and composition.

1 Spinoza, Relation, and Ratiocination

Samuel Beckett made use of Spinoza on a number of occasions, and copied the following lines into his notes of his reading of Wilhelm Windelband's *A History of Western Philosophy*: "The order of ideas [for Spinoza] is conceived as identical with order of things" (see Cordingley 2007). Spinoza considered the immanent substance, God or Nature, to express two attributes: Thought and Extension. It is apparent why such an idea would appeal to a writer: if literature is understood to involve a kind of thinking, to be a kind of thought, then an immediate connection between events that are described and some process of thinking is attractive.

Yet, there is a clear problem when one comes to consider the nature of the interaction between things and ideas in Spinoza, at least from the point of view of literature, which concerns itself with the creation of particular sensual experience. This is the problem, at the heart of the *Ethics*, of the nature of the relationship between *natura naturans* and *natura naturata*: the relation between substance as an infinite being whose essence involves existence, and modes, finite beings whose existence, at least when imagined through the first kind of knowledge given to us by our senses, appears to be contingent.

In attempting to draw out how the problem might shed light on the relationship between literature and thinking, I will consider three interconnected positions from the *Ethics*. First, how "the idea" is defined not to relate directly to words or images but to be, in effect, the process of understanding itself. Second, how thinking — that is, the first, second, and third kinds of knowledge in Spinoza — is identified with the idea of relation, which is also relevant to the existence of bodies, which are conceived through mutual relations or ratios. Finally, I will consider how it becomes possible to develop an understanding of the essence of particular things through the third kind of knowledge, and how this process of development might be understood to involve a kind of creation whose concept sheds light on processes of creation in the arts.

The Idea

Philosophers such as Edwin Curley, Pierre Macheray, and Gilles Deleuze, have long noticed that Spinoza is a philosopher who seems to have a special appeal to non-philosophers, and poets and novelists in particular.

10 Thinking in Literature

Curley lists Novalis, Heine, Coleridge, Wordsworth, Shelley, and George Eliot (see Edwin Curley's editorial comments in Spinoza 1985: p. 402), and one might add others, such as Joyce and Beckett, to this list. On an initial reading one might wonder why this would be so. There is little direct mention of the arts in the *Ethics*: music is briefly used as an example of an object that might be either good, bad, or indifferent to different people in different circumstances (Spinoza 1985: *Ethics*, IV, Preface, p. 545).[1] Yet the circle that surrounded Spinoza formed a group, *Nil Volentibus Arduum*, discussing artistic practice (Nadler 1999: p. 294), and this offers evidence of the early recognition of the possible usefulness of his system for the arts.

Still, there are key problems that emerge when one comes to think about art through the *Ethics*. If one believes that works of art function, at least in part, through the production of affects and sensations; that they form beings of sensation which produce affects in us — as Deleuze and Guattari contend in *What is Philosophy?*, for example — then how can this be reconciled with Spinoza? For Spinoza affects and sensations pertain to the first kind of knowledge, the imagination, and he clearly states that this kind of knowledge is the sole cause of error (see Spinoza 1985: *Ethics*, II, P41, p. 478). Second, if one wishes to contend that literature develops a kind of thinking, one immediately confronts the further obstacle provided by Spinoza's clear statement in Part II, Proposition 49, to the effect that images and words (which, when one remembers that images for Spinoza involve every kind of sensual material, are necessary to the production of any work of art) only concern the body and are not related to thought:

> [T]hought . . . does not at all involve the concept of extension . . . an idea (since it is a mode of thinking) consists neither in the image of anything, nor in words. For the essence of words and images is constituted only by corporeal motions, which do not at all involve the concept of thought. (Spinoza 1985: *Ethics*, II, P49, p. 486)

Yet, notwithstanding these apparent problems, I would contend that one does not have to read Spinoza against the grain to find material that might be of use to artists.

Ideas are not identified with words or images; rather, "the idea" is the very process of understanding. Spinoza insists upon this point, making it more than once, in more than one way, over a number of propositions in Part II. In the scholium to Proposition 43 he states:

---

1 References to the *Ethics* will indicate the part, the proposition, and the page number to Edwin Curley's translation of the *Ethics*.

Spinoza, Relation, and Ratiocination 11

To have a true idea means nothing other than knowing a thing perfectly, or in the best way. And of course no one can doubt this unless he thinks that an idea is something mute, like a picture on a tablet, and not a mode of thinking, viz. the very [act of] understanding. And I ask, who can know that he understands some thing unless he first understands it? I.e., who can know that he is certain about some thing unless he is first certain about it? (Spinoza 1985: *Ethics*, II, P43, p. 479)

The metaphors are extremely interesting here: a picture on a tablet, a painting, for example, is thought of as "mute," or, as Shirley translates it, "dumb" in the sense of mute (Spinoza 2002: *Ethics*, p. 273). Again, such reasoning seems initially unpromising for someone interested in art: here the image itself does not speak. Yet it is worth trying to attend to the nature of the contrast. The idea must, in some sense, speak to us directly. It is the very act of understanding and we immediately understand that we understand. The idea, then, as conceived here, already carries something of the third kind of knowledge: it strikes us immediately and intuitively. Might this mean we do not come to think, or learn to think, that rather, insofar as we understand we are already in thought?

It would no doubt be possible to attempt to understand Spinoza's point more fully by turning to the ideas of some of those who influenced his own work. The Ancient Stoics, for example, whose work Spinoza knew through his reading of Justus Lipsius who published epitomes of the Stoic doctrines on Ethics and Physics at the beginning of the sixteenth century (see Saunders 1955; Lagrée 1994). The Stoics distinguished between bodies and incorporeals arguing that while words are bodies because they pass as sound through the air or are written down, meaning or sense itself is not in the words; rather, meaning is attributed to the words and is incorporeal (see Bréhier 1997, p. 15).[2] For Spinoza the word is not adequate to or necessary to the idea, that is, ideas both exceed and precede the human signs that seek to relate them. I would argue that one can link artistic thinking to this very excess: rather than it being the kind of sign system that seeks to link signs as precisely as possible to their intended meanings, like mathematics or an ideal rational language such as that imagined by Wittgenstein in his *Tractatus*, art requires us to understand what is not

---

2 This does not mean that I understand an individual to develop sense prior to expression (prior to signs, or prior to the sensations the individual experiences as signs). Rather, expression can be thought of as being developed from a sense of the meaningful — an affect — which is better conceived of as being "external" to, rather than "internal" to, an individual. I discuss the implications of this with regard to theories of sign systems and expression below.

present in, or goes beyond the linguistic signifier, what is in the idea rather than in the word. Paradoxically, then, rather than this inhibiting someone who writes literature, it might very well be understood to open possibilities: that words might be so related that they invoke moments of immediate understanding in a reader, moments of understanding, which are intended to exceed the expression of the words, getting beyond words through words, by making use of signs — such as the music of language or powerful images, for example.

First, as we will see, feeling is not only involved in the first kind of knowledge (those images derived from the sensations) but also in the third kind (an immediate, intuitive, understanding). Second, while Spinoza states that images and words are only related to bodies and not thought, it is nevertheless clear, through his system, that there would necessarily be an idea parallel to an image, an idea parallel to a word. Parallel lines of course, at least in Euclidean geometry, do not meet. One fails to see how they might be related, unless one understands relation itself to involve the parallel, a gap, a ratio, a proportion that persists and resonates. Tradition passes on the story that Pythagoras not only discovered certain mathematical laws through ratios but also immediately applied these to the art of music.

I want to argue that for Spinoza relation itself is crucial to the generation of any kind of human thought, including thinking in the arts, which, too, proceeds through relations. That is, if we understand relation to involve a kind of linking or connection that proceeds across gaps, urging flashes of insight to emerge, to speak from ourselves to the mute tableau, as a lightening flash leaps from the sky to the ground, or a signal across a synapse.

The term "relation" itself is immediately tied to thought in Spinoza: a core meaning of the word "ratio" itself is "reason," or more generally, "thought," as in the English word ratiocination. A ratio, in turn, is a proportional relation between things. A definition in scientific terms of ratio is "the quantitative relation between two amounts showing the number of times one value contains or is contained within the other" (Oxford English Dictionary). Further, it is the ratio of speeds and slownesses that defines the particular nature of each body; or to put this another way, each body has its own logic.

Yet the indentification of ratio or relation and thought is clarified when we turn to Spinoza's definitions of the three kinds of knowledge: (1) the imagination; (2) rational logic; and (3) intuition — which comprise what we can know of the world, for Spinoza. In Proposition 40 of Part II he states that he can explain each kind through a single example that concerns proportional relations, or ratios, between numbers: for example, 1 is to 2 as 3 is to 6 as 4 is to 8, and so on (that is, each first number in the series is multiplied by 2 to reach the second number). Spinoza states:

Suppose there are three numbers, and the problem is to find a fourth which is to the third as the second is to the first. Merchants do not hesitate to multiply the second by the third, and divide the product by the first, because they have not yet forgotten what they heard from their teacher without any demonstration,[3] or because they have often found this in the simplest numbers, or from the force of the Demonstration of P7 in Bk. VII of Euclid, viz. from the property of proportionals.[4] But in the simplest numbers none of this is necessary. Given the numbers 1, 2, and 3, no one fails to see that the fourth proportional number is 6 — and we see this much more clearly because we infer the fourth number from the ratio which, in one glance, we see the first number to have to the second. (Spinoza 1985: *Ethics*, II, P40, p. 478)

The use of ratio, or proportional relation, as the material for the example here is not accidental; rather, relation, ratio, and proportion inhabit thought itself.

The first kind of knowledge commonly involves the association of ideas. Spinoza offers many examples of this when he comes to consider the nature of the affects: we connect, through the imagination, an affect or emotion with an external cause. For example, love is the affect of Joy

---

3 That is, for 1, 2, and 3: $2 \times 3 = 6$; $6 \div 1 = 6$; therefore, the fourth term is 6: i.e. 1 is to 2 as 3 is to 6.
4 Euclid (Book VII, P7):

> If a number be that part of a number, which a number subtracted is of a number subtracted, the remainder will also be the same part of the remainder that the whole is of the whole.
>
> For let the number AB be that part of the number CD which AE subtracted is of CF subtracted; I say that the remainder EB is also the same part of the remainder FD that the whole AB is of the whole CD.
>
> For, whatever part AE is of CF, the same part also let EB be of CG.
>
> Now since, whatever part AE is of CF, the same part also is EB of CG, therefore, whatever part AE is of CF, the same part also is AB of GF [see Book VII, P5].
>
> But, whatever part AE is of CF, the same part also, by hypothesis, is AB of CD; therefore, whatever part AB is of GF, the same part is it of CD also; therefore GF is equal to CD.
>
> Let CF be subtracted from each; therefore the remainder GC is equal to the remainder FD.
>
> Now since, whatever part AE is of CF, the same part also is EB of GC, while GC is equal to FD, therefore, whatever part AE is of CF, the same part also is EB of FD.
>
> But, whatever part AE is of CF, the same part also is AB of CD; therefore also the remainder EB is the same part of the remainder FD that the whole AB is of the whole CD. Q. E. D.

related to the idea of an exterior cause. In the example cited above, the Merchants might come to the correct answer via the first kind of knowledge, because they associate the response to the problem to a formula they have learnt by rote (without adequately understanding how it might work). The second kind of knowledge would be made use of by someone who understood common notions such as those described by Euclid in his *Elements*. This person has read Euclid and been convinced by, in Spinoza's words, "the force of the Demonstration"; that is, they have, through the intellect, understood a process of causation, and such a process is, in effect, nothing other than a set of necessary interrelations. Through the third kind of knowledge, however, no set of associations needs to be triggered, no logical sequence needs to be traced; rather, one understands the relation of terms immediately, with an intuitive understanding which grasps the relations involved *as understanding*. Intuition, that is, is also a kind of relation, but one in which the related terms — the thing perceived and the thing understood — involve what might almost be thought to be an identification, or to put this another way, one is adequate to the other.[5]

It remains to be seen, then, how this notion of thought as "relation" might be brought into contact with artistic practices. In discussing *Film*, Samuel Beckett's work for cinema, Gilles Deleuze contends that Beckett allows us to recognize key potentials of the filmic medium because he exhausts or negates those elements (Deleuze 1997). The same principle of exhaustion or negation might be seen in Beckett's aesthetic writings where he develops the concept of "nonrelation" in art, which he opposes to an artistic tradition that, he states, has always emphasized relation and the power of relation.

In his first novel, *Dream of Fair to Middling Women* (1932) Beckett describes an aesthetic theory that emphasizes the connections or relations between things rather than the nature of those things themselves (Beckett 1993). In a later letter to Georges Duthuit (written in 1949) Beckett outlines a somewhat different aesthetic understanding, one that emphasizes *non-relation* or the refusal to fully draw connections or relationships. Beckett states:

> As far as I'm concerned, Bram [van Velde]'s painting . . . is new because it is the first to repudiate relation in all its forms. It is not the relation with this or that order of encounter that he refuses, but the state of being quite simply in relation full stop, the state of being in front of . . . [T]he break with the outside world implies the break with the inside . . . I'm not saying that he doesn't search to

---

5 In its full philosophical sense: i.e. it involves an adequate, or complete, understanding.

Spinoza, Relation, and Ratiocination 15

re-establish correspondence. What is important is that he does not manage to. (Beckett 2006: p. 19)

In *"Peintres de l'Empêchement"* (first published in 1948) Beckett states that all works of art have involved the readjustment of the relation between subject and object (Beckett 1983: p. 137), a relation that he claims has now broken down. He announced this crisis over a decade before and prior to World War II in 1934 in another review, "Recent Irish Poetry" (Beckett 1983). Elsewhere I have argued in detail how Beckett moves from making clear links in his works, through allusion and other means, to occluding the element that would link the terms, while still offering terms that cry out to be related (Uhlmann 2006a: pp. 36–64). Such a process of occlusion, or an insistence on gaps, however, differs in degree rather than kind from other modes of artistic thinking.

That is, the insistence on gaps between relatable terms has a long history in art. Stephen Greenblatt, for example, claims that something happens to Shakespeare's artistic method around the time he writes *Hamlet*.

> Shakespeare found that he could immeasurably deepen the effect of his plays, that he could provoke in the audience . . . a peculiarly passionate intensity of response, if he took out a key explanatory element, thereby occluding the rationale, motivation, or ethical principle that accounted for the action that was to unfold. The principle was not the making of a riddle to be solved, but the creation of a strategic opacity. This opacity . . . released an enormous energy that had been at least partially blocked or contained by familiar, reassuring explanations. (Greenblatt 2004: pp. 323–4)

One kind of artistic practice, developed to a high degree by Beckett, is to leave gaps between and within the subjects who perceive and the objects that are presented. Such gaps might be understood to involve, to cite Deleuze from his essay on Marcel Proust, which will be discussed in detail below, the process of leading to thought, rather than thinking (Deleuze 2000: pp. 94–102). That is, in art the relation still has to be drawn, has not yet been fully drawn, and we need to think in attempting to bridge the gap.

Approaching Beckett's problem of the relation of subject and object through Spinoza, though moving away from Spinoza's terminology, one might consider the first kind of knowledge in Spinoza to be "subjective" knowledge: Spinoza states that the affections in our bodies and affects in our minds, which are caused by external bodies, tell us more about the nature of our own bodies than about the nature of the external objects. So too, again moving away from Spinoza's terminology, the second kind of knowledge, the intellect, which works through common notions that

16 Thinking in Literature

allow us to adequately understand general things but not particular things, might be thought to be objective.

A sophisticated understanding of this relation between kinds of thought (the imagination and the intellect) can be found in ideas attributed to the French post-Impressionist painter Paul Cézanne, who develops the concept of the "sensation" to describe thinking in painting, and argues for the possibility of a "logic of organized sensations" (Emile Bernard, cited in Kendall 1988: p. 299). While I will discuss this in more detail in the chapter on Virginia Woolf (Chapter 5), it is useful to turn to some of these ideas here in order to get our bearings.

Whereas the idea of an "impression," for the French Impressionists carries the sense of a passive reflection, with nature impressing its image on the artist who then faithfully records the moment, "sensation" involves a complex process of interaction that is more active than passive. The sensation is projected by an external nature, is registered by an internal nature; that is, the sensation is both in the image received and in the artist's response to that image. Further, a sensation analogous to that received from the world is then reprojected by the artist via a process of mental organization or composition and the brushstrokes that correspond to and build up the new sensation upon the canvas. The sensations in turn inhere in the canvas where they are able to be received by viewers. Joaquim Gasquet reports Cézanne as stating:

> The landscape is reflected, humanized, rationalized within me. I objectivize it, project it, fix it on my canvas [. . .] It may sound like nonsense, but I would see myself as the subjective consciousness of that landscape, and my canvas as its objective consciousness. (Gasquet 1991: p. 150)

For Cézanne the artist needs to become unselfconscious in order to *be* the subjective feeling of the other. This in turn develops a new interaction of the first and second kinds of knowledge around an understanding of the object.

> There are two things in the painter, the eye and the mind; each of them should aid the other. It is necessary to work at their mutual development, in the eye by looking at nature, in the mind by the logic of organized sensations which provides the means of expression. (Emile Bernard, cited in Kendall 1988: p. 299)

There is no lack of thought involved in this concept of sensation; rather, the sensation is "thought" but not necessarily conscious thought or thought mediated through language.

As we have seen, the problem with the first kind of knowledge is that

Spinoza, Relation, and Ratiocination   17

our affects merely describe the affections of our body, which, in affecting us with joy or sadness, only tell us whether a thing perceived increases or decreases our power of action. It is important to recognize, however, that artistic expression involves a thinking *of*, as much as *through*, the imagination. Art, that is, attempts to understand what Cézanne calls "the real": the experience of sensation. Reinterpreting a long tradition in thinking the nature of the relation between the lives of philosophers and their works, Bruno Clément has recently argued that philosophy, despite its protestations to the contrary, moves from the particular to the universal; that is, in Spinoza's terms, the affects of the first kind of knowledge are rendered abstract and developed into material which might be manipulated through the second kind. One might argue, again in relation to a long tradition, that art, on the contrary, achieves identification with each reader or viewer in turn affected by the work. That is, an understanding is developed not through an effort to convert things to common notions, but by making a particular experience available to others who might adapt it to their own world view.

Let us return to the subject–object relation, or gap, again. We see, through a cross reflection between the first and second kinds of knowledge, not only the other as potentially ourselves (which is still only a capacity of the imagination) but the possibility of understanding the nature of the causes that produce that other. That is, we are offered subjective and objective understandings at once: we are allowed to *be* an alien mode while grasping the causes which bring that mode about. Yet this is not done through clear, logical relations; rather, the logic of sensations developed in art requires gaps that lead to thought in the effort to bridge the gap. In doing this, however, they *imply* a unity as an analogue of Spinoza's attribute of thought (something I will discuss in more detail below): a unity which allows an overview that promises an understanding of an interrelation of viewpoints around a set of events.

I will offer an example to clarify this last point. In William Faulkner's (1994) novel *The Sound and the Fury* we are given four narratives with four narrators. The first three of these are first person and recount the "thoughts" of each narrator, while the fourth is a third-person narrator, which Faulkner later identified with himself as author. The first three are: Benjy, a mentally disabled man, fixed at a mental age of about 2 or 3, who thinks only by making associations of images, and so has no concept of time or the narrative relation this concept allows and who finds only one person, his sister Caddy, who truly loves him; Quentin, their brother, a young man who also deeply loves Caddy and who is riddled with guilt because of the events that lead to her disgrace, and who, in consequence, is about to commit suicide; Jason, their brother, who feels intense hatred towards his brothers, his sister Caddy, and Caddy's daughter (named Quentin after her uncle who some wrongly believe to have been Quentin's father), and whose resentment reaches a crescendo through the events he relates. Numerous gaps are left in the narrative and we are forced to make relations between the different fragments within the story to reconstruct the various lines of causation at play; some of these connections are made consciously and some are sensed: that is, a system of answering motifs generates resonance and harmony across or through gaps in the relation, creating the sensation both of unity and of understanding. The work challenges us to understand but does not allow us to understand through the intellect alone; rather, it leads us towards a sense, a feeling, and through the complex interrelations it establishes it creates a sense of the meaningful, which is identified with a feeling of understanding; that is, we sense the essence of what is at stake.

Feeling does not begin and end with the first kind of knowledge in Spinoza; rather, the feeling of understanding is apparent in the intuition which constitutes the third kind of knowledge, an intuition that proceeds from an immediate understanding of elements of the essence of God's attributes to the understanding of any number of other things, including particular things insofar as these are understood to be eternal modes of thinking, or essences:[6]

> [T]hough it is impossible that we should recollect that we existed before the Body — since there cannot be any traces of this in the body, and eternity can neither be defined by time nor have any relation to time — still, we feel and know by experience that we are eternal. For the Mind feels those things that it conceives in understanding no less than those it has in the memory. For the eyes of the mind, by which it sees and observes things, are the demonstrations themselves. (Spinoza 1985: *Ethics*, V, P23, pp. 607–8)

Intuition, then, also involves affect. The adequate idea, the essence, involves a felt identification of a perception and an understanding. Art, in composing relations between the first, second, and third kinds of knowledge can offer us an image of a particular essence of thinking.

In order to more fully develop this idea, however, it is necessary to consider more precisely how literature might be considered to be thought. In order to begin to do this it is useful to turn to Deleuze's understanding of thinking in literature, which he develops through readings of Spinoza and Leibniz. My contention is that rather than being understood to offer an analogue of consciousness, literature should be understood as attempting to develop an analogue of thought itself, which, as we will

---

[6] I will develop a reading of the notion of essence in Spinoza more fully in the chapter on Joyce (Chapter 4).

see below, involves representations of minds in dialogue, which exceed the representation of consciousness.

2 Leibniz's "Perception": the Incompossible, the Viewpoint, and the Composition of Sensation

Deleuze contends in *The Fold: Leibniz and the Baroque* (1993: pp. 61–3) and in the second cinema book, *Cinema 2: The Time-Image*, (1989) that the seventeenth-century German philosopher G. W. Leibniz's conception of incompossibility, as outlined in sections 414–16 of *Theodicy* (Leibniz 1990) is, "a source of all modern literature" (Deleuze 1989: p. 303). Further, in *The Fold*, Deleuze points out that Leibniz states that only novels can give us an idea of the nature of the incompossible. How, then, is Leibniz's conception of the nature of thought important to an understanding of the capacities of literary fiction? To get our bearings here we need to examine elements of Leibniz's understanding of thought.

In "Monadology. 1714," Leibniz (1992a) defines his concept of the individual as a thinking thing, the monad. Each monad is a simple substance, that is, a substance made of one part, such as a life, a soul, or a mind. Like Descartes and Spinoza, Leibniz developed a distinction between thought and matter. Monads are mental or spiritual beings, and as such they are distinguished from compound substances or bodies. All subdivisions of matter are composed of an infinity of parts and each of these parts (which are also always compounds) has an indivisible monad that corresponds to it. There is a hierarchy, however, as the monads of inanimate bodies are not considered souls: souls are only possessed by animals, and of the animals only humans have rational souls or minds. On one hand, then, you have matter composed solely of substances that are always compounds (which always include an infinite number of other compounds within them), yet on the other hand each of these distinct compounds is also represented on a spiritual or mental plane by simple, indivisible substances called monads.

Each monad reflects the primary monad: the originary simple substance that is God. Only God does not correspond to a compound substance or matter, only God is mind independent of matter. As each monad reflects the infinite Monad that is God the whole of the infinite universe is reflected or perceived within each of the monads. It is something like a hologram that, if shattered, is reputed to contain the whole image within each fragment. Yet each monad is distinct and distinguishes itself through its perceptions. While each perceives everything, each (with the exception of God) perceives most things confusedly. Its power and its nature

Leibniz's "Perception" 21

are defined by what it perceives clearly. This is understood as an internal process, but it is a peculiar kind of internal process as it is completely oriented towards the external. The monad, therefore, somehow seems to come between the dichotomy internal/external, interpreting what is other so that it can distinguish what is the same or the self; and this process is unceasing as the monad (that which is unchangeable in its single part) changes in accordance with what it perceives. To quote Leibniz from "Principles of Nature and of Grace":

> [o]ne monad, in itself and at a particular moment, can only be distinguished from another by internal qualities and activities, which can be nothing else but its *perceptions* (that is to say, the representations in the simple of the compound or of that which is outside) and its *appetitions* (that is to say, its tendencies to pass from one perception to another), which are the principles of change. (Leibniz 1992b: p. 195)

This concept of "perception," which involves the "representation" of what is outside (that is, sensation) and its nature is the thread that ties together all of what will be discussed below in relation to Leibniz: the incompossible (and its relation to causation), and the viewpoint in particular. While the relation between viewpoint and perception might seem self-evident (even with regard to Leibniz's curious "perception," which occurs within the "windowless" monad), it is less obvious how perception might be related to the incompossible. Yet this becomes much more obvious when we relate perception and sensation to fiction, and thinking in literature. Literature allows an overview that is capable of mixing various viewpoints and drawing them together into the unified perception that is the work. It does this by showing and passing between representations of the multitude of "possible worlds" that inhabit the real. I will attempt to explain aspects of this relation more fully in the chapter on Virginia Woolf.

The Incompossible

In Leibniz, the term "incompossible" refers to an understanding of possibilities that are mutually exclusive. I cannot be in two places at the same time, for example. The incompossible involves the understanding that while all things that are possible are conceived by God, only certain possibilities are realized in this world, which is the best of all possible worlds. The rule of incompossiblity affirms that "possible worlds cannot pass into existence if they are incompossible with what God chooses" (Deleuze 1993: p. 63). The fable of Sextus outlined in *Theodicy*, which Deleuze calls, "a source for all modern literature," describes a pyramid of possible worlds in which the advent of different possibilities bring into being different worlds. As all things are linked through causation, any change to a given possibility would give rise to a different world. God, then, chooses the best from among the possible worlds, and this is the world that is *realized*. The other possible worlds have a *virtual* existence, in that while they are possible they have not been brought into being: that is, they are *actualized* (their essence has been understood or adequately imagined in a different possible world by God and so there are monads which correspond to actualized essences), but have not been realized. This virtual existence of *the not realized possible*, as will be further considered below, exists only in thought, only in relation to monads, as bodies exist only as possibilities that *have been realized*. This is important to an understanding of literature as a kind of thought, as it too has the capacity to produce existences that are virtual; to create representations that have only a spiritual or mental being.

Thought and Causation
There are complex distinctions between Spinoza and Leibniz, but both Spinoza's attribute of Thought and Leibniz's concept of the incompossible relate to causation and the power to cause. The power of thinking is a productive power, the power to generate effects; that is, to make things happen, to realize the possible (which means that actualized virtuals, or those things which have been adequately imagined, might bring into being realized possibilities or "real" things). Deleuze affirms just this in relation to his reading of Proust: while literature works through the attribute of Thought, it nevertheless produces complex effects both in bodies and minds. Proust understands his work as a magnifying glass that is turned by readers upon their own souls so that they might read and interpret its workings (Deleuze 2000: p. 145). Deleuze affirms that the work of art is a machine, because it produces truths: "No one has insisted more than Proust on the following point: that the truth is produced, that it is produced by orders of machines that function within us, that it is extracted from our impressions, hewn out of our life, delivered in a work" (Deleuze 2000: pp. 146–7). No doubt these are different orders of production: the production of a God who produces all things, on the one hand, and the production made available to a mode or monad who only sees some things clearly and must struggle to adequately express or achieve the range of potentials coiled within its own essence. An important problem occurs here, then. How is it possible to create within systems (such as those devised by Spinoza and Leibniz) in which everything has been pre-determined by God? That is, if literature is to be equated with thought and thought is to be equated with creation, how is such creation possible if all the power to create rests with "God"?

Escaping from Determinism

In order to work through this problem, it is worth looking more closely at the concepts of causation developed by Leibniz and Spinoza so as to consider the different orders of causation touched upon here (that of God and that of God's creatures). As we have seen, for Leibniz, thought is related to causation. This understanding, that God must account for all possibility (by actualizing it in virtual worlds), involves necessity, determinism. For Spinoza too there is an absolute interconnectedness of things, all things must be as they are, and because God is all-powerful He therefore *will do everything* that is possible. Further, in Spinoza, the parallelism between Thought and Extension requires that everything that is Thought must also be expressed in Extension (something which is not the case in Leibniz's system, which allows for the virtual). For Spinoza, to say that something is either contingent or possible (something which we, as modes with inadequate understanding, do say) involves either an inadequate understanding of the thing's essence, or an inadequate understanding of the causes that bring that thing about:

> For if we do not know that the things' essence involves a contradiction, or if we do know very well that its essence does not involve a contradiction, and nevertheless can affirm nothing certainly about its existence, because the order of causes is hidden from us, it can seem to us either necessary or impossible. So we call it contingent or possible. (Spinoza 1985: *Ethics*, I, P33, p. 436)

Power and creation, then, are related to knowledge in complex ways. For Spinoza, the full realization of the essence of a thing requires adequate understanding.

In Leibniz, too, God is capable of all possible things, yet instead of realizing all possible things he chooses the best of all possible worlds from among all the possible worlds, and this is the world we inhabit. For both philosophers, then, though in somewhat different ways, there is a connection between thought and causation at a fundamental level. For both, too, a similar problem occurs: how can humans be understood to be free in an absolutely determined world?

The world is predetermined, but only understood as such from the viewpoint of God. How, then, can beings such as ourselves who can never adequately understand the power of the infinite causal chain be understood to be "free"? Can we freely do or create anything at all? Both Leibniz and Spinoza affirm that we do correspond to a degree of power: that is, we can create, we can produce; further, the kinds of power they describe sheds light on the nature of thinking in literature.

The determined world, then, must open up to our production, it must allow our potential and it does open out in two directions. For Spinoza, it does so in terms of *understanding* through the third kind of knowledge. That is, thought can escape towards what is but is not yet known, towards what comes into being in being "understood," with understanding here involving its creation. One might read Part V of the *Ethics* and the idea of the third kind of knowledge in this way, as an intuition that moves thought at infinite speed and which *does* allow us to know. The threat that confronts us in Spinoza involves the possibility that we may not adequately understand. We are all "eternal," Spinoza contends, but we have to endeavor, through the third kind of knowledge, to *understand* our eternal essence. This endeavor to understand is itself productive: it produces contentment and extends our knowledge of God or Nature. Still, one wonders where a failure to achieve this realization would lead. We can trace this line of thought through Part V:

> P25: *The greatest striving of the Mind, and its greatest virtue is understanding things by the third kind of knowledge* [. . .]
>
> P27: *The greatest satisfaction of Mind there can be arises from this third kind of knowledge* [. . .]
>
> P30: *Insofar as our Mind knows itself and the Body under a species of eternity, it necessarily has knowledge of God, and knows that it is in God and is conceived through God* [. . .]
>
> P31 . . . Schol.: Therefore, the more each of us is able to achieve in this kind of knowledge, the more he is conscious of himself and God, i.e., the more perfect and blessed he is [. . .] (Spinoza 1985: *Ethics*, V, pp. 609–10)

If we achieve knowledge of the eternal nature of our essence we more fully share in the productive aspects of this understanding. The mind, or thought, is the "formal cause" of this knowledge (Spinoza 1985: *Ethics*, V, P31, p. 610). Thought, then, is creative: it is capable of moving, of expanding into its essence; that is, it is capable of realizing the potential of that essence.

Whenever we create something (through science, philosophy, art) we bring into being new potentials for being. Deleuze and Guattari affirm the importance of ignorance to this process, the importance of moving towards knowledge through thought rather than simply possessing knowledge, stating:

> [O]n both sides, philosophy and science (like art itself with its third side) include an *I do not know* that has become positive and creative, the condition of creation itself, and that consists in determining by

what one does not know — as Galois said, "indicating the course of calculations and anticipating the results without ever being able to bring them about." (Deleuze and Guattari 1994: p. 128)

This creative uncertainty is opposed to a pretension to complete knowledge, a posture habitually adopted by opinion, which Deleuze and Guattari identify as the enemy of thought in *What is Philosophy?*, because it does not involve creation. It functions instead through the recognition of an already "known," which has achieved dogmatic status within a given group; an already known which is now or is becoming untrue because it is never adequate to the flux inherent in the ongoing movement of the infinite causal chain, a movement which comprises the universe and the unfolding of our essence in its unfolding.

There is a second escape route through which the determined world allows our potential: this is the virtual as it is understood by Deleuze through his reading of Leibniz. In Leibniz's system the problem of how one might explain human freedom within a deterministic world is a key concern; indeed, the subtitle of *Theodicy* is "Essays on the Goodness of God the Freedom of Man and the Origin of Evil." Still, many critics, such as Austin Farrer in his Introduction to the English edition of *Theodicy*, have found Leibniz's response (that human freedom can coexist with absolute determinism) not completely convincing. Through the doctrine of pre-established harmony each monad (and the fate contained within the essence of each monad) fits into place beside all the other monads with their complementary fates, like the pieces of an infinitely complex jigsaw puzzle. All things are pre-determined, and the fates of all are pre-determined (in an almost Calvinist sense), yet while those who are damned are damned from the beginning of time, they are damned in accordance with their own nature or essence, which leads them to "freely" commit evil (Leibniz 1990: pp. 365–8).

From the point of view of a Deleuzian reading, the problematic involvement of a transcendent God, outside his creation (unlike the immanent Spinozian God, which expresses creation), does, despite Leibniz's protestations to the contrary, seem to place tight constraints on human freedom. Yet new freedoms open up through the concept of the virtual. That is, while we cannot *realize* the possible in the manner of God, we can *imagine* the possible, Leibniz states:

> The Stoics already derived from the decrees of God the prevision of events . . . And according to my system, God, having seen the possible world that he desired to create, foresaw everything therein. Thus one may say that the divine knowledge of vision differs from the knowledge of simple intelligence only in that it adds to the latter the acquaintance with the actual decree to choose this sequence of

things which simple intelligence had already presented, but only as possible; and this decree now makes the present universe. (Leibniz 1990: pp. 342–3, § 363)

The not yet realized possible, the virtual that we actualize in imagining it *as* possible, then, does have an existence in thought, and Deleuze uses this to open the door to creation through art, as the possible worlds developed in literature (which can even include incompossible events) are understood as being productive: that is, of having real effects. This becomes clear in *The Fold*, where Deleuze insists on two regimes of causality, which he finds in Leibniz (Deleuze 1993: p. 100). He states, "The great equation, the world thus has two levels, two moments, or two halves" (1993: p. 102). On one level there is a causality that proceeds through the monad which expresses the sum of the world, and on the second, lower level, there is a causality that proceeds through bodies, which receive "the impression of 'all' of the others up to infinity" (p. 100). On the first level, within the monad, the virtual is actualized (or adequately imagined in the mind). But actualizing an event does not necessarily mean that that event will come into being through bodies; it does not necessarily mean it will become "real." Rather, the "actualized" event (an event which is possible) needs to be "realized" as a possibility on the level of bodies.

Yet read from another viewpoint, the unrealized virtual, the virtual that has been actualized within the monad in being imagined, or say, brought into being within the work of fiction, has a mental existence, a virtual existence, which involves a causal power which is a power of thought, and which, in turn, for Deleuze produces real effects.

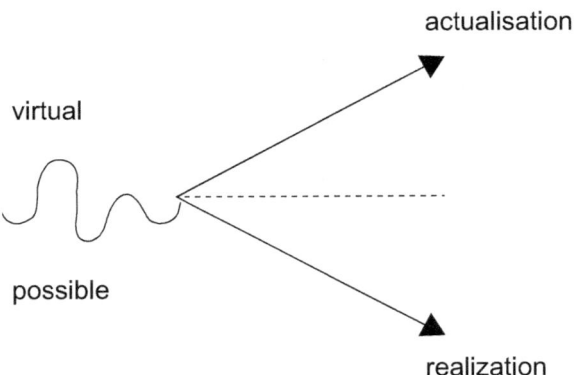

Figure 2.1 The actualisation and realization of the virtual and possible (Image from Deleuze 2006: p. 120)

While their systems are very different it is possible to see how Deleuze develops a syncretic reading, taking elements from both Spinoza (understanding) and Leibniz (the virtual) in developing his understanding of the nature of thought in literature. We can express a power of the virtual through understanding, through thought, and this is true of philosophy as much as literature, though in different ways. In the "Prospects and Concepts" section of *What is Philosophy?* Deleuze and Guattari (1994) describe the methods of science and compare them with the methods of philosophy. Science descends from the virtual to the actual by focusing upon the real event as it unfolds (the event of a chemical reaction, for example). Philosophy, on the other hand, moves in the opposite direction, from the real event back towards the virtual. It is thereby able to express an event conceptually: the event as a potentiality, a possibility. In doing this philosophy opens up or creates possibilities. The concept as a virtual event allows for the actualization of the understanding of the possibility of such events (1994: pp. 155–9). So too, in art actualized possibilities can be laid out (through design) on the plane of composition, producing affects of sense and value in the minds of readers, which in turn can have real effects upon their actions.

Viewpoint

Literature, then, involves the relation to thought of causation experienced as understanding, and the purely mental creation of the virtual as a possible world (which can nevertheless have real effects). Further, a related power of literary creation can be found in the viewpoint, which can be developed into an overview or survey of a field of possible worlds. Deleuze's interest in the fable recounted in *Theodicy*, where the Goddess Pallas leads Theodorus through rooms which describe possible alternative fates for Sextus, rooms which form a pyramid, with the best world at the top and an infinity of possible worlds beneath, can be further linked to his interest in "viewpoint." The "possible world" is a concept Deleuze develops elsewhere to describe the Other as being neither an object nor a subject, but rather "the reality of the possible as something possible" (see Deleuze 1995: p. 147). In his reading of Leibniz, Deleuze underlines how "God chooses one world among an infinity of possible worlds: [but] the other worlds also have their actuality in monads that are conveying them, Adam who does not sin, or Sextus who does not rape Lucretia" (Deleuze 1993: p. 104). "Viewpoint" is a key concept Deleuze relates to thinking in literature in *Proust and Signs*, and can be linked to the idea of "self-survey," which Deleuze describes in *The Fold* and further develops with Guattari in *What is Philosophy?* from their reading of Raymond Ruyer, who in turn draws it from his reading of Leibniz's monad. The monad is that which is capable of self-survey (and Deleuze cites Ruyer as a follower of Leibniz): this is witnessed in the problem of consciousness, to which the monad offers a response. That problem is: How is it that I see? Would I not need a third eye to see what the other two see, and might this not lead to an infinite regress? The monad offers an immediate overview of all of the micro perceptions that are affected through the eyes, which allows us to avoid falling into this abyss (1993: p. 102–3). In this way, a work of literature, which involves, to mix terms from Deleuze and Bakhtin, a dialogue between viewpoints, can offer both heteroglossia and univocity at the same time, and the task of the artist is to develop a composition that creates a unity through heteroglossia.

If literature is drawn into relation with the fable from *Theodicy* it is clearly because of the idea of possible worlds, but also because of the relation of this concept to the viewpoint: each monad expresses a viewpoint, but the possible worlds bring forth an infinity of possible viewpoints related to the same individual. The viewpoint, or monad, as I will discuss more fully below, in turn involves sensation and perception. For Leibniz, each possible world contains another monad: the Adam who does not sin is distinct from the Adam who does, and so on.

For Deleuze the power of literature in part stems from its capacity to draw together, or accommodate simultaneously, different viewpoints. Literature can accommodate incompossibles too, and this point is made forcefully in *The Time Image*, and in *The Fold*, but as well as accommodating mutually exclusive events, literature can express, in a way not so readily available to the modes of thought of science or philosophy, how the same individual might inhabit differing viewpoints:

> Each subject expresses the world from a certain viewpoint. But the viewpoint is the difference itself, the absolute internal difference. Each subject therefore expresses an absolutely different world [. . .] But the world expressed is not identified with the subject; it is distinguished from the subject precisely as essence is distinguished from existence, even from the subject's own existence. (Deleuze 2000: pp. 42–3)

The ability to mix viewpoints, to shift viewpoints, is a key capacity available to literature. There are divergences from Leibniz in Proust, as Proust establishes fragments that resemble the monads, but differ in that whereas the monads are unified by God and the pre-established harmony instituted by God, there is no such unifying agent in Proust: rather, there are fragments which are not readily drawn into a whole, fragments which are only linked "transversally" and create "food for thought" in the provocation this leads to; the provocation to create a link (Deleuze 2000: p. 111). Instead of the perfectly corresponding pieces of Leibniz's pre-established harmony, the work of art brings with it:

Leibniz's "Perception" 29

fragments that can no longer be restored, pieces that do not fit into the same puzzle . . . The language of signs begins to speak for itself . . . it is no longer supported on a subsisting Logos: only the formal structure of the work of art will be capable of deciphering the fragmentary raw material it utilizes, without external reference, without an allegorical or analogical "grid." (Deleuze 2000: p. 113)

These fragments are like the monads in that they can correspond to viewpoints, but the viewpoint is not identified with an individual (Deleuze 2000: p. 110); rather, the same individual might be inhabited by various viewpoints, with the fragments expressing the distance between one viewpoint and another within the individual.

Returning to Proust from Deleuze's reading, we see this clearly: there are a series of gaps, which force us to think. For example, we see Swann in love, his obsession with Odette, and the story of their affair, then Swann's jealously, and Odette's increasingly brazen infidelity, which seems to lead in a certain direction. Yet a gap ensues, and the next time we encounter Swann we find him married to Odette who has been transformed from courtesan to a lady of fashion and the mother of Gilberte. These are things that somehow do not follow, involving some absent process through which everything has changed: Swann is no longer the Swann we knew, Odette is no longer Odette. They do not follow, but they contain a truth, nevertheless, which allows us to see the process of time, and how this movement, this flux of time, opens up possible worlds, new viewpoints, which then inhabit individuals, supplanting or existing simultaneously with other viewpoints within those individuals, because the viewpoint "is not individual, but on the contrary a principle of individuation" (Deleuze 2000: p. 110). Following Leibniz, the shift in viewpoint would be the function of a change in perception within the monad, but in the fragmented form, we are not given, and struggle (in thought) and fail to recover, that which accounts for these shifts.

It is clear that this idea of fragmentation might be applied to works beyond Proust. Deleuze and Guattari affirm that each artist builds their own plane of composition. Yet there might be something more fundamental here: Vladimir Nabokov, or a character in a Nabokov novel, *The Real Life of Sebastian Knight*, affirms that Knight's fiction is, on the one hand, a matter of gaps, and on the other, of hidden patterns which, as one examines the fabric more closely, open out on to new levels which have to be deciphered (Nabokov 1982: pp. 30, 76–80). The play of viewpoints and the gaps between them is fundamental to the aesthetic method adopted by James Joyce in *Ulysses*: jealousy, a generative principle he identifies in *Exiles* and continues to use in *Ulysses* functions through the shifting positions of love and hate which oscillate within the self. In Virginia Woolf's *To the Lighthouse* we witness shifts across time as Lily Briscoe's perception, for example, learns to accommodate and understand relations of space and light (and relations between and within individuals) in part 3 of the novel, which could not yet be understood in part 1. So too, Woolf's work functions through the constant shifting of viewpoints, developing a univocity of thought rather than a simple stream of consciousness.

Deleuze speaks of two kinds of links in Proust: on the one hand there is "resonance," which brings together the disparate in time around an image (where time is regained, with the episode of the madelaine providing a clear example). On the other hand there is "amplitude," which establishes or underlines the reality of distance around an image. This is indicative of a kind of death; of the recognition that the individual is no longer the same individual: it involves a time lost which is experienced with the death of the grandmother, or Marcel's sense of the manner in which a given self can die, the self that loved Albertine, for example (Deleuze 2000: p. 159).

If there is a clear link between thought and the power of causation in Leibniz and Spinoza, a power linked to the making whole which occurs through a logos, a making whole which brings together all the pieces of a single puzzle, then there is a different power of causation in literature: a power of creation caused by the perception of ruptures or discontinuities in the causal chain. Memory is privileged because the experience of being through time that is felt and can be expressed in literature offers a door through to other possible worlds, to other viewpoints within the same individual:

> It is no longer a matter of saying: to create is to remember — but rather, to remember is to create, is *to reach that point where the associative chain breaks, leaps over the constituted individual, is transferred to the birth of an individuating world.* And it is no longer a matter of saying: to create is to think — but rather, to think is to create and primarily to create the act of thinking within thought. To think, then, is to provide food for thought. (Deleuze 2000: p. 111)

In his introduction to *Theodicy* Austin Farrer enters momentarily into a dialogue form in which he has Leibniz state:

> According to the truth of things, each monad is simply its own mental life, its own world-view, its own thoughts and desires. To know things as they are would be simultaneously to live over, as though from within and by a miracle of sympathy, the biographies of an infinite number of distinct monads. This is absolutely impossible. (Ferrer 1990: pp. 24–5)

While adequately representing such an absolute reality is beyond any form of human thought, Farrer's comments draw our attention to how

Leibniz's "Perception" 31

a literary image of thought, which generates its power in part from the grinding together of incommensurable parts (see Deleuze 2000: p. 123), the overlapping of pieces seemingly drawn together from different puzzles, might both provoke us into thought and imply a unity which leaves us with a sense of the meaningful. It is able to present us with fragments of viewpoints that allow us to apprehend the multiplicity and movement involved in a life: that is, it creates the possibility of that apprehension. In the first part of *Proust and Signs* Deleuze makes use of the Neoplatonic concept of "complication" to account for this. This term involves an understanding of the original state of things, a chaos from which things emerge that "envelops the many in the One and affirms the unity of the multiple" (Deleuze 2000: p. 45). He continues with regard to the character of Charlus in Proust's novel:

> The least we can say is that Charlus is complicated. But the word must be taken in its full etymological sense. Charlus's genius is to retain all the souls that compose him in the "complicated" state: this is how it happens that Charlus always has the freshness of the world just created and unceasingly emits primordial signs that the interpreter must decipher, that is, explicate. (Deleuze 2000: p. 45)

First, then, thinking in art involves the creation of complicated worlds; worlds that provoke us to interpretation. Second, we are asked to bring this interpretation into relation with our own world view; to use it in order to produce effects within our own lives; that is, to translate the complicated worlds of others from the possible worlds of fiction into what Leibniz calls our own "clear zone": the place in which we are able to understand, or apprehend a sense of the unity that underlies the multiple.

The Essence (as Composition)

We have seen how Proust's image of thought involves the understanding that "to think is . . . to interpret, is . . . to translate" (Deleuze 2000: p. 101). The viewpoint is linked to the essence: while "partial" or fragmentary, only the work of art allows the possibility of revealing an essence (or of understanding a unity). An essence is that which provokes us to interpret and provides us at the same time both with the thing to be translated and the translation of that thing (Deleuze 2000: pp. 101–2). For Deleuze the problem with interpretation in life is that we fall into errors, objective and subjective: on the one hand we tend to confuse the sign emitted by an object with that object itself. This is an error because the sign is more profound than the one transmitting the sign. On the other hand, "the sign's meaning is doubtless more profound than the subject interpreting it" (Deleuze 2000: p. 36). Art is able to overcome these errors by creating the "essence" that involves the complete correspondence of sign and meaning:

> It is the essence that constitutes the sign insofar as it is irreducible to the object emitting it; it is the essence that constitutes the meaning insofar as it is irreducible to the subject apprehending it... It is only on the level of art that essences are revealed. (Deleuze 2000: p. 38)

For Spinoza it is essences that are eternal, and it is perhaps for this reason that Deleuze and Guattari can talk of art as being that which preserves, as being the only thing in the world that is preserved (Deleuze and Guattari 1994: p. 163). It preserves, however, without doing away with movement, as movement is involved in the shifting of viewpoints, between fragments.

In "Of an Organum or Ars Magna of Thinking. 1679," Leibniz (1992c) describes how one might build an *organum* or instrument of thought. Such an instrument would allow us to understand things adequately. This instrument would be something that could be conceived through itself. That is, Leibniz contends that the cause of something (say "heat") would be the definition of that thing: if we can grasp the cause we can get to the thing.

In *Proust and Signs*, Deleuze describes literature as a thinking without an instrument, without an organum (Deleuze 2000: p. 146). He also sees Proust's challenge as involving a challenge to the logos. This, in effect, is a challenge to the idea of tracing a complete line of causation. The "dogmatic image of thought" (Deleuze 1994: pp. 103–10) leads us to the adequate idea by attempting to reconstruct such completeness: the instrument of thought is the completely understood cause itself which is applied in order to completely understand a thing in itself. Art, on the other hand, works through gaps in knowledge, fragments of sensation and perception, comprising viewpoints that are connected by transversal lines. The sign itself is a fragment, a provocation which forces us or urges us to think, to trace connections which exist but an understanding of whose functioning is elusive (Deleuze 2000: p. 129). Thinking in literature, Deleuze claims, always comes "after." That is, in literature as in life, one does not have adequate knowledge of a line of causation. There are events and gaps between them. There are signs that require interpretation. The links have to be forged, or gaps have to be leapt across, and this is done through thought.

There are important areas of interplay and overlap between philosophy and literature in relation to thought in the work of Deleuze, and Deleuze and Guattari; an interplay between the methods perceived to be utilized in, and concepts extracted from, literature, and an understanding of how philosophy might escape constraining forms and continue to

Leibniz's "Perception" 33

create. In *Negotiations*, for example, in discussing the Cinema books in an interview from 1988, Deleuze states that in working on cinema he is still doing philosophy, that it was not simply a matter of images, indicating that "concepts involve two other dimensions, percepts and affects" (Deleuze 1995: p. 137). When we get to *What is Philosophy?*, of course, percepts and affects are aligned with art, and "the concept" is defined in terms of components, which, rather than being directly linked together, involve space, gaps: the components are connected through resonance, a term which Deleuze has also tied to art in being laid out on a plane of composition.

Deleuze has stated that for him, in philosophy, constructionism should take the place of reflection (Deleuze 1995: p. 147). An example of constructionism can be found with the concept of "the image of thought" in *Proust and Signs* (Deleuze 2000) and *Difference and Repetition* (Deleuze 1968), which is constructed by bringing together fragments from different systems. These fragments are mismatched; we are given pieces from different puzzles, just like the fragments described in *Proust and Signs*, yet just as with those Proustian fragments, these overlapping but inharmoniously corresponding components resonate, generating power, the power of creation, the power of thought.

While we have outlined some of the ways in which literature might be linked with thought here, more can be done to consider the manner in which literature might be understood to *express* thought. It is necessary, then, to examine more closely the concept of expression, which again occurs in Spinoza and Leibniz and is again considered by Deleuze, as this will allow us to bring this problem into focus and tie it again to the concepts of sensation and composition.

3 Composition as the Externalized Expression of Sensation

In *Marxism and the Philosophy of Language*, V. N. Volosinov (1986)[1] develops a strong critique of the traditional manner in which the term "expression" is used, both in the philosophy of language, and more generally in philosophical idealism. He argues that there are "two trends of thought in the philosophy of language" (though the second does not interest us here). He calls the first "individualistic subjectivism" and argues it is linked to a "romantic" view of language. Volosinov criticizes individualistic subjectivism's choice of the subject as source by critiquing the conception of expression it presupposes. Individualistic subjectivism requires two elements within the concept of "expression." Expression moves from inside the speaker to outside. Thus there has to be something inside which needs to be and can be expressed: an internal something is expressible, and it is an outward objectification of this expressible which is expressed. Yet, if the expressed involves signs, then this concept of the expressible seems to imply a meaning which is prior to signs. To quote Volosinov:

> [A]ny theory of expression inevitably presupposes that the expressible is something that can somehow take shape and exist apart from expression; that it exists first in one form and then switches to another form. (1986: p. 84)

Volosinov argues that such a theory is built on spiritualistic and idealistic grounds. "Everything of real importance lies within"; the subject is the source, and language is considered the more or less inadequate messenger of the soul. A false dualism of inside and outside is in this way fabricated. This concept of expression sees expression as always proceeding from inside to outside requiring interpretation to proceed contrariwise from the outside to the inside.

Volosinov categorically states that such a theory of expression is "fundamentally untenable" (Volosinov 1986: p. 85), and he offers the following reasons:

---

[1] Who may or may not have been a mask used by Mikhail Bakhtin, see Translator's Preface, p. ix.

Composition as the Externalized Expression of Sensation 35

The experiential, expressible element and its outward objectification are created, as we know, out of one and the same material. After all, there is no such thing as experience outside the embodiment of signs.[2] Consequently, the very notion of a fundamental, qualitative difference between the inner and the outer element is invalid to begin with. Furthermore, the location of the organizing and formative center is not within (i.e., not within the material of inner signs) but outside. It is not experience which organizes expression but the other way around — *expression organizes experience.* (1986: p. 85)

Having developed this critique, Volosinov abandons the use of the term "expression" altogether. Elsewhere he tends to disparage it by associating it with an understanding of linguistics that draws upon aesthetics, stating that any "sort of expression is, at the root, artistic" (Volosinov 1986: p. 52). What Volosinov passes over here is that he has, in effect, developed, or rather, rediscovered a different concept of expression; one which involves the purely external rather than a movement from the internal towards the external; one in which expression does indeed organize experience. In the late 1960s, Gilles Deleuze, who may or may not have been thinking of Volosinov's critique,[3] describes a concept which seems very similar to that which Volosinov has identified and abandoned; one which he argues has a long tradition stretching back to the Renaissance. This concept is developed in Deleuze's (1990) reading of Spinoza and Leibniz in *Expressionism in Philosophy: Spinoza.*

Here Deleuze outlines an ontological understanding of expression which *does* understand expression as an "external" process, or at least one in which everything is laid out upon the same plane of immanence (Spinoza's Substance as it is expressed by its attributes, Thought and Extension). This surface, however, might be folded so that not everything appears visible, through processes of involution and evolution, implication and explication (see Joughin's preface in Deleuze 1990). An understanding of what might be meant by such an externalized concept of expression is important to developing a better knowledge of what is at stake in literature.

Deleuze outlines how expression is a basic concept for both Spinoza and Leibniz, one which allowed them to overcome difficulties they found in Descartes's system (difficulties which stem from cutting a

---

2 Signs, here, are not limited to linguistic signs; rather all sensations can be signs.
3 Deleuze and Guattari speak of his work in approving terms, indicating that Volosinov's book, *Marxism and the Philosophy of Language,* offers "a theory of enunciation that goes beyond the traditional categories of linguistics" (Deleuze and Guattari 1987: p. 523, n. 5).

mechanistic system off from a created world). Deleuze contends that the concept of expression allows them to, "restore a Philosophy of Nature." He states:

> In Leibniz as in Spinoza expression has theological, ontological and epistemological dimensions. It organizes their theories of God, of creatures and of knowledge. (Deleuze 1990: p. 17)

"Expression" then, both involves and explains the very process of creation, through which a perfect and absolutely infinite Being (Spinoza's Substance, God or Nature) expresses itself first through its infinite attributes and then through the infinite number of finite modes which are in turn expressed by the attributes:

> Substance first expresses itself in its attributes, each attribute expressing an essence. But then attributes express themselves in their turn: they express themselves in their subordinate modes, each such mode expressing a modification of the attribute.... the first level of expression must be understood as the very constitution, a genealogy almost, of the essence of substance. The second must be understood as the very production of particular things. (Deleuze 1990: p. 14)

The concept of expression, then, is developed to help us to understand the extremely difficult process through which Substance might work through Attributes (Thought and Extension being those we know) to produce particular things. This concept of expression is not founded upon the opposition of an internal and an external; rather, it implicates, or folds in, the idea of that which creates with that which is created: the One expresses the many through being "complicated" (or interfolded) within them. The internal and external, insofar as they are brought into play, are folded out, implicated with one another in ways that make them virtually indistinguishable.

These are challenging ideas, and move us towards highly technical lines of argument. This concept of "expression," however, is extremely important to us here, as it allows us to begin to consider how an "expression," in this case, a work of literature, might be viably understood to involve the externalization of meaningful elements throughout the work; an externalization which requires each component of the work to function as a part of an interconnected, complicated, single expression.

Expression in Beckett's Theater

In order to understand this in relation to the design or composition of works and their interaction with "intention" it is, paradoxically, useful to move from a discussion of the novel to a medium — theater — which

Composition as the Externalized Expression of Sensation 37

more clearly exemplifies what is at stake. While Samuel Beckett's apparent desire for control over the performances of his plays during his lifetime, and the subsequent ongoing insistence of the Beckett Estate that his stage directions be closely adhered to is well known, it is useful to again detail the control Beckett extended over productions of his work while he was alive. Both Kenneth Tynan — when he changed the script of *Breath* — and JoAnne Akalaitis — when she tampered with the stage directions to *Endgame* — were threatened with legal action (Bair 1990: pp. 640–1; Brater 1989: pp. 84, 107). In his letter to Akalaitis, who had changed the setting of *Endgame* to an abandoned New York subway car for her 1984 production, Beckett stated that, "Any production which ignores my stage directions is completely unacceptable to me" (Brater 1989: p. 107). Indeed, the stage directions to his plays, especially those written after *Happy Days* in 1961, have been seen to further emphasize Beckett's desire for control. Some of these plays include diagrams explaining movements of the characters, and detailed instructions on the level and pitch of voice desirable. It is almost as if the plays have been "blocked" within the text. As Enoch Brater notes: "Stage directions multiply as Beckett begins to challenge the theater's traditional function as a collaborative and interpretive art" (1989: p. 107). To quote from Deirdre Bair:

> For Beckett, the perfect stage vehicle is one in which there are no actors or directors, only the play itself. When asked how such theatre could be made viable, Beckett replied that the author had the duty to search for the perfect actor, that is, one who would comply fully with his instructions, having the ability to annihilate himself totally.
> "Not for me these Grotowskis and Methods," Beckett storms. "The best possible play is one in which there are no actors, only the text. I'm trying to find a way to write one." (Bair 1990: p. 544)

How might one account for such an apparently violent response? Clearly, Beckett's concepts of dramatic production seem antagonistic to those that have dominated twentieth-century practices, such as those developed by the Russian director and theorist Stanislavski, through which the actor is asked to look within him or herself to find the reality of the part (i.e. their own unapologetically subjective understanding) in order to express a "real" subjectivity on stage. It is important to remember, then, that a second, minor tradition of acting co-existed for a time with that developed by Stanislavski. Writing in 1911, and strongly influenced by Heinrich Von Kleist's 1810 story (or essay in story form) "On the Marionette Theatre," the English director and theorist Edward Gordon Craig, who was from time to time in contact with Virginia Woolf's Bloomsbury circle, suggested that when ruled by emotion (as is the case with Stanislavski's "realist" approach) actors lose control over their bodies and their voices, and, accordingly, what they produce is no more than a series of, perhaps interesting, accidents. As an alternative to "realism" he envisaged the "über-marionette":

> The über-marionette will not compete with life — rather it will go beyond it. Its ideal will not be the flesh and blood but rather the body in trance — it will aim to clothe itself with a death-like beauty while exhaling a living spirit. (Craig 1956: pp. 84–5)

While Craig's ideas add little to those already apparent in Kleist's short story, and while Craig dismissed his own idea of the über-marionette as "an impossible state of perfection" (Innes 1983: p. 124), and further stated that he was looking to the actors to perfect their own craft, the ideas he draws from Kleist nevertheless offered possibilities for the theatre, a certain kind of theatre, which simply could not be realized through Stanislavski's techniques. Indeed, this was something which Stanislavski himself realized. Christopher Innes notes that:

> By 1907 Stanislavski was . . . in search of a deeper kind of realism that would reflect "the life of the human spirit." But his experiments with symbolist drama . . . had been unsuccessful. The acting techniques he had developed for internalizing emotion and translating unexpressed thoughts into physical action were useless for plays that had abstract figures and no subtext . . . Maeterlinck had complained [to Stanislavski] that the mystical level of his *Bluebird* fantasy was totally missing [from Stanislavski's production]. So, prompted by Isadora Duncan . . . and impressed by the first copy of [Craig's book] *The Mask*, Stanislavski invited Craig to direct *Hamlet* for the Art Theater. (1983: pp. 149–50)

Samuel Beckett professed admiration for Kleist's story "On the Marionette Theatre" on more than one occasion and indicated that he was seeking to develop some of its insights into his own performance practice. James Knowlson tells us Beckett visited Kleist's grave in 1969, and knew lines from *The Prince of Homburg* by heart (Knowlson 1996: p. 569). He also outlines how Beckett made use of and referred to "On the Marionette Theatre" while rehearsing the production of *Happy Days* he directed at the Schiller-Theater in Berlin in 1971, in arguing that, "precision and economy would produce the maximum of grace" (1996: p. 584). Then again, in 1975, while assisting at the production of his television play *Ghost Trio*, Beckett spoke with both the principal actor Ronald Pickup, and with Knowlson about the importance of Kleist's Marionette story to understanding what he was attempting to do in this piece. As Knowlson describes it, Beckett

Composition as the Externalized Expression of Sensation   39

more or less recounted Kleist's story in total. First, he outlined how the principles of grace and harmony related to the puppets, which are detailed in the story, might be applied to the processes he was attempting to develop. Then he recounted the third part of Kleist's story concerning the bear that, in lacking self-awareness, and so human self-consciousness, therefore possesses both a more precise grace and a more comprehensive intuition with regard to the movement of bodies than any self-conscious person might (pp. 632–3).

I will develop a reading of Kleist's story below, considering how it might help us to understand how a different kind of literature, one which moves away from the inner world of an actor or a character in fiction in favor of developing affects or sensations that express an external composite world that includes but is not limited to the actors or characters (who also offer externalized expressions), is possible, and has been realized in Beckett's works and in a certain kind of literary production: one that concerns itself with developing an analogue of thought. This composite or composed expression is "univocal."

The terminology presents difficulties and it is necessary to clarify certain points. "Univocal" here, is used in analogy with Spinoza's understanding of immanence: the one Substance, God or Nature, which expresses itself in one voice. This is not to be confused with terminology adopted by Bakhtin, when he distinguishes the monological (his reading of poetry) from the dialogical (his understanding of the novel). Paradoxically, a "univocal" expression can be composed of what Bakhtin calls "heteroglossia" and does not have to be "monological" in Bakhtin's sense (see Bakhtin 1994: pp. 275–331). This is because while, in Deleuze's terms, everything in the univocal is laid out on a single plane, not everything on that plane is visible: rather, the single surface is composed of folds which appear at least from a given angle, to impose elements of discontinuity. The elements of discontinuity appear as fragments, and offer gaps, which need to be bridged, as has been discussed in the previous sections. There is no logical inconsistency, then, in speaking of heteroglossia *within* the univocal. Indeed, in Spinoza's terms this relates to the problem of the relation between *natura naturans* and *natura naturata* (or between individualized modes and the one Substance). In Leibniz's terms this relates to the interaction between ordinary monads (or individuals who only perceive certain things clearly) and the primary Monad God (who perceives all things clearly). As we have seen, the work of fiction can go beyond a single viewpoint: it works through complications and interfoldings of differing viewpoints both between and within individuals. Yet the overview, or survey, of such processes of interaction, might itself be understood to comprise a composed unity. Indeed, Bakhtin also indicates how heteroglossia in the novel can be reconciled with a single overarching intention:

[A] prose writer can distance himself from the language of his own work, while at the same time distancing himself in varying degrees, from the different layers and aspects of the work. He can make use of language without wholly giving himself up to it, he may treat it as semi-alien or completely alien to himself, while compelling language ultimately to serve all his own intentions. The author does not speak in a given language (from which he distances himself to a greater or lesser degree), but he speaks, as it were, *through* language, a language that has somehow more or less materialized, become objectivized, that he merely vetriloquates. (Bahktin 1994: p. 299)

The question of intention and its nature is begged here, and I will engage with this in the chapter on Nabokov (Chapter 6). I would argue that Beckett drew upon Kleist to better develop his works as univocal expressions: expressions which, at least ideally, would be absolutely unified within a performance, expressions which would not be diffused by carrying several discrete examples of reinterpretation (the inner meanings judged to exist by the actors) within them. That is, while the work might involve heteroglossia in the exchange between parts within the play, these exchanges are part of a univocal expression, which would be weakened by the separate interpretations which individual actors might give to their parts. The German actor Ernst Schroeder recounted something of Beckett's attitude to such processes of reinterpretation within the whole:

Of course I occasionally tried to entice a comment out of the taciturn man as to the psychology of the part. I finally told him that the actor in a rehearsal is studying not only the part, he's also studying himself under the magnifying-glass of the part. And finally, that this magnifying-glass, in this case, was especially obscured by the filter of the author. Beckett, smiling, agreed this was so. (Cited in McMillan and Fehsenfeld 1988: pp. 239–40)

The connection between the performance practitioner and Spinoza's Substance is meant analogically, but this does not mean that it involves a loose metaphor. The word analogy, used rigorously, involves the translation of a thing existing in one medium into a thing existing in a different medium. This translation, in turn, takes place through a proportional equivalence, or ratio, which is maintained across both mediums. Just as Spinoza's Substance expresses its essence through its attributes in producing its modes through Reason (ratio), or laws of causation, then, a practitioner might be understood to develop a univocal and externalized expression of a given set of ideas, images, or affects through the rational ordering and interconnection of all of the elements which are in play within the piece. Yet the overview or survey offered by the work as a

Composition as the Externalized Expression of Sensation   41

whole is not complete in the manner of Spinoza's Substance, and it does not involve absolute understanding. Rather, it implies that understanding might be *possible* and generates a *sense of understanding* that depends in part upon inducing or leading an audience or reader to thought by emphasizing gaps or the absence of continuity. The artist, then, offers an overview of thought seen from within the first, second and third kinds of knowledge, which are human rather than divine forms of knowledge but which nonetheless offer us the possibility of achieving adequate understanding of God's essence.

The question of how a performance practitioner or any other artist might develop a univocal externalized expression presents itself. Deleuze's understanding of "affect," which is also developed in part through his reading of Spinoza, helps us to see how this might be possible.

In *What is Philosophy?* Deleuze and Guattari (1994) distinguish between three kinds of thought each in its own way capable of creation: philosophic, scientific, and artistic. The three forms exist as three separate planes. The philosopher creates concepts on the plane of immanence; the scientist lays down functions on the plane of reference or coordination by creating figures or undertaking partial observations. According to Deleuze and Guattari, the artist seeks to create affects or sensations (which are not to be confused with emotions) on the plane of composition by describing percepts. The emotions that the actor brings to bear in performing can behave as a kind of interference to this process. They are interference because they do not relate to the affects which the work itself is seeking to convey. We might line these terms up here with the two understandings of expression detailed above. An affect here refers to an external expression while an emotion refers to an individualistically subjective expression. Therefore, a performance might require an actor to suppress extraneous emotion so that an audience might be carried along by the external affects produced by the work as a whole. In the worst cases what is at stake might be related to the struggle between the artistic affect and opinion. In "finding a character" a method actor might tap into a reservoir of emotions that are readily accessible; a kind of common knowledge. A familiar, easily recognizable emotion might be extracted and projected so that the audience do not sense the unfamiliar affect of the work but rather recognize the familiar emotion offered by the actor: they are thereby comforted in the belief they have grasped the "meaning" and the play fails to affect them in the least.

It is worth attempting to develop our understanding of affect more fully here. And in order to do this it is worth returning to Spinoza, in relation to whom Deleuze develops his own concept of affect. In Part 3 of Spinoza's *Ethics* an affect is defined as "the affections of the Body by which the Body's power of acting is increased or diminished, aided or restrained, and at the same time, the ideas of these affections" (Spinoza 1985:

Ethics, III, Definition 3, p. 493). In Part 2 of the *Ethics*, these affections are understood to involve our Body's perceptions of the contact it undergoes with other bodies (as for example when light strikes our eyes, a sound strikes our ear drums, something touches us, or when an image of another body occurs to us). An affect, then, is brought about through a causal chain. Just as bodies are caused by other bodies in a chain of cause and effect in Spinoza and, in parallel to this, ideas cause other ideas, so too affects (those sensations of our power increasing or decreasing which come about through the contact with other beings we encounter), develop lines of cause and effect.

One of the radical implications of Spinoza's model of causation, which extends causation into the human mind (and all other modes of the attribute of thought) as well as to all physical things (within the attribute of extension) is that it lays out a line of causation, as it were, on a surface. Spinoza himself is very clear about this idea and the implications of it. Everything is laid open to the laws of causation, the laws of nature, and this includes the human mind and what it thinks, and the human body and what it feels:

> Most of those who have written about the Affects, and men's way of living, seem to treat, not of natural things, which follow the common laws of nature, but of things which are outside nature. Indeed they seem to conceive man in nature as a dominion within a dominion . . . [Yet] nature is always the same, and its virtue and power of acting are always one and the same, i.e., the laws and rules of nature . . . The Affects, therefore, of hate, anger, envy, etc., considered in themselves, follow from the very same necessity and force of nature as the other singular things. (Spinoza 1985: *Ethics*, III, Preface, pp. 491–2)

An affect, then, in a sense similar to that applied to attributes, might be thought to be an expression, a modal expression, which, rather than coming from an inside and moving out, is both caused by what is external and becomes involved with the nature of the person through whom it is expressed (not as something which is simply "internal" to that person, but which, in effect, allows that person to perceive their self). We can see this more clearly if we turn again to Part 2, Proposition 16, where Spinoza explains how the affections we experience, the idea of being affected by something else (i.e. of coming into contact with something else) involves both the nature of our body and the body we touch. That is, the knowledge we have of anything else (the knowledge of the first kind, from the senses, for example) is really, and first and foremost, a knowledge of ourselves and how we have been affected: it does not give us a clear idea of the thing we perceive. Yet there is necessarily another way of seeing this: insofar as we do understand ourselves we can only understand ourselves

Composition as the Externalized Expression of Sensation 43

through the contact we make with other bodies. Our very thought, then, is determined from the outside.

Deleuze offers another way of understanding the same idea of exteriority through his reading of Leibniz. As has been touched upon above, a monad is distinguished from another monad by its perceptions and appetitions (Leibniz 1992b: p. 195).

What then, are some consequences of this for theater and in literature more generally? In Kleist, according to Deleuze, the self is an illusion created by the jumbling together of minute unrelated perceptions. And this confusion is primary, preceding the order that creates transcendent subjects. To quote Deleuze from *The Fold: Leibniz and the Baroque*:

> The prince of Hamburg, and all of Kleist's characters, are not so much Romantic as they are Baroque heroes. Prey to the giddiness of minute perceptions, they endlessly reach presence in illusion, in vanishment, in swooning, or by converting illusion into presence. . . The Baroque artists know well that hallucination does not feign presence, but that presence is hallucinatory. (1993: p. 125)

What is involved in such a state of affection? The affect of the work of art is unfamiliar: the kind of giddiness or uncertainty with which we are at first threatened is analogous to a kind of death. To quote Leibniz from "Monadology":

> But when there are a very great number of small perceptions with nothing to distinguish them, we are stupefied, just as it happens that if we go on turning round in the same direction several times running, we become giddy and go into a swoon, so that we can no longer distinguish anything at all. And death can throw animals into this state for a time. (1992a: p. 182)

For Deleuze art should affect rather than be comprehended, if comprehension means only recognizing the opinions that accompany the clear interpretations required of method actors, and the subjects they create, insofar as they only express themselves by showing the world commonplace, conflict-free emotions. Such emotions will in no way affect us, in no way modify our perceptions (which would involve, following Leibniz, the modification of our souls).

The automatic emotion kills the affect which such a work attempts to create: the audience fails to see beyond the familiar and so are unable to be astonished by affects which are unknown to them. The automatic emotion is safe, by definition it is not new, it is easily recognizable, whereas the unfamiliar and defamiliarizing affect is capable of taking the ground away.

44   Thinking in Literature

These are the kinds of affects Deleuze and Guattari describe in the work of Kleist, where

> feelings become uprooted from the interiority of "subject," to be projected violently outward into a milieu of pure exteriority that lends them an incredible velocity, a catapulting force: love or hate, they are no longer feelings but affects . . . Affects transpierce the body like arrows, they are weapons of war. The deterritorialization velocity of affect . . . This element of exteriority — which dominates everything, which Kleist invents in literature, which he is the first to invent — will give time a new rhythm: an endless succession of catatonic episodes or fainting spells, and flashes or rushes. Catatonia is: "This affect is too strong for me," and a flash is: "The power of this affect sweeps me away," so that the Self (Moi) is now nothing more than a character whose actions and emotions are desubjectified, perhaps even to the point of death. Such is Kleist's personal formula: a succession of flights of madness and catatonic freezes in which no subjective interiority remains. (Deleuze and Guattari 1987: p. 356)

In Kleist's *The Prince of Homburg* the eponymous character is swept away by a euphoric affect which drives him to an act of heroism, later, on being condemned to death for the disobedience that this heroism requires, he is lain low by an affect that reduces him to the most pathetic cowardice. In both cases the affect seems to come from outside: first it is caused by the battle which fills him with heroic affection and then it is caused by seeing the grave that has been newly dug for him, which suffuses him with the cowardly affection. Further, he is able to change from one role to the next in a trice in relation to the affect generated by an external situation. This is shown when a notion of fine behavior sweeps him up in an affect which would, if it were allowed to, lead him to martyrdom.

External Expression

An understanding of an "external" expression might help us to begin to judge what Beckett perceives in Kleist's "On the Marionette Theatre." In Kleist's story the narrator meets an old friend, a classical dancer, in a park and remarks that the friend seems to be spending a lot of time watching a low-brow puppet show. He wonders what attraction this could possibly have. The friend explains that some of the dance movements performed by the puppets have an extraordinary grace. Agreeing to this point, the narrator wonders why this might be, and the friend replies that this grace can be explained in mathematical terms. The puppet master does not need to control every aspect of the puppet because the movements themselves have a center of gravity, and the puppets are machines that allow a movement in a straight line to be translated in perfect ratio into a curved movement. Further, these curved movements turn about the true center of gravity: that is, they are in perfect harmony with the purely physical logic of the movement. The friend further suggests that the relationship between the movement of the puppeteer and the puppet can also be understood in mathematical terms; that is, in terms of ratios or proportions:

> [He said] ". . . there's a subtle relationship between the movements of his fingers and the movements of the puppets attached to them, something like the relationship between numbers and their logarithms or between asymptote and hyperbola." (Kleist 2003)

When asked to explain what benefits these puppets might have over human dancers, the friend indicates that the first advantage is a negative one: that it would never be guilty of self-consciousness.

Spinoza indicates that we fall into error when we confuse the manner in which causal relations proceed. This occurs when we make mistakes through the first kind of knowledge: we see some other body, for example, and think we understand it because we see it. Yet all that comes to us from that other body through our sight is an image of that other body. Furthermore, when we come into contact with that image, that image tells us more about our own selves than it does about that body itself. We fall into error, then, when we attempt to understand through an image of something. This is because an idea can only be understood through another idea; an idea cannot be understood through a body.

This notion might be seen to also be clearly exemplified in Kleist's story. The friend and the narrator continue their discussion and they begin to focus on the idea of self-consciousness. The narrator indicates that he understands very well how self-consciousness might "disturb natural grace." He then goes on to describe a young man he knows who possessed a wonderful natural grace, yet once he became conscious of that grace himself and tried to deliberately reproduce it, he simply lost the grace altogether. This happened because he saw himself in the mirror performing a graceful movement. This image of his own movement seemed to offer the first consciousness of his own grace: in Spinozian terms we could say that the image from the mirror is a body that impresses itself on the young man. The young man sees the grace, which is his own grace. He then attempts to reproduce it by repeating the movement in the mirror. This is an error because he is, in effect, attempting to understand the grace of the movement of his body through an image of that movement (what he has seen). He is then unable to reproduce that movement because he did not have any understanding of it before, and the image of the movement cannot give him access to a true understanding of the thing. We can consider this in another way. The young man is like an actor performing a part in a self-conscious manner: that is, creating his movements through imperfect understanding he falls back on clichés. On the other hand, the work which attempts to create an external expression requires an actor to lose all such self-consciousness, to allow the body, as it were, to follow its own logic without trying to impose an interpretation: to identify centers of gravity around which movements should naturally proceed. This relates closely to the importance of a lack of self-consciousness that, as will be discussed below, Virginia Woolf underlines as being crucial to the artistic process.

One might interpret the movement of the puppets and the young man when he was unselfconscious, and the bear who is the third example offered in the story, as examples of bodies which move in accord with the laws of nature which have made those bodies. There is an idea which corresponds to the idea of the body and the idea of the movement of the body, but this is not an idea of which any of these three are conscious. In order to fully understand this point, it is important to underline how Spinoza develops a distinction between the attribute of thought and consciousness. This idea, in turn, is central to the distinction I am seeking to underline here: rather than being limited to describing or representing consciousness (as, for example, in the "stream of consciousness") literature is capable of expressing thought.

In "On the Difference Between the Ethics and a Morality," Deleuze discusses the devaluation of consciousness (in favor of the attribute of thought) in Spinoza, in *Spinoza, Practical Philosophy* (Deleuze 1988: pp. 17–22). For Spinoza our consciousness itself is always based only on inadequate knowledge. We exist due to the interconnection of an infinity of causal relations: we can only sense at all, think (consciously) at all because of the incredibly complex interaction of these causes. But we are never really aware of these causes; rather, we only become aware, we only become conscious, in so far as we experience the effects of these causes. Our consciousness of what is real then, is partial and incomplete. We only ever get a mutilated view of the whole, a tiny incoherent fragment. What is truly real is what we are not conscious of: the true interrelationship of causes which allows us to experience effects. When Kleist indicates that the three examples involve a lack of self-consciousness, he allows us to understand how such an unselfconscious entity might develop a movement which is more elegant than that of a person who is consciously attempting to perform such a movement.

Drawing on Spinoza, Deleuze shows how there is a logic which is proper to bodies and this logic is pure when we attempt to simply perform movements in line with that innate logic. Spinoza also allows us to see how we cannot understand a body (which is in the attribute of extension) through an inadequate idea of that body (which is in the attribute of thought). Deleuze underlines this point in emphasizing Spinoza's insistence that "we don't even know what a body can do" (Deleuze 1988: pp. 17–18). In struggling to comprehend our bodies we develop a false or inadequate understanding of ourselves. This in turn is intuitively recognized by others and usually categorized as involving self-consciousness (when it in fact betrays an absence of genuine understanding). This further explains why, following Kleist, in order to return to an equilibrium through which our bodies and minds are perfectly in harmony, we would have to gain either perfect knowledge, or totally rid ourselves of knowledge. The puppet is more perfect because it has no consciousness: the unfallen Adam would also be perfect because he would understand his own body perfectly.

It is wrong, then, to speak of works (such as those developed by Woolf and Joyce) as involving a stream of consciousness. While consciousness might form a part of the subject of *Ulysses*, or *To The Lighthouse*, the works themselves offer analogues of thought as a whole, rather than representations of consciousness. So too, even though kinds of first person narratives are developed by writers, such as Nabokov, these rarely involve the simple representation of a single consciousness. Nabokov, in *Despair*, *Pale Fire*, and *Lolita*, for example, creates minds in dialogue with other "possible worlds" (including those within the self). In each case the multiplicity involved in the possible worlds are organized or composed into a univocal expression. Though we seem to have a single first-person narrator in *Despair*, or shifting possible worlds in *To The Lighthouse* and *Ulysses*, we realize as we look more closely that in fact we have works which are drawing elements of heteroglossia into univocal expression.

We have seen, then, how an understanding of thought in literature moves around three main terms: relation, sensation, and composition. Three terms which imply their own interconnection and the very idea of interconnectedness itself. In the chapters that follow, all three elements will come into play, though different elements will be emphasized at different times: relation in Joyce, sensation in Woolf, and composition in Nabokov.

Part II   Thinking in Modernist Fiction

This part includes three chapters related to three major novelists from the Modernist era. In each case, elements of the theoretical overview developed in Part I will be considered in relation to aesthetic ideas produced by these writers (both in their fiction and in their extra-fictional pronouncements). In this way I hope to show, rather than simply explain, how thinking can take place in literature. While the theoretical overview presented above clearly resonates and corresponds with the ideas set out in the following chapters, the former offers a general overview while the latter concerns particular aesthetic practices. The chapters focus on the three central terms identified above: relation, sensation, and composition. The overview I have developed argues that these three tendencies are crucial to thinking in literature. While each artist considered here makes use of all three elements, which in turn are all interrelated, each offers particular understandings of their nature, and particular points of emphasis.

Joyce, I argue, offers important insight into the nature of relation in fiction. Woolf is deeply concerned with sensation, and the translation of sensation from life to art, and between mediums of representation. Nabokov, as much as any writer in the modern era, brings composition to the fore in his work, and here I will consider *Despair*, a novel he described as exemplifying "the methods of composition." [1]

---

1   The narrator of Nabokov's *The Real Life of Sebastian Knight* describes Knight's novel *The Prismatic Bezel* in this way. I argue in Chapter 6, that this fictitious novel can be identified with Nabokov's own work, *Despair*.

4 James Joyce: the Art of Relation

Thought is the thought of thought.

(Joyce, *Ulysses* 2.74)[1]

Samuel Beckett's relationship with James Joyce is well documented: he wrote a well-known essay on Joyce's "Work in Progress" (his first critical publication) in 1929. Beckett had not really contemplated a career as a writer when he first met Joyce in Paris in 1928 when Joyce was 46 and Beckett was 22 (Knowlson and Knowlson 2007: p. 47). While Beckett had an equivocal relation with Joyce and his powerful presence, it is not going too far to suggest that Joyce was a father-figure to Beckett. Joycean style swamps then drowns Beckett's first novel *Dream of Fair to Middling Women*. Beckett struggled to find his own way, to somehow escape this powerful influence, and he managed this, in the end, by inverting Joyce, or moving in a direction diametrically opposed to him, something which he himself recognized, in agreeing with Maurice Nadeau's contention that Joyce was an influence *"ab contrario"* (2007: p. 47).

Many themes familiar from Joyce's fiction come to mind when these points are made: the relation between the father and son involving both identification and difference; the son's need to estrange himself from the father; the central (for Joyce) question of fidelity and infidelity, with jealously inextricably intertwined with love. The connections might be dismissed as glib if their implications had not been so profound for Beckett's work.

In letters he wrote to Georges Duthuit outlining some of his aesthetic ideas Beckett speaks of an art of "nonrelation."[2] While he does not explicitly contrast this with Joyce and his need to break away from Joyce (as he does in his comments to Driver and Shenker) it is apparent that this

---

1 References to *Ulysses* refer to Hans Gabler's edition and, as is now customary in Joyce Studies, cite the number of the episode from *Ulysses*, followed by the line numbers.
2 I have written at length of the many other influences that helped Beckett to develop his particular aesthetic, which he seemed to dimly see if not fully understand well before his post-war revelation. See *Beckett and Poststructuralism* (Uhlmann 1999) and *Samuel Beckett and the Philosophical Image* (Uhlmann 2006).

aesthetic ideal is one that also might be thought to invert Joyce's aesthetic. So, if important light might be shed on Beckett's works when considered in regard to this theory of non-relation, could new light be shed on Joyce's work by considering them in terms of "relation"?

What might be involved in such an aesthetic of relation, and how might it be thought to be formulated? Here I will attempt to establish five things that concern such an aesthetic of relation in Joyce.

First, I will examine the notion of "essence" in Joyce, which I tie to his interest in Spinoza. Second, I will further develop this reading of Joyce's interest in Spinoza in considering elements of Joyce's aesthetic method. While the aesthetic ideas expressed by Joyce in his early critical essays, and those expressed by Stephen Dedalus in *Stephen Hero* and *A Portrait of the Artist as a Young Man* have been long connected and even identified with Joyce's own works, less attention has been paid to an apparent shift in Joyce's aesthetic interests which took place between the writing of *A Portrait of the Artist as a Young Man* and *Ulysses*.[3] In his only play, *Exiles*, Joyce begins to further develop an already strong interest in relation and the nature of relationships, something which he now focuses upon and begins to formulate in part through an engagement with Spinoza and the idea of jealously. Jealousy is a privileged emotion for Joyce because it involves powerful and dynamic processes of oscillation between Spinoza's primary emotions of love and hate. In turn, the interaction of these emotions within relationships can be tied both to a theory of human interaction and a theory of artistic production.

Third, I will argue that rather than simply comprising a intellectual *tour de force*, which even Stephen Dedalus himself concedes has no truth value, the theory of identity and difference in the art and life of the artist, which Stephen outlines in "Scylla and Charybdis," might be read as offering an aesthetic theory of relationships which has powerful consequences and which might be felt to be reflected in the design of *Ulysses*.[4] Recently, McLaren has outlined the danger in reading the aesthetic theories Stephen Dedalus develops prior to *Ulysses* in an overly ironic way (a tendency which, he argues, has become dominant in the field). That is, while there is much irony in the novel, the work is not purely ironic: indeed we are more or less required to measure the aesthetic ideas Stephen Dedalus expresses against the work we read. A reading that simply emphasizes irony, then,

---

3 A number of important studies have focused on Joyce's aesthetic method as it developed through his early works up until *A Portrait of the Artist as a Young Man*. (See Aubert 1992; Gillespie 1989; Handler 1956; Riquelme 1983, 2004; Manganiello 1993; Mamigonian and Turner 2003; McLaren 2005, Slote 2002.)
4 Important studies have been written relating to Joyce's compositional methods in *Ulysses*, yet these do not touch on the ideas I will develop in this chapter. See, for example, Gibson (2002), Litz (1961), Groden (1977), and Scott (1984).

is inadequate, and, in drawing upon the evidence of the actual aesthetic design of the work, we need to attempt to gauge which claims might be felt to carry weight and which might not.

Strangely, however, with regard to "Scylla and Charybdis," rather than critics being tempted to read what are possibly serious comments in an ironic manner, problems occur because, on the contrary, readers are tempted to take Stephen Dedalus's comment that he does not *believe* his own theory too seriously (therefore hiding its real significance). I will argue below that this theory, which is, precisely, a theory of relation, is indeed important to our understanding of the novel and Joyce's aesthetic method.

Fourth, two aspects of the relationship between Homer's *Odyssey* and Joyce's *Ulysses* might be more fully examined than they have been to date. On the one hand the thematically central concerns of the *Odyssey* (the importance of hospitality and the sins of failing in hospitality; the emblems of the unstable oscillation of the stranger and the friend; the conception of the self which is related to names and appearance through the opposing ideas of identity and disguise) involve relational systems that describe a world view and a poetic logic, which are, in turn, drawn into relationship with the central concerns of *Ulysses*. On the other hand I will argue that the idea of "parallax," which haunts Bloom throughout *Ulysses*, might be systematically applied to an understanding of the relationship between the *Odyssey* and *Ulysses*.

Finally, I will argue that the importance of all of these notions of relationship and relation might be more clearly understood when drawn into contact with the logic of relation Spinoza develops in his *Ethics*. That is, all of the points to be made in this section deepen our understanding of how the concepts of relation, ratio or reason and thinking are interlinked, and crucial to the potential of art as a mode of thinking. As this concerns each of the other questions I will begin with a discussion of the importance of Spinoza to *Ulysses*.

Joyce and Spinoza

Little has been written relating Joyce to Spinoza, though his interest in this philosopher has long been known. In 1977, John Henry Raleigh sketched a connection between the central protagonist of *Ulysses*, Leopold Bloom, and Spinoza in which he suggested that Spinoza might be understood as a third archetype for Bloom (after Odysseus and Robinson Crusoe). Here, Raleigh outlines most of the evidence for Joyce's knowledge of Spinoza:

> That Joyce himself was acquainted with Spinoza from fairly early on in his career seems indubitable. In 1903 he mentioned him twice in a review of J. Lewis McIntyre's *Giordano Bruno*. Also in 1903 Joyce met Synge in Paris, and the two argued about art. Synge finally

told Joyce, who was at this time forging his ironclad esthetic in Aristotelian or Thomistic terms, that he had a mind like Spinoza, a remark that Joyce passed on, presumably with some pride, to his mother and brother. (Raleigh 1977: p. 585)

Raleigh goes on to point out Bloom's strong interest in Spinoza, who was also a favorite philosopher of his father Rudy, who left him the book *Thoughts from Spinoza* that sits on Bloom's bookshelf. Yet Raleigh seems unaware of a further reference that Joyce makes to Spinoza, in his notes to *Exiles* (which are included in Joyce 1973).[5] Joyce made these notes while writing the play in 1913 and they were first published with the Penguin edition in 1952 (see Colum 1973). Here Joyce outlines an interest in Spinoza's understanding of jealousy, alongside that developed by Shakespeare, judging both understandings inadequate:

> As a contribution to the study of jealousy Shakespeare's *Othello* is incomplete. It and Spinoza's analysis are made from the sensationalist standpoint — Spinoza speaks of *pudendis et excrementis alterius jungere imaginem rei amatae*. (Joyce 1973: p. 148)

I will consider Joyce's discussion of jealousy in his notes to *Exiles* more fully below; here I am interested in the light these comments shed on Joyce's knowledge of Spinoza. It should be noted that Joyce is not only quoting Spinoza in the original Latin here (and, moreover, quoting a passage which is rarely cited, thus indicating that it is a passage Joyce discovered through his own reading), but he is transposing elements of the sentence he quotes (I will cite the full passage and indicate the element of transposition below). This suggests that Joyce was quoting from memory rather than referring to a book that he had immediately in front of him. While circumstantial, this is strong evidence Joyce had a good knowledge of Spinoza's *Ethics*.

As I have outlined in the previous chapter, Spinoza offers a detailed definition of thinking that is centered on the idea of relation or ratio.

---

5 Since Raleigh the most sustained attempt to draw aspects of Joyce's works into relation with the ideas of Spinoza is a recent essay by Elizabeth S. Anker (2007). This links ideas of unknowability to aspects of Spinoza through a reading of the "Ithaca" episode of *Ulysses*. Anker also relates Bloom to the figure of the prophet described in Spinoza's *Theologico-Political Treatise*. Recently, interesting passing references have been made to Spinoza without being explored in detail (see Brown 2006: p. 18; and Fordham 2006: pp. 93–4). Mia McIver (2008) delivered a (as yet unpublished) paper linking Spinoza and Joyce through the concept of Legal Fiction whose outlines she traces in Spinoza's *Theologico-Political Treatise* at the XXIst International Joyce Symposium, June 15–20, 2008, at Tours, France. None of these works attempts to engage with Joyce's use of Spinoza's *Ethics* in *Exiles*.

Thought itself involves, or *is*, the relation between elements; the ratios which measure and identify things as networks of relations. As we have seen, the word "ratio" literally means "to think," and so relates to the mind, and yet a given essence is understood as a certain ratio of speeds and slowness, and so relates to the body. Understood as working in parallel by Spinoza, both the mind or thinking, and bodies have logics that inhere through these ratios or networks of relations. Further, for Spinoza it is our essence that can become eternal, our essence, then, (which others might have called the "soul") is a system of relations within the self. Indeed, the whole of the *Ethics* is built upon this logic of relations understood not simply as involving the relations of self within self, but the relationships of all things (see Spinoza 1985: *Ethics*, II, Lemmas 1–7, pp. 458–62; II, P40, p. 478; and IV, P39, p. 568).

To offer a rough summary: all interrelations, for Spinoza, necessarily involve relationships of love and hate. In effect, relationships of love draw bodies together into larger bodies (a process which increases one's power as the greater the body the more powerful the body). There is a logic of accumulation through relationship: a husband and wife, for example, might be understood as forming one, more powerful, body as they enter into relationship through marriage. So too, a nation might be understood as comprising a single body (see Spinoza 1985: *Ethics*, II, Lemma 7, p. 462). This logic might be extended to infinity, so that everything that exists might be thought to comprise one single body. On the other hand relationships of hatred sunder bodies, drawing them apart from one another and decreasing their power.

There are two aspects of this intellectual system, then, which I feel are of particular importance to a reading of Joyce's work. First, the conception of essence Spinoza develops and the manner in which he relates this to the soul. While this identification of essence and soul is not something that might be found only in Spinoza's work, it is an extremely important aspect of that work, as one of the more difficult problems with the interpretation of Spinoza's *Ethics* involves understanding his notion of eternity. That is, while our true essence is eternal for Spinoza, it is not certain that everyone will achieve or realize this essence. Our essence, then, seems to be potential: we must strive to realize or reach this potential and it is only in achieving this that we express our power to the fullest and become "eternal." Achieving our potential, however, is very difficult.

Spinoza's Essence

It is worth working through some of Spinoza's understandings both of the concept of relation or ratio and of the processes involved in achieving one's essence in order to fully understand the implications of this point for Joyce. In Part II, Proposition 7, Spinoza identifies our essence with our "conatus" or striving to continue to exist:

56 Thinking in Literature

> P7: *The striving by which each thing strives to persevere in its being is nothing but the actual essence of the thing.*
> Demonstration: From the given essence of each thing some things necessarily follow (by Part I, P36), and things are able [to produce] nothing but what follows necessarily from their determinate nature [. . .] So the power of each thing [. . .] is nothing but the given, *or* actual, essence of the thing itself. (Spinoza 1985: *Ethics*, II, P7, p. 499)

He develops this idea more fully in the scholium to Proposition 9 that follows:

> When this striving is related only to the Mind, it is called Will; but when it is related to the Mind and Body together, it is called Appetite. This Appetite, therefore, is nothing but the very essence of man, from whose nature there necessarily follow those things that promote his preservation . . . desire can be defined as appetite together with consciousness of the appetite. (Spinoza 1985: *Ethics*, II, P9, p. 500)

Essence, therefore, is now linked to Spinoza's concept of "desire" (as that which leads to one's continuing to exist). One can see how easily such an idea might be misunderstood by Spinoza's critics, especially when Spinoza goes still further in developing this chain of states of being (essence = conatus = power = will = appetite = desire) to include "virtue":

> By virtue and power I understand the same thing, i.e. (by Part 3, Prop 7), virtue, insofar as it is related to man, is the very essence, *or* nature, of man, insofar as he has the power of bringing about certain things, which can be understood through the laws of nature alone. (Spinoza 1985: *Ethics*, IV, Definition 8, p. 547)

That is, one can see how this might lead certain critics to question the moral justification of this position, which might be misread as affirming all of what we commonly call desires as good. This, however, would involve a fundamental misreading of Spinoza's system and his understanding of desire. Desire is, for Spinoza, "man's very essence" (Spinoza 1985: *Ethics*, III, Definitions of the Affects I, p. 531) but it is apparent that he does not suggest that this essence is immediately realized or that everything we do or are compelled to do involves the true desire which affirms our essence; rather, some of the things which affect us (even many of those which we seem to want), affect us in a negative way. When we are affected in a negative way, our power decreases and therefore, (as power = essence), we become less perfect; that is, we move away from our true essence. True desire is only that which involves the preservation of our own being. When we seem to want or are compelled to want (through addiction, say, or compelled reflex, or the overbearing influence of something other to us) something which takes us away from our true selves we are not acting on our desire; rather, we are passively following the desire of another body which has the potential to overcome or even destroy us. A drug addict, then, might, following this logic, completely move away from his or her real essence: that essence might even be destroyed or effaced as the former essence or desire is replaced by a second desire, the desire of self joined to an addictive agent, to persist in its being (that is, the drug addict becomes the addiction which displaces the essence which inhabited the being prior to the addiction).

Spinoza sets out the manner in which we can move from greater to lesser power and vice versa in Part III, which considers the "Origin and Nature of the Affects" (the sensations and emotions which affect us passively and actively). Midway through this Part he sets out a series of "Definitions of the Affects." When we move to greater power, we move closer to perfection: that is, we move closer to our true essence. We experience this positive change as an emotion — Joy: "Joy is a man's passage from a lesser to a greater perfection" (Spinoza 1985: *Ethics*, III, Definitions of the Affects II, p. 531). When we become less powerful, that is, when we move away from our true essence (allowing other powers to take over or efface our essence) we become less perfect, and we experience this negative change as an emotion — Sadness: "Sadness is man's passage from a greater to a lesser perfection" (Spinoza 1985: *Ethics*, III, Definitions of the Affects III, p. 531). Spinoza then links these primary emotions to a logic of relations (or relationships). "Love is a Joy, accompanied by the idea of an external cause" (Spinoza 1985: *Ethics*, III, Definitions of the Affects, Def. VI, p. 533). Opposed to this, "Hate is a Sadness, accompanied by the idea of an external cause" (Spinoza 1985: *Ethics*, III, Definitions of the Affects VII, p. 533). There, are, broadly speaking then, two kinds of affect: on the one hand there are *active* affects, which increase our power and our perfection by drawing us more closely to our essence; on the other hand there are passive affects, which decrease our power and our perfection and move us away from our essence. To put this another way, when your perfection increases the greater part of you corresponds to your true essence, whereas when your perfection decreases the greater part of you corresponds to something else which does not agree with your essence, something else which is not your essence, some parasitic being which is driving your own true being out.

Spinoza adds another link to our chain of essence by linking it to understanding, "because the Mind's essence, i.e. power consists only in thought" (Spinoza 1985: *Ethics*, V, P9, Dem., p. 601). Insofar as we adequately understand (something, our own nature, any or all things and how they go together) we increase our power. Insofar as we are unable to understand (unable, in Spinoza's terms, even to think at all) our power decreases: "Affects which are contrary to our nature, i.e . . . which are evil, are evil insofar as they prevent the Mind from understanding" (p. 601). As the power of the body consists in action, one assumes that true action involves acting in accordance with one's nature, to increase one's power, to realize one's essence (though in Part V Spinoza does not treat this question). To recapitulate the identified terms: essence = conatus = power = will = appetite = desire = understanding = acting in accordance with one's nature.

A second, though hardly secondary, process is not brought to light (or rather, glimpsed somewhat darkly, as this is a part of Spinoza's system, which many readers have found extremely obscure): that through which the essence might be expressed eternally. As I mention in the previous paragraph, in Part V of his *Ethics* "Of the Power of the Intellect, or of Human Freedom," Spinoza turns from an understanding of essence related to the Body to a consideration of essence specifically from the perspective of Mind (although Spinoza also stresses the importance of the capacity of the body, as having a body which can do a great many things involves having a mind which can actively understand, Spinoza 1985: *Ethics*, V, P39, p. 614). Yet the bodily essence of any thing is mortal: our Body, which involves a certain ratio of speeds and slowness, no longer exists when we die. This is not true of our Mind, however, or at least it does not have to be true of our Mind. We have seen that we can pass to greater or lesser perfection. It now becomes apparent that it is only the most "perfect" part of our Minds that is eternal: "our Mind, insofar as it understands, is an eternal mode of thinking" (Spinoza 1985: *Ethics*, V, P40, p. 615). It further becomes apparent that, insofar as we fail to achieve perfection we also fail to express our essence, and that insofar as we fail to express our essence, we pass away forever at death. The ignorant person is one who fails to achieve any understanding: such a person has, in effect, no remaining essence; they have, to put it another way, no soul. Such a person only exists in a passive way, only insofar as other beings act upon them. Nothing of them remains after death, because there is nothing positive, no joy, in their being. They do not act, they are only acted upon: that is, they are not free.

> For not only is the ignorant man troubled in many ways by external causes, and unable ever to possess true peace of mind, but he also lives as if he knew neither himself, nor God, nor things; and as soon as he ceases to be acted on, he ceases to be. (Spinoza 1985: *Ethics*, V, P42, p. 616)

We have to achieve our soul, then, and we do this by seeking wisdom, by understanding ourselves, God or Nature, and the modes or things that exist within Nature. Unlike the ignorant man, the wise man does not cease to be after death:

> The wise man, insofar as he is considered as such, is hardly troubled in spirit, but being, by a certain eternal necessity, conscious of himself, and of God, and of things, he never ceases to be, but always possesses true peace of mind. (Spinoza 1985: *Ethics*, V, P42, p. 617)

Spinoza stresses that becoming wise in this sense is not easy: that it is only found "rarely," finishing his Ethics with the famous sentence: "But all things excellent are as difficult as they are rare" (Spinoza 1985: *Ethics*, V, P42, p. 617).

Joyce and Essence

The understanding of essence developed by Spinoza, which has been outlined here, is of interest both to a reading of certain elements of Joyce's aesthetic method and to a reading of aspects of his works. Bloom follows Spinoza in considering that the soul is something which has to be won,[6] won through Love,[7] which is active and increases one's power in avoiding hatred and the sadness of powerlessness this brings with it. One might contrast Bloom, whom Joyce considered to be passing into eternity at the book's end (Ellmann 1983: 501), with Blazes Boylan, who Molly tells us does not believe in the soul, and who, in such a state of ignorance, indeed does not possess a soul (18.142) (just as Joyce indicates in his notes that Robert Hand, unlike Richard Rowan, does not believe in the existence of "spiritual facts," *Exiles*, 1973: p. 150).

Yet a strong interest in essence might be traced throughout all of Joyce's works. Many of the stories from *Dubliners* seem to take as their theme the process of turning away from one's true self, occluding or betraying one's essence. There are a number of stories in which we see the essences of characters being left unrealized, held back. At times this occurs because of social conventions and the timidity or lack of power they engender. Indeed elements of every story in the collection might be related to the problem of essence or soul and the obstacles to freedom that present themselves. Furthermore, these problems are often seen to stem from interrelations with others. There is the danger of being shaped by others and diverted from your own essence through encounters with them, something that is played out in different ways in "The Sisters," "An Encounter" and "After

---

6 Bloom's father Rudolph accosts him as he enters Nighttown: "What you making down this place? Have you no soul?" (15.259).
7 See the famous discussion of "love" in the Cyclops episode (12.1485). See also Ellmann (1984, 1986); and the discussion of the "word known to all men" [love]: see (3.435; 9.429–31; 15.4191).

the Race." There is a horror of interactions where the self is perverted by the felt need to distort its true image in self-aggrandizements which are fabricated precisely to meet the approval of groups, groups which, in the end, have no real love for the ones who distort themselves to gain their favor. We see this in "Two Gallants," "Counterparts," and "A Painful Case" (where again the possibility of real love is refused for the sake of convention, this time "intellectual" rather than social).

There is a thematic coherence which draws *Dubliners* together around the temptations, which result in the death of the soul: these are, broadly speaking, temptations of self-deceit; temptations that arise from the fact that communities are capable of generating false images of nobility. Mediocrity becomes a virtue or even a cure for the sense of soul-death which one might feel: this is clear in "Ivy Day in the Committee Room" where the powerful soul of Parnell is contrasted with the tired habits of those who follow.

While this is an idea that still haunts "Grace" and "The Dead," both of these stories show the community and the power of the community in a somewhat more positive light. "Grace" sets out the manner in which a group might reach out to help a friend on the way to oblivion. Yet there is the sense that the salvation from the absolute death of the soul, the salvation of following the flock and moving as one with them, might involve resigning oneself to the reduction of the self to mediocrity.[8] In "The Dead" these themes are treated with greater subtlety. Gabriel is tempted by what seem reasonably harmless vanities: he has sufficient depth and sufficient soul to avoid the pitfalls that entrap others in the story: the temptation to drunkenness that holds Freddy Malins; the temptation to monomaniacal nationalism that holds Miss Ivors; the temptation to self-aggrandizement that holds Mr Browne and Bartel D'Arcy. Yet, perhaps because of his subtlety of soul Gabriel is tormented by the failure of the idea of self that he has carefully nurtured, an idea that involves, at its center, the passionate love for his wife Gretta. He pictures this love to himself as total and all-affirming. It is the source of the joy that he projects so effectively in the company of others and which turns him into the man who can be depended on. Yet "The Dead" recounts the death of this image of self, which Gabriel has so carefully fabricated, when he comes to believe that there is another, the dead lover Michael Furey, whom Gretta has loved more passionately, with her soul rather than her body, and who has, in turn, loved his wife more passionately than Gabriel might ever do. Yet rather than the story ending with the feeling of the death of the soul, which dominates so many of the other stories in this collection, the blow Gabriel

---

8 Mediocrity in life is linked to obviousness in art: in *Stephen Hero*, Stephen speaks of "the hell of hells" as "the region ... wherein everything is found to be obvious" (Joyce 1963: p. 33).

receives opens the way to understanding. That is, rather than ultimately suffering from a powerlessness which reduces his essence, Gabriel only loses certain of the self-deceptions that have hindered him from achieving a better understanding of his own self, his wife, his countrymen, and all things. The measure of his essence is increased rather than reduced: despite the shock he has received he is drawn together with others rather than sundered from them. He is affected positively:

> Generous tears filled Gabriel's eyes. He had never felt like that himself towards any woman but he knew that such a feeling must be love. The tears gathered more thickly in his eyes and in the partial darkness he imagined he saw the form of a young man standing under a dripping tree. Other forms were near. His soul had approached that region where dwell the vast hosts of the dead. He was conscious of, but could not apprehend, their wayward and flickering existence. His own identity was fading out into a grey impalpable world: the solid world itself which these dead had one time reared and lived in was dissolving and dwindling ... His soul swooned slowly as he heard the snow falling faintly through the universe and faintly falling, like the descent of their last end, upon the living and the dead. (Joyce 1976: pp. 223–4)

The soul and its growth, is of course, the major theme of *A Portrait as an Artist as a Young Man*, yet I will not attempt to draw this out here (see Ellmann 1983: p. 145). There is some evidence that might suggest that Spinoza was in his mind and was influencing his ideas even by 1903 when he spoke with Synge. In his "Paris Notebook," following on from a discussion that makes a distinction between the kinetic and static developed in *A Portrait*, Joyce sets out his definition of comedy:

> An improper art aims at exciting in the way of comedy the feeling of desire but the feeling which is proper to comic art is the feeling of joy. Desire ... is the feeling which urges us to go to something but joy is the feeling which the possession of some good excites in us. (Joyce 2008: p. 102)

In a note to this passage Kevin Barry points out that this "diverges entirely from Aristotle's brief definition of comedy as 'an imitation of persons worse than the average'" (Joyce 2008: p. 312). We have seen how important the emotion of "joy" is to Spinoza and how it corresponds with the idea Joyce develops. For Spinoza, insofar as we understand we move from a lesser to a greater perfection and this grasping or possession of understanding produces the feeling of "joy."

Exiles and Spinoza

In his notes to *Exiles*, Joyce pays attention to Spinoza's definition of the emotion or sensation of jealousy, which is described in Part III of the *Ethics* ("Concerning the Affects"). While this is not a primary term for Spinoza, it is for Joyce.

It might be argued that Joyce takes a strong interest in jealousy because of the complexity of the relationships of love and hatred which it involves, especially if (as is the case in *Exiles*) the third party in the love triangle, Robert, who acts between the husband, Richard, and wife, Bertha, is not only potentially a lover to Bertha but already a friend of long standing to Richard. While this love triangle is the dominant element of the play, it is apparent that, at least with regard to the structure of interactions within it, the play does not simply involve a standard love triangle. The situation is complicated by Beatrice and Richard who have some feelings for one another. A second triangle, which includes Beatrice, Richard, and Bertha, then, emerges to balance the first. One might argue that this is not as fully developed as the principal triangle, and might be better thought of in terms of a sub-plot, which echoes the main action. This process of echoing might be traced still further, in still other relations. Joyce suggests in his notes to *Exiles* that "A faint glimmer of lesbianism irradiates [Bertha's] mind" (Joyce 1973: p. 156), and it is possible to imagine this idea being developed when Beatrice and Bertha enter into dialogue in Act 3. This in turn would mirror the attraction and repulsion that takes place between Richard and Robert, which Joyce also outlines in his notes:

> The bodily possession of Bertha by Robert, repeated often, would certainly bring into almost carnal contact the two men. Do they desire this? To be united, that is carnally through the person and body of Bertha as they cannot, without dissatisfaction and degradation — be united carnally man to man as man to woman? (1973: p. 157)

Further echoes of jealous bonds can be found in the reaction of Richard and Robert to Richard's son Archie. Robert wishes for a son and feels that Richard takes his own son for granted. Even Richard's relationship with his old servant Brigid carries with it the taste of jealousies: she tells Bertha in Act 3 that Richard used to tell her about his feelings for Bertha and that he would much rather share his intellectual lights with a simple woman such as her than with any "grand highup person" (Joyce 1973: pp. 116–17).

While *Exiles* has, uniquely within Joyce's oeuvre, largely been passed over by critics, it is clear that it involves a structural complexity that opens the way to the still more complex interactions of *Ulysses*. Joyce develops a meditation on relations and relationships that allows him to consider not only key elements of the nature of interactions between people, but the interactions of soul and body. In doing this he justifies Synge's contention that, with regard to his aesthetic method, he has "a mind like Spinoza's."

In Part III of his *Ethics*, where Spinoza treats the "affects," he states that while people have fallen into the habit of thinking of our minds as completely separate domains from the world of things, the workings of our minds are just as much a part of nature as anything else. Our feelings and sensations are causally determined: that is, every emotion might be understood as a mixture of simpler emotions, the three primitive or primary affects being Joy, Sadness, and Desire (Spinoza 1985: *Ethics*, III, P11, Schol., pp. 500–1). In turn these affects are connected with ideas of things outside us, thereby building up attractions and repulsions: love is the affect of joy accompanied by the idea of an exterior cause (the loved one); hate is the affect of sadness accompanied by the idea of an exterior cause (the hated one). From here Spinoza is able to treat affects in a geometrical manner: they arise through cause and effect.

As with Spinoza, there is a mathematical interest in causal interactions at an emotional level in *Exiles*. This is apparent at least in the intentions which are outlined in Joyce's notes, which begin with a distinction between soul and body: Richard, "an automystic," is aligned with the soul while Robert, "an automobile," is aligned with the body (Joyce 1973: p. 148). Joyce then goes on to consider the soul to be like the body in that it too "may have a virginity" (1973: p. 148). As with the body this virginity is lost through an act of love. This loss in turn is something of a danger: because virginity (and the power of the affect which occludes it) can never be reclaimed, a malaise is likely to set in, "a lack of spiritual energy" (p. 148). Joyce, unlike Spinoza, is an artist, and as an artist he desires not only "freedom," as we see in *Dubliners* and again in *A Portrait* and yet again in *Exiles*, but also emotional intensity. While the Stoic philosopher (whom Spinoza at times resembles) might desire apathy, something which caused Nietzsche to jeer at Spinoza (although Nietzsche had to admit that Spinoza was perhaps the only real precursor to his own work) for desiring no-more-laughing, no-more-weeping (Nietzsche 2003: p. 119), this deadening of the senses is anathema to Joyce.

The question, then, is how might this malaise be checked, how might it be overcome. Joyce's response is to emphasize the importance of jealousy. It is worth noting that in emphasizing jealousy, Joyce, as we have seen, turns to Shakespeare and to Spinoza. He does not praise the views of either (on the contrary), but it is apparent that in taking issue with them he is, in a sense, developing his ideas *through* them.

As a contribution to the study of jealousy Shakespeare's *Othello* is incomplete. It and Spinoza's analysis are made from the sensationalist standpoint — Spinoza speaks of *pudendis et excrementis alterius jungere imaginem rei amatae*.[9] (Joyce 1973: p. 148)

In *Ulysses*, Joyce via Stephen draws on Shakespeare's *Hamlet* in developing his own aesthetic theory, one which completes the project of Shakespeare in some sense by rendering more precise elements which were not fully drawn together in Shakespeare's work (at least in theory). *Othello* is also an apparent presence in *Ulysses*: the theme of cuckoldry is central to both. It is as if Joyce here is completing the study of jealousy, which was taken to a certain point by Shakespeare, through the method of affective causation Joyce finds in Spinoza. Yet Joyce is not happy with the conclusions Spinoza draws: he has only calculated from a certain standpoint, which Joyce dubs "sensationalist." This standpoint, like that developed by Shakespeare in *Othello*, emphasizes two things: first, the primary role of hate in jealousy; and second, the manner in which jealousy divides people (and so it is understood as a negative relation that occurs within an individual). Joyce, on the contrary, first wishes to put aside the idea that hatred is central to jealousy. Although, in the subtle schema he devises, it is still present, it is not dominant; rather, jealousy involves a mixture of love and hate. Second, he wishes to understand jealousy as a complex that joins people together and is experienced collectively (though not without a collective confusion). Joyce, indeed, recognizes this confusion within the processes he describes and seeks to account for them, at a theoretical level at least, by aligning himself with the (no doubt theoretically problematic) tradition of "Celtic" philosophers — Hume, Berkeley, Balfour, Bergson — which he posits as "inclined towards incertitude or skepticism" (Joyce 1973: p. 159).

We can see the importance of hatred and division to Spinoza's definition of jealousy:

> If someone imagines that a thing he loves is united with another by close, or by a closer, bond of Friendship than that with which he himself, alone, possessed the thing, he will be affected with Hate towards the thing he loves, and will envy the other. (Spinoza 1985: *Ethics*, III, P35, p. 514)

In the scholium to this proposition Spinoza states that "This Hatred toward a thing we love, combined with Envy, is called Jealousy, which is therefore nothing but *a vacillation of mind born of Love and Hate together,*

---

9 Joyce transposes elements from Spinoza's original here (though this does not alter the sense). The original reads: "*rei amatae imaginem pudendis et excrementis, alterius jungere cogitur*" (Spinoza 1914: *Ethica*, III, P35). A translation of the passage is offered on p. 65.

accompanied by the idea of another who is envied (italics in original: III, P35, p. 514). Joyce does not cite this definition, the latter part of which, I would suggest, is closely aligned with the relationships we see in *Exiles*: that is, we do witness a "vacillation of mind" throughout in all the principle characters. The element of Spinoza's discussion that Joyce chooses to emphasize comes in the final paragraph of the scholium where the slightly misquoted passage appears:

> ... he who imagines that a woman he loves prostitutes herself to another not only will be saddened, because his own appetite is restrained, but also will be repelled by her, because he is forced *to join the image of the thing he loves to the shameful parts and excretions of the other*. [I have italicized the section here that corresponds with the passage quoted by Joyce on p. 64.] (Spinoza 1985: *Ethics*, III, P35, p. 514)

It is this phrase that Joyce considers "sensationalist." His own understanding of the emotion is far different. He claims that his character Bertha "has considered the passion in itself — apart from hatred or baffled lust"; that is, she has understood jealousy in its pure form. Joyce implies that Spinoza's definition here entangles the emotion too much with hatred and lust and hints that he will disentangle it in *Exiles*. While the core notion of vacillation remains (between love and hatred) the idea of jealousy differs significantly in Joyce because it is seen from a radically different angle. It is not seen as a passive outcome of events outside our power (a chain of sad passions linked in cause and effect, which inevitably lead to a reduction of power, a sadness, in whoever is affected by it); rather, it is now seen as an emotion that might be used as an instrument, performing a function which Joyce describes in *Stephen Hero*, returning to his interest in scholasticism, as a *bonum arduum*: a "difficult good"(Joyce 1963: p. 162).

Against Spinoza, then, Joyce posits the idea that a negative affect might be applied or used to generate a positive outcome. Here jealousy is thought to be a primary state, because it is something that can stimulate regeneration: it recreates that which had been lost when spiritual virginity was lost — the burning affect of intense love felt when one first possessed the object of love. Joyce outlines this as follows:

> Separated from hatred and having its baffled lust converted into an erotic stimulus and moreover holding in its own power the hindrance, the difficulty which has excited it, it must reveal itself as the very immolation of the pleasure of possession on the altar of love. (Joyce 1973: pp. 148–9)

Jealousy, then, is understood through a theory of relationships; one which involves a belief in an intense moment of love which can only be felt once (at the very beginning). In order for love to be regained or in some sense retained, it is crucial to avoid, at all costs, falling into a malaise, a habit, with the object of one's love. Rather, one must, following Joyce, risk everything so as to recapture some of what has been lost, and to thereby unite the lover (with a vacillating bond of love–hate) as fully as possible with the loved one:

> [Richard] is jealous, wills and knows his own dishonour and dishonour of her, to be united with every phase of whose being is love's end, as to achieve that union in the region of the difficult, the void and the impossible is its necessary tendency. (Joyce 1973: p. 149)

It is still more complex than this, of course. The very word "complex" — an interfolding — expresses something of the difficulty. In the "Eumaeus" episode of *Ulysses*, Stephen uses the word "simple" in its philosophical (scholastic) sense — the concept of one indivisible thing, in this case the soul — and is misunderstood by Bloom to be talking about "simplicity" (in what Stephen terms the "marketplace" sense): yet this is a productive misunderstanding. On the one hand the complex is the simple: in that, following Leibniz and Deleuze, it is merely the simple folded in upon itself in a process through which the One expresses the Multiple. On the other hand the complex is the opposite of the simple: the complex, which moves from considering the relation of an indivisible thing to itself, to the relationship between different things, is difficult. For Joyce, with regard to the problem of how to maintain the greatest possible pitch of interrelation between people, that of *intense* love, the complex idea of jealousy is central. Jealousy confounds love and hate. More than this, however, it confounds the object of one's love with other people (and why stop at one, it can be any number: Molly Bloom's series of lovers). Nor does it work in a single direction: jealousy draws the friends of both lovers into the complex; it also draws all other objects of love — family, friends, country, belief — into the complex. The complex vacillates and remains undetermined, yet it is far from lukewarm: the laughing and the weeping never stop.

This is no doubt the reason for Joyce's personal interest in infidelities, which are well documented in Ellmann's biography: his fairly slight (and probably not completely consummated) experiments with marital infidelity; his urging of Nora to be unfaithful to him, or at least to pretend to be (how different from the standard of truth Richard demands in *Exiles*!). This interest was also played out in Joyce's reading. Thomas E. Connolly indicates that the "most heavily marked of all the books in Joyce's library"

James Joyce   67

is *Casus de matrimonio fere quingenti quibus applicat et per quos explicat sua asserta moralia circa eamdem materiam* (1893) by M. M. Matharan, a book which is "composed of 497 cases involving marital problems which range from betrothal to incest" (Connolly 1997: p. 36).

There is a powerful interest in jealousy here, then, as a sensation that is both central to and constitutive of human relationships. It seems apparent that the strong interest in jealousy explored in Joyce's only play involves a shift in, or new development of, the aesthetic methods set out in *A Portrait* and *Stephen Hero*. The love triangle and the sensation of jealousy, in turn, become important aesthetic elements that are further developed in *Ulysses*. In this way one might begin to consider Joyce's aesthetic as something which was progressively developed throughout his career.

Relational Identity

Although there are a number of traditions, not all originally from the West, which are available to Western peoples in establishing their world views, it is clear that the dominant Western ontological tradition, deriving in part from Plato, is built upon the notion of the universal. These notions are related to Plato's conception of the realm of "forms" or "ideals," which exist somehow above or outside everyday material existence. This is an understanding of being based on similarity but it also involves an abstraction from place and time: universal Man, for example, is a category to which all men from all times and places can be related. A negative aspect of this system, however, is that, while it makes claims for complete objectivity it is already contaminated by unrecognized specific social criteria. Our norms, then, are intimately tied to our cultural prejudices. We are used to universal categories: the human being as universal, and this idea has passed into criticism of James Joyce through the notion of the archetype. The archetype involves a process of modeling, through which Bloom, for example, can be understood to be in some sense modeled upon Ulysses. While this is a coherent claim, I would suggest that it leaves to one side an important aspect of the nature of the identification of Bloom and Ulysses, one built on a different understanding, the understanding of identity via relationships.

A radically different model for identity exits, and survives amongst those indigenous peoples who develop their primary understandings of identity through relations of kinship. While Western culture still carries important residual elements of this relational system, everyday Western understandings of relationship through kinship have, for the most part, become much less complex than those that persist in indigenous societies. These kinship systems are, as scholars have long argued or implied mathematical in their structure and therefore necessarily involve the kind of precise logic that inheres within mathematics more generally.[10] This logic is rational, in that the kinds of interactions outlined follow necessarily from the interrelation of elements. I am not arguing for an analogical similarity between Joyce's aesthetic of relationships and the logic of indigenous kinship relations; rather, I am claiming that the two are connected at a deeper, more essential level: they both involve the logical development of understandings of the order of human relationships. In this way both Joyce's system and those of indigenous peoples connect closely with Spinoza's contention that human emotions interact in a logically explicable manner: that like all other things they develop through laws of cause and effect. So too, the kinship systems and Joyce's system of relationships are developed through logically explicable causal relations.

This might be clarified by offering a specific example drawn from the concept of being of the Arrente (of the Central Desert regions of Australia). Here, rather than there being a general notion of the universal, and the universal concept of the individual as a particular thing (somehow divorced from the world which has brought one into existence) there is an understanding of the individual as being both identified with a still present history and individualized through systems of relationship (see Strehlow 1947; Morton 1992).

Indentifying the individual through relationship involves considering the itinerary of an individual in relation to traditions of secular knowledge and sacred knowledge — traditions which are maps of a territory over which the individual, whose identity is determined by his or her relations to that tradition, and the kinship system which exists within it, passes in accordance with a particular and unrepeatable life. You are who you are according to this world view in respect of the relations into which you enter. The relations themselves are particular, and are divided along gender lines: for a male, you have a particular conception totem, you are born into a particular skin group (there are eight for the Arrente), and your mother's brothers (as the knowledge of the male is derived patrilineally) are a particular people of a certain country, your father is of a particular people and country, and your wife's father is of a particular people and country. Your conception totem corresponds to a particular site and a

---

10 This is not to reduce human relations to mathematics: as Lévi-Strauss and others have demonstrated the systems express themselves in real human relationships, which do not necessarily directly map onto the rules set out within the systems. I simply wish to underline the point that the systems themselves develop logics which are, in essence, mathematical. (See Lévi-Strauss 1969; Weil 1969; Ascher 1991, 2004: Watson 1989; Morton 1992; Strehlow 1947; Liu 1986; White 1963.) Rather than considering kinship systems in general, the following discussion draws upon work which considers the kinship system particular to the Arrente people of Central Australia.

particular ancestor and relates you to a specific set of knowledges in relation to that place and that ancestral being (of whom you form an aspect). You are further related to the general knowledges of your people, and more closely to the knowledge of your father and your mother's brothers and your wife's father. All of these relations find particular expression in an individual as access to these knowledges needs to be won through respect of the law and the undergoing of processes of initiation. The knowledges, then, are also particular in that the relations, occurring in a certain place, have a specific set of possibilities attached to them: the possible permutations within this set of possibilities are necessarily vast (see Strehlow 1947; Morton 1992). Relational identity then, both places, and is concerned with place (although this does not mean, as the shifts involved in these permutations indicate, that a person is *fixed* in place; rather the person and the knowledge available to the person constantly shifts within this place). Relational identity, then, speaks of a tradition very different to the Western tradition of universals which displace and take the individual out of relation to his or her place, so that the center can reside only *within* that individual which is necessarily understood in universal terms, paradoxically through being emptied of any individuality. Such an empty category: the universal Woman or Man — everyman — is, in effect, No One. Ulysses, often seen as a proto-type of universal Man says, I am nobody, and escapes from the Cyclops he has blinded. Yet Ulysses is also who he is through the relationships he has entered into: these are not simply relations of kinship (the king of Ithaca, father to Telemachus, husband to Penelope, comrade in arms to the great Greek warriors of the Trojan wars, and so on) they are also relations of knowledge (which he earns and is given by the Gods) and relationships with place (his journey plays a large part in who he is).

Something very similar might be understood to emerge through *Ulysses*: Bloom does not resemble Ulysses because he is modeled upon this archetype; rather, Bloom is identified with Ulysses through the re-emergence of relationships that necessarily inhere within human existence.

Homer and Relationship

One of the dominant themes of Homer's *Odyssey* is hospitality, and two sides of the problem of hospitality emerge around the figure of the stranger. On the one hand there is the question of the proper conduct towards strangers (see Long 1970: p. 135; Gagarin 1987: pp. 293–4): Odysseus, in his travels, often appears as a stranger to others and is treated well at times (meeting with the Phaeacians, with Eumenus, with Aeolus on his first visit) and badly at other times (meeting with the Cyclops, Aeolus on his second visit, the suitors on his return to Ithaca in disguise). On the other hand there is the question of the proper conduct of guests, a theme underlined by the improper conduct of the suitors to

Penelope, who lay siege to Odysseus's home. The stranger is thought of as being protected by the gods and is even feared as possibly being a god in disguise (and, indeed, the gods do appear in disguise either in the likeness of a well-known man, or as strangers: see Gagarin 1987: p. 291; Long 1970: p. 123). Linked to these ideas is the idea of the name. The stranger is, at first, nameless, and so without relations; or rather, the stranger is a being who appears and whose relationship to those among whom he appears is uncertain. It is important, then, to treat such a stranger with respect or, at least, with caution: the as yet unknown relationship to you that the stranger embodies involves *your* fate. The stranger might be a god in disguise, or might be a figure of profound significance to you and your destiny. The ties that the stranger has to you might well be significant: as Telemachus famously states at the outset, it is a wise son who knows his own father.

Crucial to both the relationship with the stranger and the meaning of the relationship with the stranger (its significance for you) is the name. Furthermore, stories are attached to names. Yet when the stranger tells us his name and his story he might be lying, or he might be telling the truth. The name might offer us an identity (through which we can map the relationships that place the stranger in relation to ourselves and the greater world), or, on the contrary, the name might be a disguise. Odysseus is "Nobody" to the Cyclops Polyphemus, a word that, in Greek, puns upon his real name (Jones 2003: p. xxxvii). This name is a disguise and it allows Odysseus a measure of invisibility as Polyphemus complains to his countrymen that "nobody" is assaulting him. Yet when Polyphemus learns Odysseus's real name he realizes the true relationship this stranger bears to him, as he fulfills the prophecy that a man of this name will blind him (Homer 2003: Book 9, p. 123). The story of the Cyclops, like the story of Odysseus's slaughter of the suitors, involves a parable that teaches the evils that follow from outraging the laws of hospitality (see Newton 2008). Yet if this is the case, what are we to make of the story of the Phaeacians who treat the stranger kindly only to meet with punishment? Odysseus is asked for his true name and his true story, and on this occasion he gives both: why then are the Phaeacians punished for treating him well? It might be argued that when Odysseus identifies himself, and his relationships with them are known and understood, the focus of uncertainty shifts for the Phaeacians. It is no longer Odysseus and his relation to them which is unknown; what is now unknown is whether this will, at last, be the time when their hospitality will be punished by Neptune (that they may be punished they know by prophecy, when they will in fact be punished remains uncertain). In a sense then, Odysseus's true relationship to them remains unknown. They are not therefore wrong to follow the laws of hospitality.

It would be too simple to suggest that these laws are only conventions: on the contrary they describe a causal logic (see Dobbs 1987). It is not a fully determined logic as the future in the *Odyssey* is not fully determined; rather, as with quantum mechanics, it is a matter of probabilities: certain things are likely to occur given certain circumstances. The gods are capricious and fates might vary. The Phaeacians have been told they will probably be punished for their too generous hospitality to strangers, Odysseus is told he will return safely if his men refrain from killing the oxen of the sun god but he will suffer shipwreck and the loss of all his men if they kill the oxen, and so on.

In this world of causal probability the law of hospitality toward the stranger involves simple self-interest: one cannot judge simply by appearances who a stranger might be and what relationship he might bear to you. It is clear that he is an agent of fate, yet paradoxically this is clear only because the relationship he bears to you is unknown (like fate itself, like the very gods, the stranger personifies uncertainty). A name might offer an identity or a disguise, a story might reveal the truth or veil it, but what is hidden or revealed is the relationship the stranger bears to you and your fate.

Odysseus is a master of relationships and of manipulating relationships. This is one of the ways in which he is cunning: it is not a matter of working simply with conventions; on the contrary he is able to manipulate and influence events through his ability to work within the logic of relationships. The figure of Proteus is important to both *The Odyssey* and *Ulysses*: the one who is able to change shape has an impressive power, the power, precisely, over the future (which Proteus can foresee). Proteus, then, also embodies the paradox of uncertainty: the uncertain is that which has power over fate and, in revealing itself, is that which determines meaning. So the artist creates meaning by capturing uncertainty and holding it for long enough so that it might reveal something of its secrets.

Scylla and Charybdis

Since Stuart Gilbert readers have been alerted to the importance of the word "metempsychosis" that echoes through Bloom's head throughout *Ulysses*, a word that draws attention to the idea that Bloom may be a reincarnation of Ulysses. Gilbert also mentions a second echoing word — parallax — but does not develop an argument that links the two. Gilbert, did, however, already see the relation, as he draws our attention to Bloom's statement about "history repeating itself with a difference" in "Eumaeus" and suggests that this is "an unconscious allusion to the Bloom–Ulysses correspondence" (Gilbert 1955: p. 358). While metempsychosis draws upon spiritual traditions, "parallax" is a scientific term that relates, in astronomy, to the "apparent displacement, or differences in the apparent position, of an object, caused by actual change (or differences) of position of the point of observation." It is also used in a general sense to mean "change, alteration" (Oxford English Dictionary). When metempsychosis is linked with parallax we are able to see that the relationship between *Ulysses* and *The Odyssey* is not simply one of correspondence and identification; rather, they interact through a logic of relationships that presupposes alteration. In light of this, it would be worthwhile to analyze the manner in which the order of events in the episodes from *The Odyssey* are altered in *Ulysses*. For example, while episodes 1–4 of *Ulysses* correspond with episodes 1–5 of *The Odyssey*, from this point on the order of events shifts,[11] and it is likely that patterns might become apparent through careful attention to these shifts. The only point at which the episodes fall back into order, for example, comes in "Eumaeus," episode 16 of *Ulysses*, which corresponds to episodes 14, 15, and 16 of *The Odyssey*, and episode 16 of *The Odyssey* is that episode in which the son, Telemachus, at last meets the father, Odysseus, just as Stephen and Bloom at last enter into conversation with one another in the "Eumaeus" episode.

In "Scylla and Charybdis," Stephen outlines a theory of relationships, both between people and between the work of art and the world. The importance of the theory is underlined in the first episode, "Telemachus," where Buck Mulligan makes an apparently ironic reference to Stephen's theory. Asked by the English guest Haines if the theory involves some paradox, Mulligan replies:

> Pooh! . . . We have grown out of Wilde and paradoxes. It's quite simple. He proves by algebra that Hamlet's grandson is Shakespeare's grandfather and that he himself is the ghost of his own father. (Joyce 1993: 1.554–7)

Haines is somewhat confused by Mulligan's use of pronouns and needs clarification as to whether Mulligan is referring to Stephen himself or Shakespeare himself. The confusion is instructive as, while Mulligan means Shakespeare, Joyce might well mean both. So too, the irony is doubled: Mulligan means to be disparaging, but it is not clear that we are meant to side with Mulligan; rather, it is equally possible that we should be alerted to the possible seriousness of the claim precisely because its seriousness is ironically dismissed by Mulligan. If one follows this logic of double irony still further, it may be that we are being asked to take seriously the possibility that Stephen's theory is in some sense mathematical:

---

11 Episode 5 of Ulysses corresponds to elements within episode 9 of *The Odyssey*, *Ulysses* 6 = *Odyssey* 11; *Ulysses* 7 = *Odyssey* 10; *Ulysses* 8 = *Odyssey* 10; *Ulysses* 9 = *Odyssey* 12; *Ulysses* 10 = *Odyssey* 12; *Ulysses* 11 = *Odyssey* 12; *Ulysses* 12 = *Odyssey* 9; *Ulysses* 13 = *Odyssey* 6, 7, 8; *Ulysses* 14 = *Odyssey* 12; *Ulysses* 15 = *Odyssey* 10 (13); *Ulysses* 16 = *Odyssey* 14, 15, 16; *Ulysses* 17 = *Odyssey* 13–23; *Ulysses* 18 = *Odyssey* 23, 24.

a kind of algebra. In developing his *Ethics*, Spinoza made use of a "geometrical" method derived from Euclid, one which was based on the concatenations of propositions that buttress and reinforce one another, describing a line of logical causation which might be traced and tested at each move, right back to the axioms which must be asserted, but which are felt to be too fundamental in nature to allow, or require, proof. Joyce too claimed his own work was mathematical in nature (Ellmann 1983: p. 614). The word "simple" which Mulligan uses also alerts us to what recurs so often as to seem a deliberate aesthetic strategy: the interaction and correspondence of complexity and simplicity. This, translated into philosophical terms, involves the problem of the nature of relationship between the one and the multiple: the identification of some sort (which occurs in many religious as well as philosophical systems, including that of Spinoza) of all things with one thing. As we have seen, Leibniz and Deleuze consider that the solution to the problem lies within the word "complex" itself, which is etymologically related to folding, so that the simple is rendered complex by interfolding. On the one hand all being is One; on the other, there are an infinite number of individual things: there is similarity, then, or identity, within difference, or to put this another way, the complex reveals the simple, the simple the complex. Confusion is the forcing together of things that are thought to be separate, but rather than becoming meaningless, the confused offers the possibility of deeper truth (that these different things are one thing).

We can see Joyce's great themes folded into Mulligan's apparently ironic statement; rather than diminishing the importance of Stephen's theory, then, it underlines that importance. A second passage, this time within "Scylla and Charybdis" itself, involves a similar doubling, this time not involving irony so much as notions of the adherence to or dehiscence from, systems (which describe all things) through belief or unbelief in them. John Eglinton asks:

Do you believe your own theory?

— No, Stephen said promptly.

— Are you going to write it? Mr Best asked. You ought to make it a dialogue, don't you know, like the Platonic dialogues Wilde wrote.

John Eglinton doubly smiled.

— Well, in that case he said, I don't see why you should expect payment for it since you don't believe it yourself. Dowden believes there is some mystery in *Hamlet* but will say no more. Herr Bleibtreu, the man Piper met in Berlin, who is working on the Rutland theory, believes that the secret is hidden in the Stratford monument. He is going to visit the present duke, Piper says, and prove to him that his ancestor wrote the plays. It will come as a surprise to his grace. But he believes his theory.

[Stephen thinks] I believe, O Lord, help my unbelief. That is, help me to believe or help me to unbelieve? Who helps to believe? *Egomen.* Who to unbelieve? Other chap. (Joyce 1993: 9.1065–80)

The first thought that is likely to occur to most readers is to take Stephen at face value and to therefore discount his theory as intellectual pyrotechnics with no real content. This, indeed, has also been the dominant critical response.[12] Yet Stephen is asked about *belief* here, and he himself is engaging with the questions he is considering with mathematical or philosophical precision: his answer is therefore true to that precision. His theory does not require belief, unlike the vague ideas expressed by Herr Bleibtreu (a name that not only refers to a real person who really developed the theory attributed to him here, but also carries the meaning to "remain faithful"[13]), which do require belief because they cannot, in any way, be demonstrated. What can be demonstrated does not require belief or faith: faith is necessary only in the face of that which cannot be demonstrated. Stephen's theory is not developed through faith, but through logic and his thoughts underline this point, linking belief to the servants of faith ("egomen" being monastic functionaries in the Greek Church, Oxford English Dictionary), and unbelief (or doubt) to the devil (a tradition that will be discussed in more detail in Chapter 6 on Vladimir Nabokov[14]). There are hints that the reader should be left in two minds about Stephen's comments about his theory, then. A surface reading would encourage us to ignore it entirely, yet a second reading asks us to think of it as being of the utmost seriousness because it involves not only a system which might explain elements of artistic production, but one which is logically demonstrable.

---

12 See, for example, Zack Bowen (1984) "Ulysses," in *A Companion to Joyce Studies*, "Unlike the aesthetic theory of Portrait, Stephen's Hamlet theory is presented tongue in cheek; he is not even sure if he believes it himself, and his ideas are further undercut by the mocking tone of some of the narration" (p. 475).
13 In response to the Shakespearean objection voiced by Eglington "what's in a name," with regard to Stephen's theories concerning the use of Shakespeare's brothers' names in his plays, Stephen offers, among other things, another question, "Why did he take them rather than others?" (Joyce 1993: 9.984).
14 I am in disagreement then, with Gifford and Seidman's note on this passage (Gifford and Seidman 1974: p. 204), in which they take "Egomen" to principally refer to the literary journal, *The Egoist* (which, in any case, did not begin publication until 1914, i.e. ten years after the first Bloomsday).

That we are meant to take the theory seriously is underlined by the second mention of Oscar Wilde in relation to it. This might make us think of Wilde's own "theory" with regard to Shakespeare, set out in *The Portrait of Mr W. H.* (Wilde 1958), which is directly referred to earlier in the episode, and a detailed comparative reading of these two works would no doubt prove instructive. Like Stephen's theory, Wilde's is developed through fiction rather than as an academic publication and so the truth value of the argument is left in suspension, but just as Stephen's theory might be taken to reflect real understandings developed seriously by Joyce, Cyril Graham's theory concerning Shakespeare's love for the beautiful Mr. Willie Hughes, which is invented by Oscar Wilde in his book, echoes events in Wilde's own life. A series of identifications are in play: the work is already interrelated with the life and it is this very process of interrelationship that is at the heart of Joyce's theory.

Yet I feel there are still stronger reasons for taking Stephen's theory seriously, reasons which themselves underline the importance of relationships to this episode and to the book as a whole. First, one might consider the structural and numerical importance of this episode. It is episode 9 of 18 episodes: a position of apparent importance. The importance of the number 9, as Joseph Campbell and Henry Morton Robinson point out in their reading of *Finnegans Wake* is underlined by Dante in the Vita Nuova: "Beatrice in a Nine, because the root of nine is three, and the root of Beatrice is the Trinity" (cited in Campbell 2005: p. 44). According to Vincent Foster Hopper:

> With the adoption of 10 as a complete cycle, the number 9 comes into prominence as "almost complete." Troy was besieged for 9 years and fell on the tenth. Odysseus wandered 9 years and arrived home on the tenth. The 9–10 relationship is very common in the *Iliad* and the *Odyssey*, which both indicate a much earlier stage of number symbolism than the most ancient of Babylonian tablets. (2000: p. 10)

There are still further structural hints, within this episode, that our understanding of it as being either serious or in jest is itself being called into question: "Do you think it is only a paradox," the Quaker librarian asks, adding, "The mocker is never taken seriously when he is most serious" (Joyce 1993: 9.541–2). During his discussion Stephen has two consistent auditors: Eglington and Mr. Best. The Quaker librarian moves in and out of the room in accordance with his other duties. Yet there are two other listeners, the poet A. E. who only remains for the beginning of the discussion and Buck Mulligan who only appears towards the end of the discussion. These two characters serve to frame the dialogue: A. E. offers a figure of the serious one, even the overly earnest one — his own work is linked with a pious belief in occult wisdom (something that is underlined at 9.279–86). This arch-seriousness seems somewhat offended by Stephen's methods and his theory, which he takes to be overly concerned with Shakespeare's unidealized, physical, personal life (when one, in line with the seriousness of the neo-Platonism A. E. draws upon, should rather be concerned with the ideal abstract elements of Shakespeare). In consequence, although he makes his excuses, A. E., an abstract, ideal, figure rather than a real person, and follower of Madame Blavatsky's *Isis Unveiled*, rather rudely and pointedly walks out on Stephen:

> A tall figure in bearded homespun rose from shadow and unveiled its cooperative watch.
>
> — I am afraid I am due at the *Homestead*. (Joyce 1993: 9.269–71)

In stark contrast Buck Mulligan brings a complete lack of seriousness to the discussion when he joins it. This is so much the case that Mulligan's position as arch-mocker is clearly contrasted with that of Stephen. Mulligan is seen a "lubber," a clown, who lacks the wisdom of the fool, and mocks only for the sake of mocking (Joyce 1993: 9.1106–9). Stephen, then, rests between two positions: that of the archly serious follower of ideal systems, and that of the arch-skeptic, whose mockery takes away all ground of meaning and leaves only puerile merriment. Therefore, while we cannot take him absolutely seriously, neither can we dismiss his theory as pure mockery: like jealousy, which is built upon the vacillation between love and hate, Stephen's thoughts vacillate between sense and nonsense, thereby avoiding the pitfalls of each position, in negotiating his way between Scylla and Charybdis.

Stephen sets out a theory of relationships. The correspondences indicated by Joyce include for Scylla "Aristotle, dogma" and for Charybdis "Plato and mysticism" and the "Technic" for the episode is "dialectic." There is a further vacillation, then, between the scientific (or physical materialism or realism) and the spiritual (or metaphysics as idealism). This vacillation, and the technique (dialectic), which allows Joyce to negotiate it, comes into being and is identified with relationships. These relations are both human and real and abstract and ideal; further, they concern life and art both in real and ideal ways. When A. E., disgusted by Stephen's insistence on the importance of real relationships (rather than concentrating on purely abstract relations), demands that Stephen explain what useful discovery Socrates learned from his shrewish wife Xanthippe (Joyce 1993: 9.232–4) promptly answers, "Dialectic" (Joyce 1993: 9.235). Dialectic, of course, is Socrates's principal method of discovery and this, as it is developed by Plato, offers one of *the* primary contributions to Western thought. Stephen's comment, though, is more than simply a joke: there is an important element of seriousness within it.

The dialectic involves two parts in Plato, but with Hegel it involves three. There are many references to the trinity through this episode. The apparent final word delivered by Eglington in dismissing Stephen's theories is that he has done nothing but offer us a "French triangle" (which Gifford and Seidman [1974] gloss as an adulterous relationship "man-wife-lover" [p. 203]). Eglington makes the pronouncement that Stephen is "a delusion," "roundly," an adverb that, I would contend, alludes to hermeneutics, which seeks to close circles of interpretation. In place of the perfect closed circle, Stephen here offers a series of vacillating (because they are necessarily involved with jealousy) triangular relationships. There are many manifestations of such triangular relationships in this episode. The principle audience for Stephen are Eglington, who is drawn as a wise bachelor, the virtuous older man of the Platonic dialogues and Platonic love, and Mr. Best who (despite the fact that his real-life model would have been 32) is drawn as a beautiful youth of the Platonic dialogues and Platonic love: "the dour recluse [Eglington] . . . and the douce youngling, minion of pleasure, Phedo's toyable fair hair" [Mr. Best], (Joyce 1993: 9.1138–9). We have a pair of "lovers" (of wisdom, but the ambiguity that confuses spiritual and physical love is everywhere felt) at the center of the episode, then. Stephen moves between them as the third corner of this dialectic triangle.

Everywhere where there is a pair of lovers (a younger and an older) here there is a dialectic third term that intervenes and develops a jealous vacillation. Young Shakespeare is paired with his seducer Ann Hathaway (with the mature Shakespeare coming between them); Shakespeare is paired with Mr. W. H. (with the Dark Lady moving between); the shadow of Oscar Wilde and Alfred Lord Douglas falls over the image of Shakespeare and W. H. (with the world coming between them); Mulligan mockingly imagines Bloom and Stephen as lovers (thereby coming between); Shakespeare and Stephen might also form such a pair (with any of the numerous skeptical interlocutors, A. E., Eglington, Mulligan, Haines) coming between.

Yet the relationship of older masculine lover or teacher to younger feminine lover (the boywoman, 9.254) or apprentice (the schoolman and the schoolboy, 9.56–7) is only one figure of relationship. In this case it is a relationship of knowledge ("knowing" in both senses), an exchange which initiates and energizes, but which carries a stigma: the stigma of the boar which wounds Adonis as the young Shakespeare's masculinity is usurped by the seducer Ann Hathaway; the stigma of adulterous relations such as those in which Shakespeare is thought to indulge in London; the stigma of homosexuality; the stigma of relations with a Jew for Stephen; the stigma of being a favorite of a widely loved master as Stephen would fain be with Shakespeare.

This relationship of teacher–apprentice is involved both with the figures of the masculine and feminine (though does not exhaust them, as the

78 Thinking in Literature

husband–wife pairing can, as we have seen with Socrates and Xanthippe, involve a rivalry or discord: a struggle for dominance which gives rise to dialectic) and with the father and son. Stephen turns from thoughts of the schoolman and the schoolboy to a meditation on the trinity: the Father, the Son, the Holy Ghost (Joyce 1993: 9.61–4). There are elements of identification, then, between these two sets of relations and this is seen through the manner in which knowledge might also pass from the father to the son. Yet this is a paradoxical and curiously unidirectional flow of knowledge. The knowledge, earned through suffering, which belongs to the master/father/writer cannot be understood by the master/father/writer; rather, it can only be understood by the apprentice/son/reader. Hamlet's father is a ghost who cannot profit from the wisdom he has earned, he is only a voice heard by his son. So too, Shakespeare returns to Stratford, "untaught by the wisdom he has written or by the laws he has revealed" (Joyce 1993: 9.477–8) yet he is heard by his spiritual "sons" (in this case Stephen, but one assumes this might be generalized to any who come after who feel themselves spiritually related to Shakespeare):

> He is a ghost, a shadow now, the wind of Elsinore's rocks or what you will, the sea's voice, a voice heard only in the heart of him who is the substance of his shadow, the son consubstantial with the father. (Joyce 1993: 9.478–81)

The relationship between the father and son can be confused with that of schoolman and schoolboy, but is not simply reduced to this confusion: it is a strong relationship which brings much more than mere echoes of the relationship of lovers and it is central to both this episode and the book as a whole. That the father son relationship developed by Bloom and Stephen, echoing that of Odysseus and Telemachus is one of the principal structures upon which the book is built is self-evident. Here the relationship is further echoed through the relationship of Hamlet and his father, and Shakespeare and both his son and his father, but also through the relationship between Shakespeare and "the son of his soul" Hamlet (the artist and the creation), which is further echoed by the relationship between Joyce and his creation.

The logic of relationships, then, moves across the boundaries between soul and body, art and life: one set of relationships (those which pertain in a given life) in some sense, however deviously (the creative work, as we have seen through the discussion of Leibniz in Chapter 1, involves the manipulation of possibilities) determine a second set (those purely mental relationships at work in a work of art):

> Is it possible that that player Shakespeare, a ghost by absence, and in the vesture of buried Denmark, a ghost by death, speaking his

own words to his own son's name (had Hamnet Shakespeare lived he would have been prince Hamlet's twin), is it possible, I want to know, or probable that he did not draw or foresee the logical conclusion of those premises: you are the dispossessed son: I am the murdered father: your mother is the guilty queen, Ann Shakespeare, born Hathaway? (Joyce 1993: 9.174–80)

The relationship between the father and son is privileged here for a number of reasons. First, it is distinguished from the relationship between the mother and the child. Mother love is that very rare thing, for Stephen, a perfectly symmetrical two-way bond (Joyce 1993: 9.842–3). "Mother love" might mean the love of the mother for the child or the love of the child for the mother: the relationship is stable because it is natural and undeniable and "true" for this reason. The love of the father and for the father, however, is quite a different thing. Whereas mother love is undeniable in the sense that a real identifiable woman gives birth to a real identifiable child, it is a, "wise son who knows his own father." The relationship between father and son therefore is "mystical," it is based upon uncertainty and therefore requires faith:

Fatherhood, in the sense of conscious begetting, is unknown to man. It is a mystical estate, an apostolic succession, from only begetter to only begotten. On that mystery and not on the Madonna which the cunning Italian intellect flung to the mob of Europe the church is founded and founded irremovably because founded, like the world, macro and microcosm, upon the void. Upon incertitude, upon unlikelihood. *Amor matris*, subjective and objective genitive, may be the only true thing in life. Paternity may be a legal fiction. Who is the father of any son that any son should love him or he any son? (Joyce 1993: 9.837–45)

Whereas the mother–child relationship might provide the only true duality in human relations (though it is mirrored by that between the dead and the living, 9.1037–8), because it is true in a physical sense, the relationship between the father and son always involves a third term, a third party which comes between as the cause of both identification and jealousy between them. This third term in the Holy Trinity is the "Holy Breath" (Joyce 1993: 9.61), a purely spiritual or mental entity. This spiritual entity not only passes from father to son (as a son becomes a father) but between the artist and the creation. The only begetter of Shakespeare's *Sonnets* is Mr. W. H., and while Mr. Best makes an error when he states that the Sonnets are written *by* Mr. W. H., Joyce, in allowing Best to say this, does not (1993: 9.522–30). The subject — Mr. W. H. — forms the works in the artist's mind: they are caused by the relationship he embodies with

Shakespeare which has crystallized in Shakespeare's mind, and in order to continue and deepen this relationship Shakespeare creates the Sonnets which will work upon this relationship and so, in a sense, the poems are written both for and by Mr. W. H.

As in life there is a constant slippage between real physical relationships and spiritual or metaphysical relationships, which is crucial to the complexity of the argument here. It is difficult to unfold these complexities without doing real damage to the fabric. It must be emphasized that the distinctions male and female; husband and wife; father and son; body and spirit slip from the concrete to the abstract, from the real to the ideal and in becoming ideals they no longer refer to real men and women but to insubstantial entities, spirits, which would not exclusively pass, for example, into male bodies. *Hamlet*, we are told, is being performed in Dublin with a woman in the lead role (Joyce 1993: 9.517), just as men become women (and vice versa) in Shakespeare.

The image of the artist is woven and unwoven by artists who, although modifying it, take on the form of those who come before. Just as physically we change our molecules while maintaining, following Spinoza, the ratios or relations which comprise the essence of our physical bodies, so too "the artist" is always part of a greater spirit, a ratio or set of mental or spiritual relations which continues the being of art and both creates and is drawn from the image of all artists.

> As we, or mother Dana, weave and unweave our bodies, Stephen said, from day to day, their molecules shuttled to and fro, so does the artist weave and unweave his image. And as the mole on my right breast is where it was when I was born, though all my body has been woven of new stuff time after time, so through the ghost of the unquiet father the image of the unliving son looks forth. In the intense instant of imagination, when the mind, Shelley says, is a fading coal, that which I was is that which I am and that which in possibility I may come to be. So in the future, the sister of the past, I may see myself as I sit here now but by reflection from that which then I shall be. (Joyce 1993: 9.376–85)

These comments are misunderstood by Best, who considers them to relate only to Shakespeare, when Stephen means them to involve spiritual essences which link one artist to another: "He [Shakespeare] is in my father. I am in his son" (Joyce 1993: 9.390). The logic of relationships then, involves complex processes of identification and difference. Metempsychosis is posited here, just as it is posited throughout *Ulysses*, but here as throughout the book it is always to be understood in relation to parallax. There is a recurrence, then, but what recur are the relationships into which we enter: it is the relationships which continue the form or the

James Joyce 81

spirit of human endeavor even though they change and involve variation. It is still more complex than this, as Stephen wishes to invoke not only a spiritual causation or continuation from spiritual father to spiritual son, but also an intermixing of lines of causation, so that physical causes inform and create the mental causes which emerge in art (and vice versa as the worlds created by art inform and create our lives). This is apparent in the penultimate words of the episode where Stephen imagines himself as a hierophant (an expounder of sacred mysteries). If he is a priest of this kind he makes his altar "from wide earth" (Joyce 1993: 9.1221): he creates the spiritual reality from the physical realm. One passes into the other, male being (identified here with the spiritual) and female being (identified here with the physical) become further identified in the artist who resembles "an androgynous angel" (an image which Mulligan finds highly amusing) (9.1052). Yet, more than this, the artist is the one who is able to imagine all possible relationships, to identify with all of the beings created in their art which are all drawn from some aspect of their own self:

> The boy of act one is the mature man of act five. All in all. In *Cymbeline*, in Othello he is bawd and cuckold. He acts and is acted on. Lover of an ideal or a perversion, like José he kills the real Carmen. His unremitting intellect is the hornmad Iago ceaselessly willing the moor in him to suffer. (9.1020-4)

The relationship which is common to all artists, then, is the capacity to embody all in all, the capacity to exhaustively be each of the points of relationship within a given set of relations: the one who loves, the one who is loved, the one who betrays, the one who is betrayed. Is this, perhaps, why the artist for Joyce is also the one in exile (as Shakespeare is thought to be in banishment here, (Joyce 1993: 9.1000), as Odysseus and Bloom are in banishment)? Is he a stranger in exile because in a constant state of doubt, because there is no simple relationship of love, because love always involves the possibility of betrayal, and can only renew itself with that which might also destroy: jealousy? I would suggest that it is both more and less than this. The artist is like God in that both are "all in all." Yet the artist is also like every human being. We enter into any number of relationships, yet these relationships are drawn from a certain number of possible relationships which have been since people have been. Yet in all of our relationships we are constantly meeting ourselves (9.1041–50). Stephen meets Synge in Paris and each meets his own image (9.580), the brothers and friends Stephen meets are "whetstones" (9.977), they serve to allow him to think, they serve to allow him to experience the betrayal that will throw him back upon himself (9.976–1010). The brother is the one one opposes so as to become oneself, the one one befriends in order to understand what it means to have an enemy. Exile is the result because the artist realizes the separation of the self from others paradoxically through identification with all possible points of relationship: a stranger wandering the earth and entering into relationship with the world. It is very much like the logic of Leibniz's monads: god is doubtless in all of us (9.1049–50) but we are only in ourselves and can only meet ourselves in the others we face (9.1046). So too it resembles Spinoza's understanding of affect or sensation that allows us to recognise how we only know others through the effects they have on us. What we have in common is that we share a logic of relationships.

This, I would argue, is the meaning of Stephen's claim in *Stephen Hero* that, "For Stephen art was neither a copy nor an imitation of nature: the artistic process was a natural process" (Joyce 1963: p. 154). Nature proceeds and reproduces itself through a logic of relationships. This is a kind of thinking that involves both repetition and difference. We, as much as the Arrente people of the Central Australian Desert, are identified through relationships that recur and have continued to recur from the beginning of time, but these relationships also vary and are particular. The process of identification has two aspects, then: it involves that which is particular as well as that which is general and both of these aspects form the relationships themselves, which are at once generalized (a father, a mother) and specific (my father, my mother), objective and subjective. The specific and the general, then, are both presupposed through the idea of relation. Joyce, in relation with Spinoza, allows us to understand this idea, which relates not only to his own particular work, but also to the work of art in general, in all its complexity.

5 Virginia Woolf: the Art of Sensation

If the particular aesthetic method Joyce develops through *Exiles* and *Ulysses* allows us to understand the general sense in which the concept and practice of relation generates thinking in literature, how might certain of Virginia Woolf's aesthetic ideas help us to understand the complex interplay between perception, possible worlds, the incompossible, viewpoint, sensation, and thinking in literature?

As we have seen in Chapter 2, above, the idea, derived from Leibniz, of "possible worlds" is, for Deleuze, related to all fiction, but it has been explicitly related to the work of Virginia Woolf by a number of critics (see Henry 2003: pp. 71–92; Ferrer 1990: p. 36, 156; and Banfield 2000, who links Woolf to Leibniz via Russell). In this chapter, then, I will focus on the idea of sensation, as it emerges in Woolf's work. Sensation is the central concept in the list of interlinked concepts listed here for two reasons: first it connects and informs the other concepts, and second it involves a kind of thinking that is proper to the arts.

With regard to the first point, sensation is that which precedes and informs the composition of a series of mutually exclusive (incompossible) perceptions, which are incompossible because they pertain to distinct individuals, into a unity. For example, Lily Briscoe's sensations in *To the Lighthouse*, like those of Woolf herself, draw together (relate) and compose disparate, even incompossible, perceptual elements (sensations), so as to create an idea of the real. Sensation involves perception, both making it possible and calling it into being: what we perceive is what announces itself to our perceptions through sensation. Leibniz accounts for the multiplicity and unity of possible perceptions in the concept of the monad. The monad is a possible world, defined by what it perceives clearly. The infinite monad (God) perceives all things clearly, yet human minds only perceive some things clearly. Fiction, as we have seen in Chapter 2, can to an extent account for, or represent, something of this paradoxical relationship between the individual and the world: allowing us to understand how the world involves the interaction of multiple viewpoints which both converge and diverge.

This divergence and convergence announces itself to readers in Woolf's particular form of writing, in works such as *To the Lighthouse* (Woolf 2000a) through the, at times, rapid shifting between the perspectives, or points of view both of different characters and within single characters. That is, "sensation" furnishes the multiplicity of perceptions which coalesce into these viewpoints, and, as we have seen in Chapter 2, the same complicated character might fold several viewpoints within their "self." This style might be in part understood to develop from Woolf's desire to capture "reality" as fully as possible. So too, it results from her understanding that art can develop a kind of thinking proper to itself, as, as noted with reference to Baumgarten in the introduction, the aesthetic involves perception.

The problem of how to capture reality through art (how to do justice to or adequately imagine the real) is something that preoccupied her, and can be witnessed in a famous exchange between Woolf and Bertrand Russell at a dinner party in December 1921. At the table Woolf complained to Russell of the lack of reality, the lack of purity, of what they were then experiencing (the dinner party itself):

[Woolf] All this is mush; & you can put a telescope to your eye and see through it.

[Russell] If you had my brain you would find the world a very thin, colourless place he said.

[Woolf] But my colours are so foolish, I replied.

[Russell] You want them for your writing, he said. Do you never see things impersonally?

[Woolf] Yes, I see literature like that ... But I have a feeling that human affairs are impure.

[Russell] God does mathematics ... It is the most exalted form of art. (Woolf 1980a: p. 147)

This exchange is fascinating in that it seems to involve simultaneous understanding and misunderstanding between Woolf and Russell. Russell indicates that the way in which he sees the world (through mathematical and philosophical generalizations) renders that world in some ways colorless: the abstract impersonal imposes itself and overrides the particular personal. Woolf, effacing herself (in a way that is consistent, as we will see below, with her own understanding of the nature of the artistic process), calls her colors "foolish." Russell then, implicitly agreeing that these colors are "foolish" (though their understanding of this term might well vary) further suggests that Woolf requires color, or the particular, for her writing (implying that he understands literature to be primarily concerned with such particular color).

He then asks her if she ever sees things "impersonally": that is, in an abstract, ideal light, removed from the personal. Woolf replies that *she sees literature like that*, and it is worth pausing on this point. Her understanding of literature, then, does not involve recounting or representing the purely particular; rather, it is impersonal, a kind of thinking (involving a logic or set of proportional relations). Moreover, this is something she contrasts with everyday human affairs, which, she suggests, lack reality and are impure. Insofar as she requires "color," then, the particular, this particular is understood as interfolded with an impersonal unity. Whether or not they are completely in agreement is open to question, but Russell's final point continues the exchange in an interesting way. "God does mathematics"; or God expresses the particular through general, abstract sets of relations. "[Mathematics] is the most exalted form of art"; or art, in its highest form, would also be that that expresses the particular through the general. Yet does Russell also mean that this kind of relation to the general is not possible in other less "exalted" forms of art? This is unclear from what is left of this exchange, yet the claim that literature, and art more generally, can think, is one that can be affirmed through Woolf's writing and her aesthetic method.

Through a detailed examination of the concept of sensation which she draws from painting, and applies to her own writing, this chapter will set out to examine how Woolf's interest in artistic process, and specifically her interest in painting, develops into a logic of sensations that allows us to see the strong interfolding of the particular into the general fabric. Woolf's interest in painting, and her anxiety as to how her descriptions of painting in *To the Lighthouse* would be received by painters, and in particular her sister Vanessa Bell and her friend Roger Fry, is well known. In underlining the importance of sensation and the kind of logic particular to sensation which might be exploited by the arts in order to understand the real, I will focus on two aspects of this idea in this chapter. First, how the understanding of the interlinked ideas of "sensation" and "rhythm," which Woolf develops might be drawn into relation with aesthetic ideas explored by the great French painter Paul Cézanne and described by Roger Fry in his critical writings. In doing this I will seek to underline how this logic of sensation involves a logic that is both proper to art, and also underlines how art, like other forms of thinking such as mathematics, can contribute in crucial ways to our understanding of the real. Second, by considering her 1934 essay *Walter Sickert: A Conversation*, I will draw these ideas into relation with Woolf's anxiety about entering into dialogue with the visual artists and aesthetic theorists in the Bloomsbury group, emphasizing how this connects to the idea of self-consciousness and its necessary absence in art that she develops.

Sensation, as we have seen, is linked to perception, which is at the heart of Leibniz's understanding of thinking. The question of translation between the arts, in effect, sheds further light on the concept of sensation and what is proper to it both prior to and through its composition into a work of art. So too, as we have seen in Chapter 3, the question of self-consciousness is crucial to an understanding of the expression of sensation within an artistic composition.

Sensation and Aesthetics: Banfield and Bloomsbury

In chapter 6 of her impressive book, *The Phantom Table*, Ann Banfield (2000) draws out numerous points of relation between Woolf's writing and the ideas of Roger Fry. I am in broad agreement with the contention that Woolf moves towards an aesthetic theory which was "discovered by Fry in Cézanne" (2000: p. 293), and, indeed, Banfield has done as much as any critic since Jane Goldman and Allen McLaurin to emphasize and underline aspects of the nature of the dialogue between Woolf and Fry. Like McLaurin, however, Banfield does not move very far back from Fry's reading towards the ideas of Paul Cézanne. Rather, her thesis requires that she find a way of identifying, at least to an extent, Fry's thought with that of British Analytic Philosophy of the early twentieth century, and the work of Bertrand Russell in particular. This is often convincing in part, especially, for example, with regard to how Russell's interest in Leibniz resonates with Woolf's development of possible worlds in her fiction. Yet while Banfield certainly does more than enough to show that the ideas of Russell, and the Cambridge Apostles and G. E. Moore before him, were an important point of reference for both Fry and Woolf, at times she goes too far in wishing to circumscribe a process of identification, so that Fry's thought and Woolf's thought become simply versions of an analytic philosophical position applied to the visual arts and literature. Banfield's arguments are difficult to ignore insofar as they underline how the voices of Russell, Whitehead, and perhaps Wittgenstein enter into dialogue with those of Fry and Cézanne in Woolf's writing, yet at times she glosses over the real differences between the kinds of thinking which take place, on the one hand in a work of analytical philosophy and on the other in a work of art and art criticism. While, as we have seen in the previous chapter, elements of relational logic which participate within a work of art can be mathematical in character, a "logic of sensations" also involves other elements, which are often used to different purpose, and so it cannot be simply identified with analytic logic. As Fry states in *Cézanne*, "What is here called intellect is not, of course, a purely logical function" (Fry 1927: p. 71).

Banfield draws out the importance of the notions of "logic" and "relations" in both analytical philosophy and in Fry's writings on Cézanne, but wants to instantiate an overly precise correspondence between the kind of logic found in visual art and that in mathematics (as understood by analytical philosophy); that is, between the *function* of relations in art and the *function* of relations in analytical philosophy. She states: "Artistic form . . . is subject to logic, like scientific laws" and proceeds to quote Fry from *Cézanne*, describing the artist's "sensual intelligence." She then concludes that "The logical form discovered has the status of a scientific law which approximates to some fact" (Banfield 2000: p. 279). The problem here is that of developing an overly precise identification between different systems of thought, collapsing the distinction between "things perceived" and "things known" set forth by Baumgarten and cited in the introduction (p. 1). While Fry indeed, borrowing his terms from Cézanne, talks of a "logic of sensations" (2000: p. 276), this is not to suggest that this logic is simply identical with an analytical or mathematical logic. The idea that there are differences between kinds of logic and forms of expression is something Cézanne insisted upon. He told Joachim Gasquet, "There's a logic of colour, damn it all! The painter owes allegiance to that alone" (Gasquet 1991: p. 161).

While it is true that the artist needs to refine or develop the logic of sensation she or he puts to use in making a painting or writing a novel, the process of refinement does not necessarily follow the same steps or tend towards the same end as the "process of simplification" through which, according to Banfield via Russell, the analytical philosopher develops a scientific language. In buttressing her argument Banfield makes use of the following quotation from Russell: "Ordinary language is totally unsuited for expressing what physics really asserts, since the words of everyday life are not sufficiently abstract. Only mathematics and mathematical logic can say as little as the physicist means to say" (cited in Banfield 2000: p. 283). While this may be true in relation to Russell's idea of scientific language, it by no means squares with the manner in which Woolf makes use of language, or Cézanne makes use of visual motifs and color.

As will be drawn out below in a reading of Woolf's essay on Walter Sickert, for Woolf, "conversation," or everyday language itself, is capable of accomplishing things that a more overtly rational form would be unable to accomplish, and it does this through its very capacity to be *imprecise*. That is, while conversational language might not be proper to scientific enquiry, it does not follow that a logic of sensations, drawing upon color and visual material, or even such apparently mathematical material as the motifs of geometrical forms, can be identified with a scientific language. The forms created in Cézanne's art are never pure geometrical forms. Banfield herself recognizes this in citing a passage from Fry's *Cézanne* where this point is explicitly made as Fry insists that, "the apparent continuity of the contour is illusory" and that there is a movement from an extreme simplicity of form to extreme complexity (Banfield 2000: p. 284).

That is, Cézanne's expression, the "logic of sensations" involves an insistence upon a specificity of thought to painting, one that can be translated, but only by making use of materials proper to the medium into which it is translated. This is a point which Woolf herself insists upon in *Walter Sickert: A Conversation* (Woolf 1934: pp. 23–4). Literature, like painting, is an art which interests itself in the logic of sensations: our experience of the world directly through the senses, and the sensual understanding developed through language, mathematics, "scientific language," and so on. The logic of sensations would itself involve a sign system, but this would not necessarily be identical with that of language; rather, just as Charles Sanders Pierce considered sign systems to exist in nature as much as in human language, the visual arts makes use of signs (color, form) which exist alongside human language.

In short, then, there are types of thinking. They are all "thought," and Cézanne's logic of sensations partakes of our human cognitive capacities as much as scientific language does: yet there is a difference of degree. Banfield cites the dinner party conversation between Virginia Woolf and Bertrand Russell outlined above where Russell told Woolf that if she had his mind she would see the world mathematically, as colorless matter. While Banfield notes that Woolf disagreed with much of this, she still manages to conclude that Woolf must have (through the influence of Fry, perhaps) moved closer to Russell's position (Banfield 2000: p. 262). It might, on the contrary, be argued that these different ways of seeing, that of the philosopher and that of the artist, do nothing but confirm the novelist's intuition that there are different ways of thinking; that there are different minds with different dispositions; different lives with different rhythms, and that these differing dispositions allow or require different types of engagement with the matter of being. That is, Russell was a certain type of person, an analytical philosopher, whereas Roger Fry had a different disposition, one which led him, despite his close association with analytical philosophers among his friends in the Cambridge apostles, towards the logic of sensations possible through painting, rather than to a more mathematical logic, even while, when thinking of things analytically, he might find himself in agreement with those of his friends with more purely philosophical dispositions.

The question of disposition is one which occurs throughout Woolf's works: *The Waves* (2000b) might be understood to picture how "types," or people attracted to particular capacities of the human organism (which are not infinite in number, for Woolf, but break rather, into a reasonably small number of types), understand similar sets of experience in differing ways. To put this another way: she shows how multiple viewpoints, or possible worlds, can co-exist, even in contradicting one another, and yet comprise a coherent expression of the same unified reality. So too, as will be discussed below (see p. 109), she understands there to be various types of artists: the "literary" painter, and the painterly writer, being examples of possible types. In this way one might recognize something of a difference between Fry and Woolf. Whereas Fry considers that there is a proper way to do things: a *genuine* logic of sensations for example, which allows him to consider Van Gogh an inferior artist because he does not develop the same conception of form as Cézanne (Fry 1927), Woolf contends, more generously, that there are types of art. The literary painter is not worse than the "pure" painter: rather, he or she is a different type of painter, one who thinks in a different way, and who, therefore, is capable of different things (see Woolf 1934).

Style, Rhythm, and Sensation

What kind of thinking, then, might be understood to be proper to art? The importance of "rhythm" to an understanding of Virginia Woolf's aesthetic practice has long been known, with a passage from a letter to Vita Sackville-West of March 16, 1926 (Woolf 1980b) having often been cited by critics. Yet it is worth quoting again from this letter, which was written while Woolf was working on *To the Lighthouse*, to begin to get our bearings:

> As for the *mot juste*, you are quite wrong. Style is a very simple matter; it is all rhythm. Once you get that, you can't use the wrong words. But on the other hand here am I sitting after half the morning, crammed with ideas, and visions, and so on, and can't dislodge them, for lack of the right rhythm. Now this is very profound, what rhythm is, and goes far deeper than words. A sight, an emotion, creates this wave in the mind, long before it makes words to fit it; and in writing (such is my present belief) one has to recapture this, and set this working (which has nothing apparently to do with words) and then, as it breaks and tumbles in the mind, it makes words to fit it: But no doubt I shall think differently next year. (Woolf 1980b: p. 247)

There are two processes at work here. First, rhythm is created by external sensation; and second, writing seeks to recapture this sensation. A good deal of light can be shed on these comments by considering the ideas of the French post-impressionist painter Paul Cézanne, who was a major influence on Roger Fry, and, as I will argue here, on Woolf herself. Cézanne developed a powerfully coherent understanding of the role of "sensation" both within the artistic process and as a process of thinking. The word "rhythm" is not one that occurs in Cézanne's letters or in the reported conversations with him in which he described his aesthetic methods (see Gasquet 1991; Kendall 1988; Cézanne 1976). A related term, "harmony" does occur in these sources, however, and in a manner quite similar to that seen in Woolf's description of rhythm Cézanne discusses the problem of reproducing the harmony of a sensation encountered in the world:

> [Borély] "Isn't painting a matter of producing a harmonious impression? And what if I want to celebrate light like this?"

90 Thinking in Literature

[Cézanne] "I know what you mean; there is a languid glow which I will not be able to emulate on canvas; but what if I could create this impression by means of another, corresponding one, even if it meant using bitumen [i.e. the darkest available pigment]!" (Cited in Kendall 1988: p. 296)

In his important study of Woolf, Allen McLaurin considers the nature of sensation in literature and painting. While he suggests that literature and art must distinguish themselves from sensation (McLaurin 1973: p. 189), he concedes, following Roger Fry, that there is a purely physiological process (which Fry disparages) at play in painting, such as the direct sensation of color, for example (1973: p. 193). For McLaurin, this immediate physiological process cannot be conveyed in literature, yet he argues that literature is nevertheless able to create, through the development of formal relations, an analogous sensation, similar to the process that Cézanne describes to Borély. McLaurin argues that Woolf attempts to develop a kind of painting in literature in order to better convey the "jar on the nerves, the thing itself before it has been made anything" of immediate sensation that Lily Briscoe describes in *To the Lighthouse* (Woolf, cited in McLaurin 1973: p. 189).

While I am in broad agreement with many of the points McLaurin makes in his fine study I would also wish to underline the manner in which rhythm itself, as Woolf insists in her letter to Vita Sackville-West, both comes from sensation and immediately conveys sensation. That is, first, for Woolf, rhythm comes from external sensation as "A sight, an emotion, creates [a] wave in the mind." Second, the rhythm of a sentence, whether silently sounded in the head or read aloud, has a physical presence. That is, unlike the meaning of the words which are attributed to sounds, the sounds themselves and the patterns they form in being linked together are purely material, corporeal: bodies which pass as sound waves through the air, or are silently sounded as verbal images by the neurons within the brain. As material things, they are, like music, capable of producing purely physiological effects upon readers. If this idea were to be more fully explored, one might consider the manner in which such a rhythm of words can carry with it or create a voice or voices, which in turn are caused by the bodies of individuals. A rhythm or style in this sense is closely linked to the material being of the voice. In fiction it might be the voice of a character or a narrator, but ultimately it has always emerged from an individual and those things which have passed through that individual: those discourses which animate and help to form that individual on one hand, but also the purely physical bodies which have come into contact with and affected that individual, generating the sensations which are transformed, among other things, into a rhythm embodied in a voice.

Virginia Woolf 91

"Rhythm" is an important term in Roger Fry's critical writings, and is discussed by Woolf in her biography of Fry. In Fry rhythm is a difficult concept that also seems to be understood to correspond with the personal style of an artist. It must be found if the work is to cohere, but it presents certain dangers: one has to be attuned to the correct rhythm (the rhythm proper to the work), and one cannot allow the rhythm to harden into a habitual form. In *Roger Fry: A Biography*, Woolf discusses Fry's use of the word in his essay "Art and Life":

> Art and Life are two rhythms [Fry says] — the word "rhythm" was henceforth to occur frequently in his writing — [Woolf quotes Fry:] "and in the main the two rhythms are distinct, and as often as not play against each other ... What this survey suggests to me is that if we consider this special spiritual activity of art we find it no doubt open at times to influences from life, but in the main self-contained ... I admit of course that it is always conditioned more or less by economic changes, but these are rather conditions of its existence at all than directive influences. I also admit that under certain conditions the rhythms of life and of art may coincide with great effect on both; but in the main the two rhythms are distinct, and as often as not play against each other". (Woolf 1976: p. 214)

Later in her biography Woolf praises Fry both for his power to stimulate and his power to suggest. She offers two examples of passages she considers to "break off heavy with meaning" and "go behind the picture" being discussed. The first of these concerns rhythm. Fry states: "There is great danger in a strong personal rhythm ... unless [the artist] constantly strains it by the effort to make it take in new and refractory material it becomes stereotyped." The second quotation from Fry also concerns the development of an aesthetic method: "You cannot imitate the final results of mastery without going through the preliminaries" (Woolf 1976: p. 228). Passages such as these are elusive, yet certain of their implications can be clarified through consideration of some of the key ideas of Paul Cézanne, the painter with whom Roger Fry's career as a critic is most closely associated.

In short, the first idea, "rhythm," can be illuminated by a related term, drawn from Cézanne, the "sensation"; while the second idea, of "going through the preliminaries," corresponds with Cézanne's assertions that the painter is comprised of two parts, the eye and the mind. While it is possible to work without the mind, in the manner of the best Impressionists, such as Monet whom Cézanne says had "the most prodigious eye since painting began" (Gasquet 1991: p. 164), the kind of art Cézanne is seeking to develop involves the processes of organizing and understanding what the eye has perceived. Emile Bernard quotes Cézanne as follows:

> There are two things in the painter: the eye and the mind; each of them should aid the other. It is necessary to work at their mutual development, in the eye by looking at nature, in the mind by the logic of organized sensations which provides the means of expression. (Kendall 1988: p. 299)

In her biography of Fry, Woolf describes Fry's development as a critic and a painter. His first passion was for the art of the Renaissance, and this, in effect, made his own art appear somehow old fashioned. Rather than this being due to a failure to remain up to date, it reflected Fry's feeling that something important was missing from the art of his time that seemed, as he wrote in 1902, "paralysed by the fear of failure" (Woolf 1976: p. 160). What was missing, in part, was a full understanding of the classical heritage, which, for Fry, was being ignored in line with

> a sophistical theory of aesthetics, which denies them the full use of the pictorial convention. The arbitrary rule that they have formulated is that they may leave out anything they like in a given scene, but that they must not introduce forms which do not happen to be there, however much these might increase the harmony or intensify the idea. (Woolf 1976: p. 110)

Although Fry is here discussing English painting in 1902, the arbitrary rules he describes no doubt owe a great deal to French Impressionism. A review of the 1876 Impressionist exhibition described the painters' goal as follows: "to render with absolute sincerity the impression that features of reality have made rise within them, avoiding compositional adjustment or any attenuation" (cited in Shiff 1998: p. 14). All of this helps to explain the powerful effect Cézanne's work had upon Fry, both when he first saw it in 1906, and then when he began to look at it in much greater detail while preparing the first post-Impressionist exhibition at the Grafton Gallery in 1910. While he had exhibited as an Impressionist and had been influenced and taught elements of technique by Claude Pissaro, as Fry outlines in his study (Fry 1927: p. 35), Cézanne was not satisfied with certain of the tenants of Impressionism. He wanted to bring Classicism to Impressionism; that is, he wanted to marry the kind of formal quality apparent in the classical schools of painting to the impressionist emphasis on working direct from nature (see Goldman 1998). He wanted to emphasize the structure of an image and to create that structure in the process of painting.

In painting, that structure comes from composition and the system of relations built up within the picture by answering motifs. The compositional relations are echoes and repetitions of form, or balancing elements: as Cézanne told his son, "the whole thing is to put in as much rapport as possible" (cited in Maloon 1998a: p. 74). These elements are apparent in the overall design of the painting, but Cézanne also understood the brushstroke itself, the small repeated "touches," which build up the image as forming part of the motif. This is apparent in the use Cézanne made of the term "sensation," and it is this idea, which can be seen to be developed in *To the Lighthouse* and *The Waves*.

Cézanne's Sensation

The "sensation" is a many-sided concept for Cézanne. He used it to refer to the brushstroke itself and the repetition of brush strokes, as is apparent through the famous story of his falling out with Paul Gauguin because Gauguin copied his brushstroke. Cézanne was reported as saying:

> Oh, this guy Gauguin! I had a little sensation, just a little, little sensation . . . But, you know, it was mine, this little sensation. Well, one day this guy Gauguin, he took it from me. (Cited in Shiff 1998: p. 26)

Yet Cézanne also spoke of the sensation in much more general terms. Emile Bernard reported the following conversation:

> "By a perspective I mean a logical vision; in other words one which has nothing absurd about it."
>
> "But what will you base your perspective on, Master?"
>
> "On nature."
>
> "What do you mean by that word? Our human nature or nature herself?"
>
> "Both."
>
> "So you understand art to be a union of the world and the individual?"
>
> "I understand it as personal apperception. This apperception I locate in sensation and I require of the intellect that it should organise these sensations into a work of art."
>
> "But what sensations are you referring to? Those of your feelings or of your retina?"
>
> "I don't think you can distinguish between the two; however, as a painter, I believe in the visual sensation above all else." (Kendall 1988: p. 289)

While critics such as John Rewald and Richard Shiff have written on the difficulties which are at times involved in determining the extent to which the reported conversations provided by Bernard and Joachim Gasquet among others have been altered in being dramatized, they also consider that the core ideas, which can be further verified in Cézanne's letters, remain clear (see Rewald in Gasquet 1991; and Rewald in Cézanne 1976; Shiff 1991). Among these, for Shiff, is the idea that the sensation involves the interaction of two natures: internal human nature, or that of the artist, and external nature or that of the world perceived. The exchange between these two natures is ongoing: rather than the mind of the artist seeking to impose classical order on nature by applying some iron-cast intellectual formula to it, the artist brings tentative formulas that are open to ongoing modification in the face of nature itself (Shiff 1991: pp. 20–1). Gasquet, whom Shiff considers close to the mark with regard to this (1991: p. 21), reports Cézanne as follows: "Yes, we need a system. But once the system is established, work from nature. One has a system all arranged, then one forgets it: one works from nature." (Gasquet 1991: p. 169)

Cézanne's "sensation," then, is a remarkably mobile concept. As touched upon in the first chapter, whereas the idea of an "impression" carries the sense of a passive reflection, with nature impressing its image on the artist who then faithfully records the moment, "sensation" involves a complex process of interaction which is more active than passive. The sensation is projected by an external nature and is then registered by an internal nature. To put this another way, the sensation exists both in the image projected by the world and in the artist's reception of that image. Further, a sensation that develops an analogue of what has been projected by the world is then mentally organized or composed by the artist. Finally, the artist re-projects the sensation via the brushstrokes that correspond to and build up the analogous sensation on the canvas. The sensations then rest within the canvas where they are able to be received by viewers. In a passage cited by Fry (Fry 1927: p. 68) in his study of Cézanne, which I have already quoted, Gasquet reports Cézanne as stating: "The landscape is reflected, humanized, rationalized within me. I objectivize it, project it, fix it on my canvas [. . .] It may sound like nonsense, but I would see myself as the subjective consciousness of that landscape, and my canvas as its objective consciousness" (Gasquet 1991: p. 150). The individual is the monad, or human mind, perceiving clearly and rationalizing a part of the great unity of nature. The artist then composes and recreates that perception, in turn generating new relations with those who view the work. As outlined in Chapter 1, then, art is able to combine the subjective and objective with intuition in drawing together Spinoza's three kinds of knowledge.

The world, then, can be drawn into the painting, even in unexpected ways. In a letter to Emile Bernard of 1888 Vincent Van Gogh wrote of the apparent clumsiness of some of Cézanne's brushstrokes:

Figure 5.1 Cézanne painting from Nature (photo c. 1890s)

I thought about Cézanne, especially in regard to his touch, which is so inept in certain studies — skip the word inept, given that he probably executed those studies when the mistral was blowing. Since, half the time, I have to cope with the same difficulty, it dawned on me why Cézanne's touch is sometimes so sure and sometimes appears clumsy: it's his easel shaking. (Cited in Maloon 1998b: p. 171)

While Allen McLaurin, apparently oversimplifying a point he renders much more complex earlier in his book, states that, "language and art gain their value by their difference from sensation, by their escape from the tyranny of immediacy" (McLaurin 1973: p. 189), he nevertheless goes on to show that Woolf develops a form capable of creating this very immediacy; "the jar on the nerves" of which Lily Briscoe speaks. Like Fry, McLaurin tends to undervalue and disparage purely physiological effects in art (in *Cézanne* Fry criticizes both Vincent Van Gogh, and music, for their reliance on the physiological). Yet through his reading of Fry, McLaurin does underline how the sensation can be generated, created, through the formal relation of elements within a work. For Cézanne, as we have seen, there is no attempt to escape from sensation; rather, the process of creation is inexorably entwined with the sensation: the sensation, indeed, is that which is conveyed to the canvas, it *is* the brushstroke, and McLaurin has noted how, for Woolf, the brushstroke is equated with the sentence (1973: p. 197). Further, as we have seen, there is no naïve conception of pure immediacy or lack of thought involved in this concept of sensation; rather, the sensation is "thought" but not necessarily thought mediated through language; not necessarily conscious thought. This too is clear in the comments Woolf makes with regard to rhythm, where the process of recapturing the rhythm that has been first sensed through nature ("a sight, an emotion") in writing "has nothing apparently to do with words." It is, instead, a felt thought: it is sensation and nothing other than sensation, even though it is conveyed or translated by another medium: be it "bitumen" for Cézanne, or for Woolf, some thought (induced by the sign or series of signs that is sensation) prior to words,[1] which the mind "makes words to fit." What is at stake, then, is a process of translation in art, from the medium of the world, that part of the unity of nature clearly perceived by the artist, to the medium of art. That is, sensation itself, as cognitive scientists (Damasio) and philosophers (Deleuze; Nussbaum) have come to affirm, deserves to be understood to be thought, as much as language is thought.

Such a reading, of sensation as thought, is, I would contend, consistent with Cézanne's understanding, which, in turn, is consistent with Leibniz's relation between the Monad (God, or the idea of everything) and the monads (perceiving minds). I would further contend that Cézanne's theories, as a number of critics have noted, are developed by Roger Fry, and further adapted by Virginia Woolf: especially in *To the Lighthouse* and *The Waves*.

Fry's Sensation and Composition

Fry begins using the word "sensation" long before he becomes aware of Cézanne. In an unpublished article of 1894, "The Philosophy of Impressionism," he outlines the manner in which Impressionism moves away from an attempt to depict things, by instead rendering the flux of sensations, which are understood as appearances (Fry 1996: pp. 13–14). The term "sensation" here has a different sense to that given to it by Cézanne. Whereas the "sensation" of the Impressionists relates to the

---

1 As I outlined in Chapter 1, this does not mean that expression requires something prior to itself; rather, the external sensation already is expression.

appearance of things, Cézanne, as we have seen, brings the appearances, or sensations offered by external nature, into dialogue with the internal nature of the artist; that is, the painter is no longer all "eye" as with the Impressionists, but now also mind, an organizing mind, which orders or composes these external sensations through recourse to its own internal sensations. These internal sensations in turn echo the sense of form apparent in the answering motifs and perceived harmony of nature. Again, one thinks of Leibniz here: the monad reflects part of the great Monad that is all in all, not merely in perceiving a section of the whole clearly, but in partaking of the same reason or ratio that determines the nature of the whole. Writing in his essay "Post Impressionism" of 1911, Fry ventures that Cézanne took this step, a step away from mere recording to reinstating the kind of expressive form that had been lost to modern art, "almost unconsciously" (1996: p. 109). In doing this, Fry contends that Cézanne went beyond appearances in creating *the real* in his pictures. In his full length study of Cézanne, Fry moves away from this notion of the unconscious, indicating that Cézanne represents an almost miraculous coming together of a rigorous intellect and a "sensibility of extreme delicacy" (Fry 1927: p. 70). He recognizes the discomfort with the word "intellect" and offers a rare footnote in which he justifies the term:

> What is here called intellect is not, of course, a purely logical function. All apprehension of formal relations depends on the special sensibility of the artist . . . an artist's sensibility to form appears as having two almost distinct functions according as it is applied to the correlation of all the separate forms in a design, and as applied to the detailed texture of form, its minor variations and play of surface. In comparing these two one is tempted to use the word intellectual of the former . . . (Fry 1927: p. 71)

Fry, then, has separated the terms somewhat, using "sensation" to apply to the data received from external nature, and an intellectual "sensibility," for the apprehension and organization of this that is applied by the internal nature of the artist. The understanding of the process involved, however, is identical with that described above through Cézanne's descriptions of his own endeavors. Elsewhere in this study, indeed, Fry recognizes that these two domains might be understood, in Cézanne's terms, to correspond through the sensation: "[Cézanne] alone was sincere enough to rely on his sensations and abandon all efforts at eloquence or emphasis" (Fry 1927: p. 72).

Woolf's Sensation
In a letter to Roger Fry of April 1924, Virginia Woolf states that she is reading a biography of Cézanne. While she does not indicate whether this is Vollard's 1914 biography, or Gasquet's book, which appeared in 1921,

Vollard's biography is held in her and Leonard's library. While Woolf would have known of Cézanne's notion of sensation through Fry, then, she also clearly knew of his key ideas through her own reading.

In the final section of To the Lighthouse, Lily Briscoe is described finally beginning to solve the problem posed by external nature, the image that confronts her, which has been held suspended over the many years since the time recounted in the opening section of the novel. At last she begins:

> With a curious physical sensation, as if she were urged forward and at the same time must hold herself back, she made her first quick decisive stroke. The brush descended. It flickered brown over the white canvas; it left a running mark. A second time she did it — a third time. And so pausing and so flickering, she attained a dancing rhythmical movement, as if the pauses were one part of the rhythm and the strokes another, and all were related; and so, lightly and swiftly pausing, striking, she scored her canvas with brown running nervous lines which had no sooner settled there than they enclosed (she felt it looming out at her) a space. Down in the hollow of one wave she saw the next wave towering higher and higher above her. For what could be more formidable than that space? Here she was again, she thought, stepping back to look at it, drawn out of gossip, out of living, out of community with people into the presence of this formidable ancient enemy of hers — this other thing, this truth, this reality, which suddenly laid hands on her, emerged stark at the back of appearances and commanded her attention. (Woolf 2000a: pp. 172–3)

This passage brings to mind the conversation between Woolf and Russell, and the shadows of Leibniz that Banfield and others have found in their shared interests: the desire to move beyond "mush" to the real; the real that can be revealed by attending to the logic that inheres within sensation. So too, not only the emphasis on sensation (which begins this passage and infuses it through the rhythm of the brushstrokes) but also on moving from appearance to reality bring Cézanne sharply to mind here. The links are even more fully apparent if one looks at the drafts of To the Lighthouse, where the link that Cézanne makes between the sensation that is felt and the sensation that is conveyed by the brushstroke and now comes to life on the canvas is underlined through the repeated use of the words "sensitive" and "sensibility":

> Her preparations were made; her palate spread; & now
>
> With a curious physical sensation of ~~leaping~~, . . . she laid the t made
>
> The first quick decisive stroke. It flickered brown over the pure

white canvas ... attaining by degrees, a

~~dancing~~ rhythmical ~~sensitive~~ movement, as if the

brush itself were ~~a~~ one sensitive ~~proboscis of instrument of some~~

some sensitive weapon ~~in the inspired~~ with nerves ~~of its own~~

she ~~scribbled~~ scored her canvas ~~over with~~ with light brown

~~sl~~ lines ~~wavering, whose~~ which ~~extreme~~ sensibility froze into

~~whose~~ sensibility ~~enclosed described the~~ at once settled into

something ~~formidable~~ permanent. (Woolf 1983: p. 256)

As with Cézanne, then, there is a complex interaction around the idea of sensation: sensation is projected by external nature and seen, and the process of seeing itself (which involves the viewpoint or rather a series of viewpoints) is a natural process for organizing sensation, but then it needs to be further organized by the internal nature of the artist. The process of organization, the understanding or compositional thinking required of the "mind" of the artist, has been that which has been in suspension, for Lily, between part one and part three of the novel. Once it has been organized or understood the sensation is transferred to the touch, or brushstroke, with each rhythmical touch constituting a sensation, laying down a series of related sensations in turn on the canvas, which might then be experienced or confronted by a viewer.

The process of ordering sensations, then, is something that concerns the artist, but it also concerns the viewer. Everyone has sensations, what is required, however, both with the creation of the work and with any response to the work, is that those sensations be given solidity in being properly composed within the work. The following quotation is attributed to Cézanne by Gasquet, with Cézanne here discussing the portrait he is in the process of painting of Gasquet's father:

[E]very brush stroke I make is a little of my blood mixed with a little of your father's blood, in the sunshine, in the light, in the colour, and that there's a mysterious exchange which goes from his soul (which he doesn't know about) to my eye, which recreates it and in which he will recognize himself ... if I am a painter ... Every stroke, there on my canvas, must correspond to a living breath, to the light over there on his whiskers, on his cheek. (Cited in Gasquet 1991: p. 212)

This problem, of how to properly connect the work by drawing together the relations between motifs, is the very one which confronts Lily:

> It was a question, she remembered, how to connect this mass on the right hand with that on the left. She might do it by bringing the line of the branch across so; or break the vacancy in the foreground by an object (James perhaps) so. But the danger was that by doing that the unity of the whole might be broken. She stopped; she did not want to bore him. (Woolf 2000a: p. 60; see also Woolf 1983: p. 93)

The problem of establishing relations in the work is immediately linked with the problem of establishing relations in life, connections with other people. Mr. Bankes has seriously engaged with her picture, and to Lily, who is used to being patronized, this involves both on the one hand having something which is very important to her taken from her (she hates the violation of her unfinished work being seen) and on the other being exhilarated by being able to share in an almost unimaginable intimacy, one which is not simply sexual but related to the emotional intellect which Fry has seen in the work of Cézanne. Mr. Bankes's genuine engagement with her work has opened to her a power of the world, "which she had not suspected, that one could walk away down that long gallery not alone any more but arm-in-arm with somebody" (Woolf 2000a: p. 60). The metaphor here links the interaction around the work with immediate human intimacy. What allows this as a possibly is a corresponding effort on each side: Lily's effort to relate, and Mr Bankes's effort to understand what is being related. Woolf, then, underlines how the artistic process involves not only sensation but the composition of relations that are found within and between distinct sensations (or viewpoints). What is represented, then, is not merely the pure sensation (the perception of the monad) but a logic of sensations (Leibniz's idea of the mind as a particular kind of monad that is able to organize or think about its perceptions). This logic involves not only the relation of the self of the monad, but the complex relation to the world that comprises the actualization (or adequate understanding) of the monad, through the composition.

Interestingly, in the draft of *To the Lighthouse* transcribed by Susan Dick, the relation between the work and human relations is stressed in a way which is toned down considerably in the finished version. In the draft Lily's thoughts emphasize a feminine movement from art toward the kinds of relations which were then thought to be more "proper" to women: human relations. She thinks:

> But here was somebody who made it seem possible to paint a
>
> picture; &, returning to the normal relationship again; not

of women & trees, but of women & human beings, she ~~would~~ was

~~have thanked him for~~ n̂ot his extraordinary magnanimity,

~~would have~~ which was so rare, so in her experience, &

~~how odd it was~~, sometimes to be which lightened the whole

of her horizon — for here was a man . . . who ~~did not~~

would let one talk to him. (Woolf 1983: p. 93)

In the finished version, this idea is largely cut from Lily's account, replaced by the image of walking arm in arm down a gallery. It is Mrs. Ramsay who is the artist of human relations, and Lily, in the end, offers the possibility of allowing women to develop relationships in art which are not inferior to human relations, which rather, allow a fuller understanding of relations of all kinds.

The Waves: Sensation and the Composition of Viewpoints

The challenge to relate in art involves the challenge to both open up and order sensations in ways which are unexpected and revealing, and in *The Waves* the idea that this challenge involves the viewer as much as the artist is emphasized. Bernard mourns Perceval, and suffering the raw sensations of this recent bereavement he removes himself from the "usual order" of the world, an order in which things belong within the inexorable sequence of everyday life. Bernard cannot bear this usual order and goes to an art gallery to escape it:

> Yes, but I still resent the usual order. I will not let myself be made to accept the sequence of things. I will walk; I will not change the rhythm of my mind by stopping, by looking; I will walk. I will go up these steps into the gallery and submit myself to the influence of minds like mine outside the sequence. (Woolf 2000b: pp. 104–5)

The world attempts to force the mind to follow its order, and Bernard resists this. The key word "rhythm" recurs here, related to a sense of self which, in its disordered state directly perceives something hidden beneath the surface of the everyday sequence, and the paintings allow Bernard to explore this space:

> Let them lay to rest the incessant activity of the mind's eye, the bandaged head, the men with ropes, so that I may find something unvisual beneath . . . Mercifully these pictures make no reference; they

do not nudge; they do not point. Thus they expand my consciousness of him and bring him back to me differently. (Woolf 2000b: p. 105)

The relations drawn in the works are not the straightforward connections of "the sequence," where one thing follows another in a simplistic line of causation. Rather, they are relations which remain elusive, which one needs to struggle to grasp, but from the beginning it is apparent that these are deeper, hidden or sacred relations. In Chapter 2, the importance of causation to thinking in the arts was discussed, but this chapter has attempted to further illustrate how this idea needs to be understood in a nuanced way in the arts with regard to its manner of thinking the real. That is, causation involves gaps and relations across gaps in differing but ultimately related viewpoints. The key word "sensation" will return in the passage immediately following that just cited, but here it is linked to the core of life, the kinds of violent shocks which Woolf described elsewhere as involved in moments of being or exceptional moments, jolts on the nerves which are at once a kind of understanding (an immediate fearful understanding, an apprehensive recognition) and elusive, drawing one on to try and translate the nonlinguistic apprehension into a medium that will preserve it (either through interpreting and defining what has been felt, or in creating an object which can in turn convey a sensation approximate to that which has been felt). Here, art takes the place of religion in that it offers a means of coming into contact with this sensation. She outlines the nature of these moments in "Sketch from the Past" in a passage that resonates with the notions of pattern and meaning we will consider in detail in looking at the work of Nabokov below.

> [T]hough I still have the peculiarity that I receive these sudden shocks, they are now always welcome; after the first surprise, I always feel instantly that they are particularly valuable. And so I go on to suppose that the shock-receiving capacity is what makes me a writer. I hazard the explanation that a shock is at once in my case followed by the desire to explain it. I feel that I have had a blow; but it is not, as I thought as a child, simply a blow from an enemy hidden behind the cotton wool of daily life; it is or will become a revelation of some order; it is a token of some real thing behind appearances; and I make it real by putting it into words. It is only by putting it into words that I make it whole; this wholeness means that it has lost its power to hurt me; it gives me, perhaps because by doing so I take away the pain, a great delight to put the severed parts together. Perhaps this is the strongest pleasure known to me. It is the rapture I get when in writing I seem to be discovering what belongs to what; making a scene come right; making a character come together. From this I reach what I might call a philosophy; at any rate it is a constant idea of mine;

that behind the cotton wool is hidden a pattern; that we — I mean all human beings — are connected with this; that the whole world is a work of art; that we are parts of the work of art. (Woolf 2002: p. 73)

At first Bernard is pessimistic that any real connection will be made for him by the work, that any real comfort or understanding will emerge as he considers a painting of the Madonna by Titian. He believes the violent sensation he is feeling will remain cut off from the rest of the world:

> Behold, then, the blue madonna streaked with tears. This is my funeral service. We have no ceremonies, only private dirges and no conclusions, only violent sensations, each separate. Nothing that has been said meets our case. We sit in the Italian room at the National Gallery picking up fragments. I doubt that Titian ever felt this raw gnaw. Painters live lives of methodical absorption, adding stroke to stroke. (Woolf 2000b: p. 106)

As he continues to contemplate the work, however, Bernard becomes less certain. Something in the work, or many things, the emotional intelligence behind the relation of the elements within the work, the forms, the colors, in turn gnaw at him, in some way echoing, or revealing an unexpected and barely understood harmony with the gnawing of the violent sensation left him by Perceval's death. He realizes he has not understood the picture, that he cannot simply dismiss it as failing to do justice to what he is feeling, that its sensations are entering into him and working on him directly, beneath and despite of any logical assessment he might be capable of bringing to bear through language and conscious reflection.

> Yet that crimson must have burnt in Titian's gizzard. No doubt he rose with the great arms holding the cornucopia, and fell, in that descent. But the silence weighs on me — the perpetual solicitation of the eye. The pressure is intermittent and muffled. I distinguish too little and too vaguely. The bell is pressed and I do not ring or give out irrelevant clamours all jangled. I am titillated inordinately by some splendour; the ruffled crimson against the green lining; the march of pillars; the orange light behind the black, pricked ears of the olive trees. Arrows of sensation strike from my spine, but without order. (Woolf 2000b: p. 106)

That order, that is, is not immediately perceived, it does not follow a linguistic linear sequence; rather, it works subtly and directly through a logic of sensations. The sensations have, despite Bernard's skepticism, been planted, a connection has been made and the seed of a dimly apprehended order has begun to work itself upon his system.

Yet something is added to my interpretations. Something lies deeply buried. For one moment I thought to grasp it. But bury it, bury it; let it breed, hidden in the depths of my mind some day to fructify. After a long lifetime, loosely, in a moment of revelation, I may lay hands on it, but now the idea breaks in my hand. (Woolf 2000b: p. 106)

Again it is a problem of translation between, in this case, the medium proper to art and the medium proper to life. The problem of translation between forms or rhythms was something that greatly occupied Woolf and in some senses structured her relationships with her circle, the Bloomsbury group, which contained so many painters and theorists of artistic practice. It seems as if in some way she wanted to translate for them.

As I note above a number of critics have drawn links between Leibniz and Woolf (see Ferrer 1990; Henry 2003; Banfield 2000), particularly in relation to the idea of possible worlds and the manner in which Woolf seems to shift between these viewpoints in developing her fiction. The idea of sensation is crucial to the process in two ways.

First, the sensation of the artist is that which allows the development of an overview of disparate possible worlds. The apparently discrete possible worlds comprised by individuals need to be composed into a unity. This unity is first felt before it is organized or understood through the kind of logic of sensation described above. We see this process illustrated in the example of Lily Briscoe, but here she stands for all artists and in particular Woolf. As is well known, Woolf began to think of *To The Lighthouse* with a sketch of two rooms connected by a corridor (Lee 1999: p. 469). Each room already comprises an overview, or set, of possible worlds (the world with Mrs. Ramsey; the world without Mrs. Ramsey), yet it is not possible to have both sets *at the same time*. Of course, the passing of time is the corridor through which one set of possible worlds communicates with another set. The world with Mrs. Ramsey and the world without Mrs. Ramsey are drawn into a unity through processes that begin with sensation and are realized through the composition of those sensations.

Second, in *The Waves*, Bernard first begins to come to terms with his situation through his contemplation of the organized sensations he encounters in the gallery. That is, he feels the meaning in the works, which, through the composition of intense sensations they have effected, render him, at last, composed. This is a second kind of use of sensation as it does not now involve a composition across possible worlds (that is, reconciling lived existence to the passing of time); rather it now involves a correspondence between a work of art and a viewer, which, in turn, effects a composure of disparate sensations within a self, which, due to grief had found itself in disarray. Death has caused a former state of being or feeling to become incompatible with a present state, yet through the composition of sensation the seemingly incompatible parts of one's self are again drawn together: they are composed, or, to put this another way, understood through the creation of thought possible in art.

What is crucial here is to recognize that art, and in this case *To The Lighthouse* and *The Waves* offers a type of thinking. What we need to attempt to trace is the nature of this thinking, or some of its attributes. We have seen how it comes from sensation, is organized, and emerges as sensation. What might equally be recognized in the passages cited above in which Lily Briscoe begins to paint, is how the ideas themselves, the thoughts themselves, only take their genuine form as they emerge upon the canvas. The practice itself, the process of painting, of putting touches on the canvas is as crucial to the thinking as the internal reflection or the initial apprehension of sensation. So too, while a writer of Woolf's type might first hear a rhythm which she then translates into words, the words themselves complete the thought in embodying the original rhythm and attributing sense to that sensation.

Self-consciousness

An idea which has been expressed by numerous artists and theorists, with Deleuze and Guattari returning to the notion in recent years, is that art does not represent nature; rather, it creates alongside nature. Emile Bernard reported that Cézanne, for his part, stated that, "Painting from nature is not copying the object; it is realizing one's sensations" (Kendall 1988: p. 299). Gasquet, in turn, cites Cézanne as stating that, "Art has a harmony which parallels that of nature" (Gasquet 1991: p. 150). Fry discusses this kind of "realization" in his reading of Cézanne's portrait of M. Geoffroy, citing the sixteenth-century Italian art critic Giorgio Vasari in support of the idea that the painting is no longer "mere imitation" but "life itself," which he, in turn, suggests to be, "another way of expressing Cézanne's idea that the artist is the means by which nature becomes self-conscious" (Fry 1927: p. 71). This process of rendering nature self-conscious is a complex one, which involves an interplay with the mind, which organizes and projects the sensations received from nature.

In order to render an objective consciousness on the canvas, the artist needs to develop an unselfconscious or modest approach. We have seen the importance of this process to composition in art in Chapter 3. For Fry the process of creation necessarily involves "humility" and he suggests that "all artists of the highest order have to pass through this state" (Fry 1927: p. 29): that is, the artist needs to efface the self, or at least the opinions and direct interpretations that are generally associated with the self, in order to achieve the work. The mind of the artist, as it is understood by Cézanne, then, rather than interpreting nature, translates nature; he is quoted by Gasquet as follows:

> The artist is nothing more than a receptacle of sensations, a brain, a recording machine . . . A damned good machine, fragile and complex,

above all in its relationship to other machines . . . But if he intervenes, if he dares to meddle voluntarily with what he ought to merely be translating, he introduces his own insignificance into it and the work is inferior . . . His whole aim must be silence. He must silence all the voices of prejudice within him, he must forget, forget, be silent, become a perfect echo. And then the entire landscape will engrave itself on the sensitive plate of his being. (Gasquet 1991: p. 150)

Similar ideas can be traced in Virginia Woolf's description of the artistic process developed by Lily Briscoe, and more generally in her own aesthetic writings. Both in "The Window" and "The Lighthouse" Lily Briscoe is represented as self-effacing, with a lack of self-confidence linked to an acute sensitivity to the dominant cultural opinion, expressed by Charles Tansley, that women are unable to create at the same level as men (Woolf 2000a: p. 54). She is forced to be humble, and like Roger Fry, who, as Woolf noted, had difficulty selling his work, she resigns herself to creating works that might never be seen, canvases that will be rolled up and stored to gather dust. Yet, as Woolf would already have known from her reading about Cézanne, such humility if coupled with an intense concentration on the process of creation, can be important components to the achievement of art. This model of creation is validated and even mythologized by the story of Cézanne, who remained obscure throughout his life-time.

In Gasquet's book, we are given a scene involving Cézanne painting a portrait of Gasquet's father, and discussing his methods with the father and son in the process. Here the idea of concentration and self-effacement are highlighted as principles of the artistic process. Obscurity allows fuller concentration on the works and leaves the artist free from the temptation to become self-satisfied. Without these impediments the artist can continue to strive, to try again in a different manner. To cite from Gasquet:

My Father:

But the boy tells me that you don't have the standing you deserve.

Cézanne:

He can say what he likes . . . As for me, I have to stay in my house, see nobody, work . . . My standing, indeed! . . . That would mean being pleased with myself. And that I never am. That I will never be. I can't be. (Gasquet 1991: p. 208)

Woolf was clearly aware of this aspect of Cézanne's legend, and drew upon it in linking Fry to Cézanne. In the letter of 1924 in which she tells Fry she has been reading a biography of Cézanne, she links Fry, through his failure to achieve popular acclaim, with Cézanne, in a way that also makes us think of Lily Briscoe: "So if you never sell a picture till you're 70 you will only be like Cézanne — but I hope you are selling" (Woolf 1980b: p. 29).

More than this, however, humility seems to be necessary to the proper creation of the work, whose emergence is only possible when true self-effacement is achieved. As with Kleist, as we have seen in Chapter 3, in order for nature to become self-conscious in the work, the artist cannot be self-conscious; rather, it is suggested, "conscious thought" must somehow be suppressed so that another kind of thinking can take hold, akin to Cézanne's "thinking machine" of sensation:

> What was the problem then? She must try and get hold of something that evaded her. It evaded her when she thought of Mrs. Ramsay; it evaded her now when she thought of her picture. Phrases came. Visions came. Beautiful pictures. Beautiful phrases. But what she wished to get hold of was the very jar on the nerves, the thing itself before it has been made anything. Get that and start afresh; she said desperately, pitching herself firmly again before her easel. It was a miserable machine, an inefficient machine, she thought, the human apparatus for painting or for feeling; it always broke down at the critical moment; heroically, one must force it on. She stared, frowning. There was the hedge, sure enough. But one got nothing by soliciting urgently. One got only a glare in the eye from looking at the line of the wall, or from thinking — she wore a grey hat. She was astonishingly beautiful. Let it come, she thought, if it will come. For there are moments when one can neither think nor feel. And if one can neither think nor feel, she thought, where is one? (Woolf 2000a: pp. 209–10)

Rather than complacently dismissing these concepts of "rhythm" and "sensation" as "romantic" (in the now commonplace sense of foolishly naïve), we need to recognize, as Woolf, Cézanne, and the Romantics themselves recognized, that they are linked to facts of perception. In a diary entry of 19 December 1920 Woolf compares Fry to Coleridge in a somewhat slighting way: "I think [*Vision and Design*] reads rudimentary compared with Coleridge. Fancy reforming poetry by discovering something scientific about the composition of light" (Woolf 1980a: p. 81). Woolf is no doubt referring to a passage in chapter 14 of Coleridge's *Biographia Literaria* of 1817 in which he describes how he and Wordsworth recognized two powers in poetry: first the power to excite sympathy by "faithful adherence to the truth of nature," and second the power "of giving the interest of novelty" through the inventions of the imagination. Recognizing that various effects of light apparent at sun-set or through moonlight could modify a familiar landscape, they realized that these two powers could be combined. Two kinds of "nature" poetry were then developed by the poets in response to the recognition of these facts of perception. First, there is the poem of supernatural theme (such as Coleridge's "Rime of the Ancient Mariner"), which works on the fact that we all, when confronted with hallucination or some other kind of altered state of perception, believe fantastic visions to be real. This kind of poem exploits this perceptual mechanism by presenting fantastic visions as if they were real in order to excite the kinds of sensations in a reader that altered perception might engender. The second kind of poem, developed by Wordsworth in the *Lyrical Ballads*, focuses upon and requires us to closely examine the nature of everyday characters and events. In both cases, then, rather than this aesthetic theory passing through naïve formulas or simplistic conventions, it becomes apparent that such thought is built upon theories of perception, sensation, and psychological insight. Such theory, that is, takes perception and its affects as a point of departure.

In order to *translate* a perception or a sensation, it follows that one has to leave that sensation in an "uninterpreted" state. The conscious self interferes with this process because it strives to impose its interpretations. The artist's mind must organize the sensations, so as to translate it in such a way that something akin to the original sensation can be re-projected, but that mind cannot be self-conscious.

Such ideas are not only there in Cézanne and Fry, but also in the work of another of Woolf's contemporaries, Edward Gordan Craig, who was also linked at times with Bloomsbury. As we have seen in Chapter 3, Craig drew on the aesthetic theories of another Romantic writer, the German playwright Heinrich von Kleist in developing a theory of the actor as *"über-marionette."* It is worth revisiting this idea here, to further develop our understanding of what is at stake. Craig complained that actors were too self-conscious in their performances, that they must replace this with an absolute lack of self-consciousness such as would be conveyed by a body in trance. Actors "must create for themselves a new form of acting" (Craig 1956: p. 61), "The über-marionette will not compete with life — rather will it go beyond it. Its ideal will not be the flesh and blood but rather the body in trance" (1956: p. 84). Christopher Innes states that Craig saw the major vice of actors to be "the display of personality" (Innes 1983: p. 123), which got in the way of the expression of the work. In order to properly convey the work, to translate its sensations, "the actor had to have total physical control, which precluded personal vanity" (1983: p. 123).

Like Lily Briscoe, the artist must be humble, must not *be* at all, in a sense. As Hermione Lee has shown, this notion of the unselfconscious artist as key to the production of art was something which interested Woolf a good deal, especially towards the end of her life. Lee contends that

Woolf's last novel, *Between the Acts*, ends where one of her last projected books of criticism, *Reading at Random* begins:[2] that is, with a meditation on the notion of the importance of anonymity in art (Lee 1999: p. 738).

Translating Sensation: Literature and Painting

In 1934, Woolf published a pamphlet on the English painter Walter Sickert, entitled *Walter Sickert: A Conversation*. This work returns to a question that has been begged throughout this paper: the relation between the arts of painting and writing, and how sensation might not only be translated across the mediums of art and life, but how it might be further translated between artistic mediums. This process is of fundamental importance for this study as it emphasizes the nature of that which is itself translatable: the sensation. Sickert told Woolf, "I have always been a literary painter" (Woolf 1934: p. 26; see Lee 1999: p. 632). It is apparent, however, that what is at stake in this relation between painting and literature needs to be clarified.

Cézanne, for his part, condemned a certain kind of "literary" painting. He told Gasquet:

> I don't like literary painting. To write below a person what he's thinking and what he's doing is to admit that his thought and his intention are not conveyed by the drawing and the colour. And wanting to force nature to say things, making trees twist and rocks frown, as Gustave Doré does, or even painting it like da Vinci, that's literature too. There's a logic of colour, damn it all! The painter owes allegiance to that alone. (Gasquet 1991: p. 161)

Yet, the rejection of the literary is not as straightforward as it might appear. Cézanne here equates "literary" painting with the over-explanatory, the merely illustrative: the kind of painting which too obviously directs a viewer's interpretation. Fry's study of Cézanne, however, makes clear that the relations between Cézanne's art and literature are more complex. Fry underlines how Cézanne, in his early work, came to painting with an imagination which was already steeped in poetry, and, rather than seeking to draw upon external nature (as he was to later do), he at first attempted to draw upon his imagination. Fry states:

> He worked . . . to find expression for the agitations of his inner life, and, without making literary pictures in the bad sense of the word, he sought to express himself as much by the choice and implications of his figures as by the plastic exposition of their forms. (Fry 1927: p. 9)

---

2 A book that would, among other things, explain to painters what it meant to be a writer (Lee 1999: p. 737).

Hermoine Lee outlines in her biography how Woolf came to write *Walter Sickert: A Conversation* (Lee 1999: pp. 632–3). Clearly, the problem of how one might begin to consider positive relations between literature and painting when her visual artist friends where hostile to the very idea of "literary" painting, is one which preoccupied her. No doubt Woolf was encouraged in this project by Walter Sickert himself, yet the sense of difficulty in establishing this relation would have been exacerbated for her by her attraction to, and sense of distance from, the kind of visual aesthetic intelligence developed by her artist friends, and Vanessa Bell, Duncan Grant, Clive Bell, and Roger Fry in particular. Lee, indeed, alludes to the feelings of ridicule she exposed herself to in developing the idea that there might be such a thing as a worthwhile "literary" reading of a painting.

Some of the anxiety inherent in the process makes itself felt in the form of this piece. While the dialogue form was a well-known technique within art criticism (see Shiff 19991: p. 16), Woolf chooses to write a "conversation" rather than a "dialogue." The dialogue, with its echoes of Plato and the history of philosophy, is a serious form, one in which questions are dissected and analyzed until the truth is at last discovered. Woolf opposes "the conversation" to this: while it is still a matter of entering into a kind of dialogue, where contrasting positions might be brought into comparison, the conversation is not serious; rather, it is impure, "it runs hither and thither, seldom sticks to the point, [and] abounds in exaggeration and inaccuracy" (Woolf 1934: p. 5). Yet while conversation might only "haunt the borders" of the true silence that is at the core of any art, this borderland is nevertheless "a region of very strong sensations" (1934: p. 12). Furthermore, towards the end of her essay, Woolf hints that this kind of impurity inheres in any major work of art, so that, in effect, the conversation allows us to see the kinds of hybrid forms that can emerge in the arts. The apparent lack of seriousness that Woolf develops reveals a deeper seriousness, and an impatience with forms of criticism that do not countenance the necessarily impure mixtures that emerge both in life and art.

> Undoubtedly, they agreed, the arts are closely united. What poet sets pen to paper without first hearing a tune in his head? And the prose writer, though he makes believe to walk soberly, in obedience to the voice of reason, excites us by perpetual changes of rhythm following the emotions with which he deals. The best critics, Dryden, Lamb, Hazlitt, were acutely aware of the mixture of elements, and wrote of literature with music and painting in their minds. Nowadays we are all so specialized that critics keep their brains fixed to the print, which accounts for the starved condition of criticism in our time, and the attenuated and partial manner in which it deals with its subject. (p. 24)

This quotation brings us back to the question of rhythm and offers more detail as to how we might understand it. Further, when one reads this essay in the light of Lee's biography, it becomes strangely apparent that the conversation described involves not a true dialogue but two parallel dialogues, one of which, indeed, might well be a monologue. In the set piece of the conversation we are given a number of heterogeneous elements. We begin with small talk about traffic lights, which leads to speculative fictions on the invention of the art gallery in England. From here we are entertained with a fanciful myth, linked with natural history, of an insect that lives on color alone. Yet as the conversation progresses, we meet a point at which two "groups" at the imagined dinner party diverge (and they are never really reconciled, with each developing their separate conversations). When one speaker ventures, as Woolf herself does in the piece as a whole, that Sickert's paintings could be read to involve stories — biographical stories in that each of the characters portrayed have, folded within them but somehow visible on their faces, all of their life story presented to us in the pictures; or fictional or novelistic stories, as the characters seem to be set in action, and cause the viewer to want to make up stories about them — the experts in painting laugh, and turn to one another, discussing the pure forms within the paintings, the kinds of relations between geometrical and chromatic motifs described by Cézanne, and in Fry's criticism, for example. This group then proceeds to "talk" among themselves, but without words, as words are not adequate to fully convey this level of meaning, which Woolf's narrator concedes is at a deeper and truer level. A second group, however, cannot follow these experts. The second group are privileged Englishmen and women, who are habituated to talk and cannot escape from the implications of words.

As we have noted, Lee shows how Woolf was dismissed as naïve for wanting to make a link between literature and painting. With this in mind, then, one tends to read the "groups" as involving Virginia's painter friends as the experts on the one hand, and herself, more or less alone, on the other. The conversation between the talkers, who consider that painting, and Sickert's in particular, can be biographical and novelistic, seems really to involve a dramatization of a monologue within Woolf's own head. The "real" conversation, then, that between different people, involves the complete failure to communicate that is witnessed between the experts and the talkers. Yet the form itself works upon us, putting us in a scene that we picture and sense: the scene of an interesting dinner party among intelligent and amusing friends. It disarms us: we are urged to leave our weapons at the door for the evening, and, in the course of the evening, we imbibe substances that, if our nature is favorable to such processes, might work upon us and change our minds.

At the heart of this are a few ideas concerning the relation between literature and painting. While it is recognized that the two forms part ways at a given point and that painting is not writing, it is asserted that they indeed have much in common: the painter writing, the writer painting. What is important, however, is that neither compromise her or his art in looking to the other for guidance: the writer cannot succeed in "painting" by pure description; rather, metaphors hidden at the heart of individual words are brought into contact to suggest rather than describe visual effects (Woolf 1934: pp. 23–4). So too, the painter is not literary in the sense that the images are explained by some story or life history; rather, the painted image includes such stories and histories in virtual form, curled within even while visible on the surface. Just as with Deleuze's understanding of Leibniz's folds of being (discussed in Chapter 2), the stories have to be unraveled, unfolded; what is given is the immediate truth of a moment, a moment that reveals elements towards a meaning of an entire life (1934: pp. 10–19). Here Woolf makes us think of Cézanne, who admitted the possibility of the revelation of the truth about a life in painting, in the work of Velasquez, if not in his own work.

In Gasquet, Cézanne describes how he wants to express the reality of his self, by first rendering that self unconscious, merging it with the subject he paints through "suggestions of shadow and light." That is, rather than attempting to "trace the truth" over the "preconceived" person he paints, he wants to get to the truth of his own self: "to present it as it is." Gasquet then interrupts to ask Cézanne about Velasquez. Did he not paint true portraits?

> Ah! Velasquez, that's another story. He took his revenge [...] here was this man painting away in privacy [...] Some idiot [...] drags him along to the king ... In those days they had not invented photography ... Do my portrait [...] Velasquez became the court photographer [...] He was a prisoner [...] He took a terrible revenge. He painted them with all their blemishes, their vices, their decadence ... His hatred and his objectivity became one ... He painted the king and his buffoons the way Flaubert presented his Homais and Bournisien ... Velasquez bears no resemblance to his portraits, but look how Rembrandt and Rubens are always there, you can recognize them under all the faces. (Gasquet 1991: p. 215)

While Woolf, then, argues for the possibility of an art like that of Velasquez, one might suggest that she herself paints more like a Rubens or Rembrandt: recognizable under the surface of her characters and the situations they encounter. Yet she insists on the idea that there are *kinds* of artists: that artists have different gifts and different ways of working. Yet in each case the artist must begin with a relation to sensation (a viewpoint or series of viewpoints) which must then be translated or composed into a work capable of conveying that sensation (which can, in effect, be conveyed in various ways using various mediums). If one sees Cézanne as a kind of poet, as Fry does, one might read Velasquez here as that rare thing: the true, objective biographer, a species which Woolf considers more likely to emerge in painting than in writing, given the various compromises the writer of biography is required to make (Woolf 1934: pp. 12–13). Yet the painter as novelist is a somewhat different beast (1934: pp. 13–14).

It is possible, however, to link all this with well-known insights Woolf expressed elsewhere — the idea of "moments of being" — which allow us to see something in common between portrait painting, at least, and fiction. The moment of being Woolf describes is a moment of pure and intense sensation. It is intense because it involves the folding within of pure potential. All life, or at least a clue to its meaning, is condensed into a moment, is held within that moment. In writing one seeks to recapture such a moment or to approximate the intense sensations it produces, by other means. Such a moment, however, because it is folded in, might in turn be unfolded, teased out, either in interpretation, or in the stories which surround that moment, leading up to and away from it. This is the kind of "story" Woolf, or her avatars, find in Sickert, stories which are implicit within a captured moment, which carry a power to make a viewer want to enter into it and tease out its implications. Lily Briscoe is striving to capture such a moment, to fold relationships within a canvas. So too, Bernard is seeking to unravel the secret within a canvas that seems to include, folded within it, something which speaks to his own life. *To the Lighthouse*, of course, is also structured around such moments: James's failure to reach the Lighthouse in part one and his finally achieving it in part three provide motifs that are echoed throughout in the stories of the parents. So too, Lily Briscoe's attempts to finish her painting echoes Woolf's own biography, not least in her own tense relationship with painting and painters, where she wanted to be among them, apparently paradoxically, by folding back into herself to the point of that self becoming anonymous.

Yet the paradox is only apparent as, as we have seen, the composition of the sensation (the viewpoint or series of viewpoints) requires a thought capable of developing an overview: moving across and between possible worlds in developing a univocal survey of them.

6 Vladimir Nabokov: the Art of Composition

In 1999, Nabokov's biographer Brian Boyd published *Nabokov's Pale Fire: The Magic of Artistic Discovery*, a book which defends, often compellingly, an astonishing thesis. While Boyd backs away from the idea that he has found the "absolute meaning"[1] in this book, stating that he might be proved wrong in the future, he in no way backs away from the idea that, in Nabokov at least, the promise that there *might* be such a meaning is real, and further that Nabokov's novels often work with structures built around puzzles to be solved (puzzles, which, in effect, can be solved). The implications of Boyd's arguments are challenging, in that they force us to reconsider what a work of fiction might do: how it might function, and how it might be designed to function; that is, insofar as they relate to an idea of how fiction might work at the level of design or composition.

In this chapter I will begin to consider some of the implications of the problem of intention Nabokov's work brings urgently back into focus, by drawing out elements of the interrelations between intention, influence, inspiration, intuition, and interpretation. All of this relates in turn to what I call the composition of externalized expression in Chapter 3. I will consider the extent to which Nabokov's works in particular, and works of fiction more generally that attempt to think about the world, might be understood in relation to an understanding of the analogue as a particular kind of relation between a work of fiction and an understanding of that which constitutes the real, an understanding built up through that kind of interpretation which seeks out the traces of composition (or that which draws together apparently disparate parts into a unity which generates a sense of meaning).

In this Chapter, I will profit from and build upon the critical insights offered by Boyd in developing my own reading of Nabokov's novel *Despair*, which was written in Russian as *Otchayanie* in 1932 and translated by Nabokov into English in 1936, and published in England in 1937 (see Proffer 1968). As such, it might be considered Nabokov's first English novel. In doing this I will show how Nabokov's method, which he partly describes in *The Real Life of Sebastian Knight* (as exemplifying

---

1 See Boyd (1999: p. 116) and Kernan (1987: p. 114).

"the methods of composition") and further describes in correspondence related to "The Vane Sisters," had, as Nabokov hints in *Strong Opinions*, already been developed prior to World War II (Nabokov 1990: pp. 102–3) and, indeed, form a crucial part of the overall composition. Further, and more importantly, I will show how this method of composition involves externalized expression, as viewpoints or sensations are related through intra- and inter-textual references, leading us towards a sense of meaning.

Boyd and *Nabokov's Pale Fire*

In *Nabokov's Pale Fire* Boyd (1999) argues that there are "solutions" to various problems, which are posed within various layers of *Pale Fire*, solutions that resemble the solutions to chess problems, and moreover, that these can be tested through criteria of "falsifiability" (based on an analogy with the scientific models developed by Karl Popper). Further, Boyd claims that, while no Nabokov novel can be seen as a template for any other Nabokov novel, that "they all operate through compounded connections and ramified relationships, and that they all have a shared foundation of ideas and attitudes" (1999: p. 253). That is, he argues that this process of problem setting occurs within many of Nabokov's novels: that Nabokov "repeatedly refers to 'solutions' to his novels" (p. 256).

In working towards this conclusion Boyd develops a description of Nabokov's aesthetic method which underlines the importance of techniques which Nabokov himself clearly outlined in relation to the design of his short story "The Vane Sisters." This story was submitted to the *New Yorker* in 1951, yet was rejected by the editor Katharine White, who was normally a great supporter of his work. Upset by the rejection of a story that he felt had brought his aesthetic method to a new level of perfection, Nabokov wrote to White to carefully explain the composition of this story, which includes an acrostic in the final paragraph, which reveals a hidden depth within it. He wrote:

> Most of the stories I am contemplating (and some I have written in the past — you actually published one with such an "inside" — the one about the old Jewish couple and their sick boy ["Signs and Symbols"]) will be composed on these lines, according to this system wherein a second (main) story is woven into, or placed behind, the superficial semitransparent one. (Cited in Boyd 1991: p. 195; and Boyd 1999: p. 214)

Boyd argues that Nabokov applied similar processes of composition, through pattern and problem setting, to many of his works. Boyd suggests that this method involves conceiving of the works, in part, as puzzles to be solved. In developing this idea he draws a close analogy between

Nabokov as a writer of fiction and Nabokov as a writer of chess problems (Boyd 1999: pp. 10–11; see Nabokov 1989a: pp. 289–93). His reading of *Pale Fire* proceeds along these lines. In many ways Boyd's argument is compelling and adds significantly to our understanding of Nabokov's aesthetic method. It is apparent that patterns do emerge as one looks for them in Nabokov's fiction. Yet I would argue, against Boyd, that even while one might approach ever closer (or as close as is critically possible) to an absolute meaning in Nabokov, the final terms of that meaning remain unknown, and that this too is intended.

In support of his contention that Nabokov's fiction is layered, and that it requires reading, re-reading and re-re-reading to uncover these layers, Boyd cites Nabokov's descriptions of reality, a word which elsewhere Nabokov describes as only having meaning within quotation marks:

> I can only define [Reality] as a kind of gradual accumulation of information; and as a specialization. If we take a lily, for instance, or any other kind of natural object, a lily is more real to a naturalist than it is to an ordinary person. But it is still more real to a botanist. And yet another stage of reality is reached with that botanist who is a specialist in lilies. You can get nearer and nearer, so to speak, to reality; but you never get near enough because reality is an infinite succession of steps, levels of perception, false bottoms, and hence unquenchable, unattainable. (Nabokov 1990: pp. 10–11)

This clearly supports Boyd's theory of the hidden patterns within *Pale Fire* and other of Nabokov's works: the closer one looks the more one finds. Yet the passage, too, might be read as a challenge to the idea first teasingly suggested by Nabokov himself in *The Real Life of Sebastian Knight* (Nabokov 1982: p. 151) that the fiction of his character Sebastian Knight (and by implication Nabokov's own fiction) might provide, or offer to provide an "absolute meaning." For while reality is approached it is never attained; that is, while absolute meaning is promised it remains nonetheless out of reach. Further, this approach towards reality involves degree. In *Pale Fire* the figure of Gradus and his gradual quest for Kinbote offer a kind of ironic inversion of this pursuit of knowledge. "Gradus," in Latin, is one of those peculiar words with two apparently contradictory senses: on the one hand the word refers to a step-by-step approach (as Jacob Gradus inexorably makes his way from Zembla to New Wye), and "degree" is associated with this meaning, which Boyd emphasizes in his reading, yet on the other hand it means a fixed position, a "station, position, ground" (which reminds us of the limitations of Gradus's doctrinal communism), and Boyd neglects this sense. The figure of Gradus, then, offers *both* an image of the kind of gradual accumulation one needs in order to move closer to reality and the image of the kind of fixed world

view which renders any genuine movement towards reality impossible.
What kind of relation, then, between the work of art as a composition of patterns and sensations, intra- and inter-textual relations and the real world, does all of this presuppose?

Nabokov's Fiction as an Analogue of the Real

Critics have underlined how important scientific models were to Nabokov, yet rather than being trained in scientific modes of thought, Nabokov was a brilliant autodidact. Perhaps because of this his scientific thought is marked by certain peculiarities. In *Speak Memory*, which appeared in its final form in 1967, Nabokov states:

> The mysteries of mimicry had a special attraction for me. Its phenomena showed an artistic perfection usually associated with man-wrought things. Consider the imitation of oozing poison by bubblelike macules on a wing (complete with pseudo-refraction) or by glossy yellow knobs on a chrysalis ("Don't eat me — I have already been squashed, sampled and rejected") . . . "Natural selection," in the Darwinian sense, could not explain the miraculous coincidence of imitative aspect and imitative behaviour, nor could one appeal to the theory of "the struggle for life" when a protective device was carried to the point of mimetic subtlety, exuberance, and luxury far in excess of a predator's power of appreciation. I discovered in nature the nonutilitarian delights that I sought in art. Both were a form of magic, both were a game of intricate enchantment and deception. (Nabokov 1989a: p. 125)

While Nabokov had a strong interest in scientific enquiry, and developed a formidable body of knowledge within the corner of lepidoptry in which he took an interest, he brought his own understanding of the real to it, one which owed as much to his artistic frame of mind as to his close observations of nature and understanding of scientific theory. What is of interest here is the particularity of Nabokov's understanding of mimicry in nature, which allowed him to draw a clear analogy between creation and composition in nature and creation and composition in art, with both kinds of composition understood to involve thinking and understanding and the composure these bring. Boyd underlines a similar point in quoting Nabokov: "Does there not exist a high ridge where the mountainside of 'scientific' knowledge joins the opposite slope of 'artistic' imagination?" (Nabokov, cited in Boyd 1999: p. 145). Nabokov is arguing here, against the strong opinions of many scientists, that nature, like art, is a *meaningful* composition of interrelated elements. It does not matter that most scientists and many non-scientists would dismiss Nabokov's understanding of artistic creation in the natural world as erroneous, what matters is the extraordinary complexity this understanding of the real allows Nabokov to bring to bear in composing his fictitious worlds as analogues of his particular understanding of the real. This in turn would allow for an understanding of art in which art could be thought to produce not a simple representation of nature, but a composed understanding that offers an analogue of natural creation; that is, not a conventional depiction of reality, but imagined worlds whose formal composition of interrelations offers an analogue of real interrelations. Just as nature's depths can be read through carefully tracing and relating the surface signs it conveys in a multiplicity of sites, so too depths in Nabokov's imagined worlds emerge through a similar externalized expression which "hides" its meanings on the surfaces both of the text itself, and the intertextual and contextual relation into which it enters.

For Nabokov, then, the real world is full of patterns of connection, and these patterns link into a warp and weft that not only makes the texture of being, but imbues that being with meaning, a meaning, moreover derived from its formal composition that situates the works as agents within the real world. Such a view allows the compositions of fictional worlds that mimic this play of pattern, drawing meaning out of connections that seem hidden and unexpected, but which are able to be verified through close attention to the composition and correspondence of details, which in effect lie on the surface either of the text itself, or other texts and contexts to which it refers. In turn these details themselves reveal the hand of the one who means, the one who, in French, is said to want to say, or intend (*vouloir dire*). Expression and intention, on this model, are inseparable: that expression has meaning, that signs emerge and are understood, means that meaning has been intended, and in affirming this the work of art does no more than offer an analogue of the real for Nabokov.

One might posit, then, following Nabokov, an analogical reality in art distinct from a conventional realism. One of the contentions of this study is that the works considered here (while in many ways extremely different), and works of art that attempt to think about the world more generally, often attempt to construct an analogical reality. An examination of the composition of this kind of created reality would reveal not only an image of thought as they each understand it but, in parallel, an analogue of what that artist understands to be "the real" or a given aspect of it. In this way the work might be seen not only to implicate itself within and operate through thinking (in creating the kinds of virtual or mental existence discussed in Chapter 2), but to further enter into dialogue with the material or real. In all cases this is because each artist works with a model of external expression: just as the world in being folded in upon itself, reveals gaps that have to be bridged through interpretation, so too does the work of art. Yet both allow this interpretation through the correspondence of material (the series of viewpoints that comprise the sensation) in relations that resonate and imply or convey a sense of meaning that unifies the whole.

Intention, Irony

One of the major problems involved in removing the "talon-like claws" from around the word "real" in Nabokov is that of coming to terms with the role of irony in his writing. Indeed, the problem posed for interpretation by Nabokov's use of irony is something a reader becomes aware of in Nabokov's published interviews as much as in his fiction. When you read or listen to interviews with Nabokov[2] you are immediately struck by the tone of his comments, which seem to be both categorical and heavily ironic. Surely some of these comments are too outrageous to be taken seriously? Indeed, Boyd's close reading of *Pale Fire* has shown both how at times apparently ironic statements *can be* taken seriously: "Whenever we hear something called 'pointless' in Nabokov, we should look for the hidden point" (Boyd 1999: p. 87), and how at other times certain apparently emphatic comments can be taken to be signposts to a hidden counter-meaning and therefore require an ironic reading. Boyd has shown how the second strategy works in *Pale Fire* in the manner of the magician who insists that we look at something so that the trick which goes on behind might take place. Clearly, then, Nabokov can and does have it both ways: that which might at first seem ludicrous may well be meant to be taken seriously, while that which is stated in apparent seriousness might be *meant* to be recognized as a statement made in error. We then have the problem of the regress of irony: we are offered an appearance, but do we interpret that appearance on simple face value? That would surprise us. Rather, we seem to be required to link the appearance with the transparencies before, behind and beyond these appearances. Yet everything we need to order our understandings is available to us on the folded surfaces or layers of the appearance (though this appearance also relates out beyond the text to other texts and contexts).

This is also, in effect, a matter of composition, and indeed exemplifies Nabokov's method of working with layers, or interfolded surfaces, which he composes in mirroring lines that throw back reflections and distortions. Writing in *Speak Memory* Nabokov states:

> The spiral is a spiritualized circle. In the spiral form, the circle, uncoiled, unwound, has ceased to be vicious; it has been set free. I thought this up when I was a schoolboy, and I also discovered that Hegel's triadic series (so popular in old Russia) expressed merely

---

2 Excerpts from BBC interviews to which one might listen were at one time posted on the BBC website. Interviews with Nabokov are published in *Strong Opinions* (Nabokov 1990).

the essential spirality of all things in their relation to time. Twirl follows twirl, and every synthesis is the thesis of the next series. If we consider the simplest spiral, three stages may be distinguished in it, corresponding to those of the triad: We can call "thetic" the small curve or arc that initiates the convolution centrally; "antithetic" the larger arc that faces the first in the process of continuing it; and "synthetic" the still ampler arc that continues the second while following the first along the outer side. (Nabokov 1989a: p. 277)

In Nabokov's fiction it is possible to conceive of the thesis as being equivalent to the understanding of something from a fixed or particular point of view. This often involves how a character views a set of events with which he or she is involved: how Humbert understands the events recounted in *Lolita*, how Hermann understands the events in *Despair*, or Kinbote the events in *Pale Fire*, for example. This is, in effect, the representation of a subjective "reality" that is most clearly seen in those novels which make use of the first person (surface one). An antithesis would then be how others view that self and/or, the "objective" truth (facts revealed to us through the narrative) related to what the self thinks: what Lolita thinks of Humbert, what the world thinks of the resemblance of Hermann and Felix, or of Kinbote's reading of Shade's poem (surface two). A synthesis would involve the relation of the thesis and antithesis (by an ideal reader) that involves or produces a third principle: an analogue of "reality" which only becomes apparent when one considers the composition of the work as a whole. Again, this model supports the claim made above that art can partake of each of Spinoza's three kinds of knowledge. Yet further, each level within this process generates irony, which, in effect, is nothing other than the recognition of the disparity between one view and another, a second view of something that does not necessarily correspond with the first view. The interaction or struggle between the thesis and the antithesis generates, or provides the ground for one layer of irony: that which emerges through the differences apparent between what we are told within the thesis and what we are told within the antithesis. A second level of irony emerges within the synthesis, which brings together and understands the nature of the interaction between the subjective and objective, an understanding tied to a recognition or apprehension of the univocal composition of the whole that corresponds with what might be called the real.

The Real Life of Sebastian Knight

While *Despair* is the first of these novels that Nabokov translated into English (in 1936), *The Real Life of Sebastian Knight* is the first work which Nabakov wrote (in 1938–38) in English. No doubt because of this it offers what might be read as instructions to readers on how to approach

Nabokov's novels. That is, the works of Sebastian Knight and the descriptions his critic and biographer (his unnamed half-brother) offers of these works point us toward particular strategies which seem to relate closely to strategies which are discernable in Nabokov's own novels. Most critics state that *Dar* (*The Gift*), completed before *The Real Life of Sebastian Knight*, is his greatest Russian-language novel; that he had perfected his aesthetic method and style in Russian by this time. Yet *Dar* only appeared in mutilated form in the Russian émigré press, due to certain tendencies of self-censorship within that community (see Boyd 1990: pp. 441–3). And now Nabokov was forced by history to begin again in another language, addressing an audience he could only expect to be completely unfamiliar with any of his previous works and likely to be oblivious to the subtleties of his methods. *The Real Life of Sebastian Knight* might be read as a kind of apology or prologemena to future works (and future translations of existing works), offering readers materials with which to understand the scope of his artistic ambition.

One of the key ideas in *The Real Life of Sebastian Knight* is that the worlds described in Knight's novels are worlds in which all of the elements are drawn together into a meaningful expression: that the "reality" of the worlds described are realities which generate meaning; that the works ask you to draw connections and follow the threads of connections which will reveal hidden meaning, even *the* hidden meaning, to those able to perceive the composition of the whole. Further, the novels are understood to be analogues of the real itself which is understood (as it is in Deleuze's reading of Leibniz and Spinoza in Chapter 3) as composing an externalized expression which both urges and answers interpretation:

> The answer to all questions of life and death, "the absolute solution" was written all over the world he had known: it was like a traveller realizing that the wild country he surveys is not an accidental assembly of natural phenomena, but the page in a book where these mountains and forests, and fields, and rivers are disposed in such a way as to form a coherent sentence; the vowel of the lake fusing with the consonant of the sibilant slope; the windings of a road writing its message in a round hand, as clear as that of one's father; trees conversing in dumb-show, making sense to one who has learnt the gestures of their language . . . Thus the traveller spells the landscape and its sense is disclosed, and likewise, the intricate pattern of human life turns out to be monogrammatic, now quite clear to the inner eye disentangling the interwoven letters. And the word, the meaning which appears is astounding in its simplicity: the greatest surprise being perhaps that in the course of one's earthly existence, with one's brain encompassed by an iron ring, by the close-fitting dream of one's own personality — one had not made by chance that

simple mental jerk, which would have set free imprisoned thought and granted it the great understanding. Now the puzzle was solved. (Nabokov 1982: p. 150, ellipsis in original)

At first glance all of this would seem to draw us readily into line with Kernan's reading, cited in Boyd, which asks whether we are meant to find an "absolute meaning," or solution in Nabokov. Yet the book Sebastian's brother is describing is called *The Doubtful Asphodel*,[3] and what is striking about it is that it seems to give us such meaning, yet this absolute vanishes as we approach. The narrator describes reading Knight's book, and the sensation of feeling the solution is about to be revealed, which is then confronted by the feeling that this solution has slipped past us, is out of reach:

> The man is dead and we do not know. The asphodel on the other shore is as doubtful as ever. We hold a dead book in our hands. Or are we mistaken? I sometimes feel when I turn the pages of Sebastian's masterpiece that the "absolute solution" is there, somewhere, concealed in some passage I have read too hastily, or that it is intertwined with other words whose familiar guise deceived me. I don't know any other book that gives one this special sensation, and perhaps this was the author's special intention. (Nabokov 1982: p. 151)

This doubt is somewhat different to the post-modern "uncertainty," which Boyd critiques in *Nabokov's Pale Fire*: this is a doubt from whose shadow emerges the shadow of a certainty. This passage could be read as confirming Boyd's thesis: the meaning is there, if only we can find the code allowing us to find what is concealed in the expression of the intra- and inter-textual surfaces of the work. On the other hand, the passage could be read as affirming that the sense of doubt that remains in this process of searching is itself part of the author's intention: that the reality whose analogue is offered in the works is one which involves in the end an always receding horizon of doubt, like Popper's theories, which only describe what is currently known but will always be overwritten as we move further, but will never, foreseeably, offer a final word. In short, it does not so much convey a certainty as to a specific meaning, but the sensation that something here is meaningful. The composition, then, involves the marshalling into relation of perceptions which generate this sense of meaning (which Nabokov, equally, feels in Nature itself).

---

3 An asphodel is a flower from the Lily family and is often associated with the narcissus.

The Springboard of Parody

Alfred Appel has made use of another of the aesthetic hints offered by *The Real Life of Sebastian Knight*: the idea of "the springboard of parody" which Appel draws upon in his reading of *Lolita*, but which he shows might be applied to many of Nabokov's works (see Appel 1967). Appel underlines the following sentence:

> As often was the way with Sebastian Knight he used parody as a kind of springboard for leaping into the highest region of serious emotion. (Nabokov 1982: p. 76)

The narrator here is describing a particular novel by Knight, *The Prismatic Bezel*, which is "based cunningly on a parody of certain tricks of the literary trade" (Nabokov 1982: p. 76). This novel is then described and it transpires that it involves a parody of the detective genre which considers a play of identities with an apparently murdered man revealing himself as not murdered, as being merely in disguise. The play of parody leads to a dream reality in which the deeper reality of the characters is revealed (1982: pp. 78–9). These elements might remind us of *Despair*, the novel Nabokov wrote before *Invitation to a Beheading* and *The Gift*. The resemblance becomes further apparent when the narrator (having determined that *The Prismatic Bezel* is a book that could be understood to reveal or consider ideas of "the methods of composition," in which different approaches to the telling of a story are harmoniously fused to show a deeper level of complexity) goes on to describe Knight's next novel, *Success*, as one which considers "the method of fate." If *Success*, with its "method of fate" reminds us of the working backwards of fate which draws together Zina and Fyodor in *The Gift*,[4] *The Prismatic Bezel*, with its "methods of composition," reminds us of *Despair*, a novel written by a narrator who shows us he is able to write in many hands and begins chapter 3 with "How shall we begin this chapter. I offer several variations to choose from" (Nabokov 2000: p. 45).

It might be argued that if the idea of "the springboard of parody" is relevant to many of Nabokov's novels, as Appel has claimed, then it is particularly relevant to *Despair* which most closely resembles *The Prismatic Bezel*. The question might also be asked, in light of the clear outlines of aesthetic methodologies offered in *The Real Life of Sebastian Knight*, as to whether Nabokov is justified in his claim, made in *Strong Opinions*, that he had completely developed his aesthetic methods by the 1930s (Nabokov 1990: pp. 102–3).

---

4 Both begin with parody: *Despair* of the detective genre and *The Gift* of biography, just as *Pale Fire* involves a parody of the academic edition.

If this is the case then perhaps, rather than being seen as a dim precursor to later achievements (an interpretation encouraged by Nabokov himself in his 1965 Foreword to the revised translation of *Despair*), *Despair* might be thought to be an important work, one in which Nabokov-Sirin's aesthetic methods have already been developed to an extremely high degree; one which might be seen as something other than an interesting failure (as Boyd 1990 contends in *Nabokov: Russian Years*). Indeed it might be one which allows us to see, perhaps more clearly than other of his works, the importance of composition to his aesthetic method. Such composition, as we have seen in Chapter 3, allows the development of a properly univocal expression across disparate, even apparently confused or insane, sets of perceptions, providing an overview of various possible worlds. Further, as Nabokov's first attempt at an English language novel (given he translated it himself), it should, perhaps occupy a much more important place among Nabokov's English-language works.

Despair: "the methods of composition"

As we have seen above, *Despair* might be closely related to what Nabokov calls the "methods of composition." Nabokov's understanding of the concept of composition itself in fiction, then, might be drawn out through a close reading of this novel and the methods Nabokov uses in constructing it (which he continues to use from this time on). In *Vladimir Nabokov: The Russian Years* Boyd (1990) underlines how Nabokov-Sirin was already keenly aware of potential audiences beyond the small Russian émigré literary community already familiar with his works. As a struggling professional writer looking to support his young family he wanted to see his novels translated into the major European languages of German, French and English, so that they might generate some viable economic return. It would not be surprising, then, if he began to include inter-textual and contextual references that would appeal to these potential readers. His second novel, *King, Queen, Knave* already involved (German) characters outside the émigré community and *Laughter in the Dark*, similarly moved beyond the narrow confines of the world of Russian émigrés. *Despair*, in its English language version also involves numerous allusions which might be thought to have been placed there to appeal to the sphere of reference of non-émigré readers. This very idea, indeed, is parodied in *Despair*:

> [...] let other nations, too, translate it into their respective languages, so that American readers may satisfy their craving for gory glamour; the French discern mirages of sodomy in my partiality for a vagabond; and Germans relish the skittish side of a semi-Slavonic soul. Read, read it, as many as possible, ladies and gentlemen! I welcome you all as my readers. (Nabokov 2000: p. 134)

If carefully composed patterns revealing a deeper meaning, such as those indicated in *The Real Life of Sebastian Knight*, are to emerge in *Despair*, they are likely to be traced, as Boyd has shown with regard to *Pale Fire*, at the level of allusion, or inter-textual relations. Certain references in *Despair* are more or less explicitly underlined within the text itself: the references to Dostoevsky's *Crime and Punishment* and *The Double*; to Conan Doyle's Sherlock Holmes novels; to the popular crime fiction writers Edgar Wallace and Maurice Leblanc are well known (see Nabokov 2000: p. 106). Less attention has been paid to the reference to James Joyce's *A Portrait of the Artist as a Young Man*: when Hermann lists possible titles for his novel he considers "A Portrait of the Artist in a Mirror" (2000: p. 167).

Apart from these explicit relations, however, there are layers of more subtle allusion, both to works of popular culture and high culture, and it is possible to trace certain themes through this web of relations, themes which indeed seem to form a discernable pattern, which in turn indeed leads us towards a surprising idea.

A "Pleasing Plot"

Nabokov's foreword to the 1965 edition of *Despair* is filled with strange hints and asides: in short it seems to be offering clues to patterns within the novel that reveal its overall composition. While the tone of the foreword is apparently dismissive, elements within it seem to indicate a deeper structure at play in the work. Nabokov claims, apparently flippantly that "plain readers," or those not interested in applying external theories to the work (such as those developed by Marxists and Freudians, whom he criticizes here), "will welcome its plain structure and pleasing plot — which, however, is not quite as familiar as the writer of the rude letter in Chapter Eleven assumes it to be" (Nabokov 2000: p. 10). Following Boyd's logic, the double emphasis on the "plain" nature of both the reader and the structure should alert us to the possibility of irony here. The writer of the letter is the painter Ardalion, who is both cousin and lover of Hermann's wife Lydia, though Hermann remains ignorant, or pretends to remain ignorant of their affair throughout. Ardalion accuses Hermann of developing a hackneyed plot: staging one's own death in order to receive insurance money. The plot, of course, and its role within the overall composition, is much more complex, yet this is not the point to Nabokov's aside: rather, in indicating that Hermann's plot is not as familiar as is made out, Nabokov causes us to consider the extent to which Hermann also varies or diverges from those stories of doubles, pulp crime fiction and murder that seem to inspire *him*.

While Nabokov explicitly names certain sources, there are at least two important occasions in *Despair* where popular culture texts are referred to but not explicitly named. The first occurs when Hermann alludes to a film he has seen which concerns doubles, and makes use of the same actor in split screen:

> On the screen I have seen a man meeting his double; or better to say an actor playing two parts with, as in our case, the difference of social standing naively stressed, so that in one part he was a slinking rough, and in the other a staid bourgeois in a car — as if, really, a pair of identical tramps, or a pair of identical gents, would have been less fun. (Nabokov 2000: p. 23)

The second refers to the book which Lydia reads, a book Hermann has purchased for her at a railway station: "some rotten detective novel with a crimson spider amid a black web on its cover" (Nabokov 2000: p. 29). On both occasions the source texts seem deliberately difficult to trace and generalized to the extent that they might be taken to represent a genre rather than specific works. Yet on both occasions there are sufficient clues to link the references to particular works, yet only if one is prepared to accept a degree of distortion in the process of transference; that is, if one is to argue that rather than borrowing directly Nabokov deliberately distorts certain key sources.

The identification of sources, then, in these cases is doubtful, though it is unclear as to whether the doubt indicates that any attribution of allusion will be erroneous, or that the sources have been deliberately distorted. Within the compositional strategy that involves lining up mirrors that both reflect and distort that Nabokov adopts, it is apparent that distortion is an end point of Nabokov's analogical expression, and so a strong case might be made too for the distortion of allusions.

On the Screen

A number of important references to cinema occur throughout *Despair*. In the foreword Nabokov playfully claims to be uncertain as to whether Hermann ever made "that film he proposed to direct" (Nabokov 2000: p. 11). Readers will search in vain for a direct reference to Hermann's desire to direct a film. Yet a list can be made: one of the narrative techniques Hermann adopts in beginning chapter 3 is mimicking the techniques of cinema (2000: p. 46). Hermann also attempts to convince Felix that he is a film actor and this is why he requires a double (pp. 72–83). He copies melodramatic behavior from films when lying to Lydia, "spectres of red melodrama reeled" (p. 121). So too the novel ends with Hermann pretending to convince the crowds who have come to witness his arrest that all of this is a movie, and that they should restrain the police and allow him to escape as part of the plot. As Nabokov added this final passage when he revised the translation of *Despair* in 1965, it is possible to read this as an allusion to the end of the 1950 Billy Wilder film *Sunset Boulevard*, where the aging actress, Norma Desmond, who is about to be arrested for murdering her hired lover, Joe Gilles, comes to believe, in her lunacy, that the film crew who have come to film the arrest for the newsreels are in fact part of the film crew for her come-back into feature films (p. 176).

Yet perhaps the most telling allusion to film relates to the film which was among the most famous "double" movies at the time Nabokov wrote *Despair*. Hans Heinz Ewers had written a novel drawing upon the legend of Faust, E. T. A. Hoffmann, and Edgar Allan Poe called *The Student of Prague*. This, in turn, was made into a film on two occasions before Nabokov wrote *Despair*: first in 1913,[5] and again, to more telling effect, in 1926.[6] The latter film stars Conrad Veidt (who also starred in *The Cabinet of Dr. Caligari*) as the impoverished student Balduin, who is visited by the Devil in the guise of a travelling money lender Scapinelli who offers Balduin 600,000 gold pieces in exchange for his choice of anything in Balduin's room. Given he has few possessions Balduin readily agrees, but Scapinelli then summons Balduin's reflection from the mirror. Balduin for a time appears prosperous and attempts to woo the Comtesse Margit until his double begins to haunt him, taking his place in a duel he had sworn on his honor to the Baron, Margit's father, not to take part in, and killing the fiancé of Margit. Balduin then falls into ruin before, to the backdrop of a wild wind-storm, he drunkenly breaks into Margit's room where, after she has fainted, he confronts his double one last time. After a period of pursuit in the high wind and amid the alleys of the town, he returns to his old room and shoots and destroys his double, shattering a mirror, only to realize that in shooting and killing his double he has also shot and killed himself.

As this summary makes apparent there are as many, if not more, differences than similarities between this and Hermann's story. Yet the play of resemblances and differences is one of the more evident themes in the novel with Hermann arguing with Ardalion about the possibility that there might be resemblances, and seeming most confused and deranged when he wanders the streets of Tarnitz in chapter 4 seeing

---

5 *Der Student von Prag* (Germany, Deutsche Bioscop GmbH: Released 1913). Directed by Stellan Rye and Paul Wegener, based on a novel by Hanns Heinze Ewers from a story by Edgar Allan Poe. Starring Paul Wegener (Balduin), John Gottowt (Scapinelli), Grete Berger (Komtesse Margit), Lyda Salmonova (Lyduschka), Lothar Korner (Graf von Schwarzenberg), and Fritz Weidenmann (Baron Waldis-Schwarzenberg).

6 *Der Student von Prag* (Germany, Sokal-Film GmbH: Released 1926). Written and directed by Henrik Galeen, based on a novel by Hanns Heinze Ewers from a story by Edgar Allan Poe. Cinematographers: Günther Krampf and Erich Nitzschmann. Starring Conrad Veidt (Balduin), Werner Krauss (Scapinelli), Agnes Esterhazy (Comtesse Margit), Elizza La Porta (Liduschka), Fritz Alberti (Graf Schwarzenberg), Ferdinand von Alten (Baron Waldis-Schawarzenberg, Margits Vetter und Verlobter), Erich Kober (Student), and Max Maximillian (Student).

only resemblances. A reference to Pascal (whom Hermann insists he has never read, having merely pilfered the quotation from some secondary source) alerts us to similarities (Pascal 1958: paragraph 133, 39).[7] However, another passage nearby in Pascal (in this section of the *Pensées*, which deals with the nature of similarities and differences) emphasizes the *differences* between things:

114

Variety is as abundant as all tones of the voice, all ways of walking, coughing, blowing the nose, sneezing. We distinguish vines by their fruit, and call them the Condrien, the Desargues, and such and such a stock. Is this all? Has a vine ever produced two bunches exactly the same, and has a bunch two grapes alike, etc.?

I can never judge of the same thing exactly in the same way. I cannot judge of my work, while doing it. I must do as the artists, stand at a distance, but not too far. How far, then? Guess. (Pascal 1958: p. 36)

While being aware of the differences, then, it is worth indicating some points of connection between *Despair* and *The Student of Prague*. Hermann meets Felix in *Prague* in chapter 1, and, when talking of film technique on page 46, he remembers this meeting again, making mention of Prague while rerunning "his life on my private screen" (Nabokov 2000: p. 46). Just as with the film of the doubles Hermann discusses on page 23 the doubles in *The Student of Prague* are distinguished by clothing: the double retains the clothes of an impoverished student which Balduin was wearing when Scapinelli summoned his image from the mirror (just as Hermann's helping Felix to his feet reminds him of "Narcissus fooling Nemesis by helping his image out of the brook," 2000: p. 21), while the now wealthy Balduin dresses as a member of the haut bourgeois. So too, the high wind at the end of the film brings to mind the winds that howl throughout *Despair*, echoing from the narrative present in which Hermann writes back into the past he describes. This wind is further connected with another theme, the theme of damnation which runs through the film and, more tellingly, is sown throughout *Despair* through a complex set of allusions I will discuss below.

Given the popularity of *The Student of Prague* it is likely that this film would have been called to mind by Nabokov's first readers. A final point might be made about film, however. The references to the film versions

---

7 See *Despair* (Nabokov 2000: p. 73). The passage from Pascal is as follows: "Two faces which resemble each other make us laugh, when together, by their resemblance, though neither of them by itself makes us laugh."

of doubles and the doubles of popular fiction, which I will discuss below, both indicate that Hermann is acting under influence, that he is highly suggestible, and that the popular forms of representation he disparages have in fact taken charge of certain of his thought processes. While Ardalion is no doubt also viewed ironically, it is interesting how he makes a distinction between the *differences* emphasized by high art and the cheap *resemblances* emphasized by popular forms:

> You forget, my good man, that what the artist perceives is, primarily, the differences between things. It is the vulgar who note their resemblance. Haven't we heard Lydia exclaim at the talkies: "Oo! Isn't she just like our maid?" (Nabokov 2000: p. 44)

The reference to the maid, here, indeed, makes us wonder if this is not also part of Hermann's distorted perceptions which are polluted by a mania for finding resemblances or having them appear. Is the maid in the novel a real character, or has she been suggested by models from fiction? Is Hermann himself, like Don Quixote and Dostoevsky's underground man, a character formed by fictions?

Excitement

Popular fiction is equally if not more important to the play of representations which form the texture of the composition of *Despair*. There is a suggestion that the entire story Hermann recounts has been copied or counterfeited from a popular novel describing the murder of a double. Hermann describes finding just such a novel at a railway station and purchasing it for Lydia who was addicted to entertainments of this kind.

> Once I brought back from a railway journey some rotten detective novel with a crimson spider amid a black web on its cover. She dipped into it and found it terribly thrilling — felt that she simply could not help taking a peep at the end, but as that would spoil everything, she shut her eyes tight and tore the book in two down its back and hid the second, concluding, portion; then, later, she forgot the place and was a long, long time searching the house for the criminal she herself had concealed, repeating the while in a small voice: "It was so exciting, so terribly exciting; I know I shall die if I don't find out —"

> She has found out now. Those pages that explained everything were securely hidden; still, they were found — all of them except one, perhaps. Indeed, a lot of things have happened; now duly explained. Also that came to pass which she feared most. Of all omens it was

the weirdest. A shattered mirror. Yes, it did happen, although not quite in the ordinary way. The poor dead woman. (Nabokov 2000: pp. 29–30)

The final paragraph here smells strongly of parody: the queer syntax and the clear indication of a puzzle to be solved drawing to our attention that there might indeed be a puzzle here, though in the very next paragraph Hermann, who finally finishes his narrative on April 1, tells us outright that he is in the process of making April fools of we, his readers.

It is difficult, then, to know what if anything we should take seriously. Yet the August 1930 issue of the crime fiction magazine *Excitement* not only includes a spider on a web (though not a crimson spider, and not a spider alone) it also includes a short story called "The Man who Forged

Figure 6.1 August 1930 issue of the crime fiction magazine *Excitement*

Himself."[8] Published in New York, and distributed through Europe by a Covent Garden-based company, *Excitement* would have been sold at Railway stations, and appeared before Nabokov wrote *Despair*. It is a magazine and not a novel, so again there are as many distortions as there are reflections involved.

There is a strange repetition of variations of the word excitement whenever this mysterious book is mentioned. Lydia says it is "so exciting, so terribly exciting" (Nabokov 2000: p. 30). When imagining his own face as Lydia might see it (whom he also erroneously imagines to be perfectly faithful to him) Hermann quickly turns to describing the resemblances between his face and that of Felix, assuring the reader that he is doing this dispassionately: "No, I am not getting in the least excited; my self-control is perfect" (2000: p. 34). On the next page he admits that he has taken Lydia's book and is reading it. Overhearing the word "dull," we are shown Lydia again reading the book: "'What's dull?' inquired Lydia, lifting her eyes and holding one finger on the interrupted line" (p. 52). Certainly, it is not the book, which is the opposite of dull; rather, it must be something in her everyday world. Later Hermann tells us that he is a proficient writer of fiction:

> How many novels I wrote when young — just like that, casually, and without the least intention of publishing them. Here is another utterance: a published manuscript, says Swift, is comparable to a whore. I happened one day (in Russia) to give Lydia a manuscript of mine to read, telling her that it was the work of a friend; she found it boring and did not finish it. To this day my handwriting is practically unfamiliar to her. (Nabokov 2000: pp. 73–4)

This passage is revealing in a number of ways. The idea of the whore and Lydia occur in uncomfortable proximity, hinting that Hermann is lying to himself about his knowledge of his wife's unfaithfulness. The phrase "practically unfamiliar" indicates a real sense of pain in Lydia's contemptuous dismissal of his work, one which is explained away by the belief that she really must not have known that this was in fact his own work. In sum, there is an indication of jealousy: Hermann is jealous of those hack works which excite Lydia, who is bored by his own highbrow art. Might the work of art which Hermann sees in his murder of the double plot be, in part, an attempt to compose an exciting work, a work which would be exciting to Lydia?

Hermann certainly takes the opportunity to develop his exciting story

---

8 For details of the contents of this and other magazines see the following website and scroll down to *Excitement* v20 #6, August 1930: http://www.philsp.com/homeville/fmi/t744.htm#A15781

for Lydia, when he invents the tale that his long separated, virtually identical brother wishes to kill himself so that Hermann might benefit from his life insurance, and, indeed, this story does grip Lydia's imagination in the way his earlier works clearly did not:

> Lydia hugged my leg and stared up at me.
>
> "His plan is as follows." I went on, in a bland voice: "My life, say, is insured for half a million. In a wood, somewhere, my corpse is found. My widow, that is you—"
>
> "Oh, stop saying such horrors," cried Lydia, scrambling up from the carpet. "I've just been reading a story like that. Oh, do please stop—"(Nabokov 2000: p. 120)

Here at last, boring Hermann (who perhaps only imagines that he and his wife have an extraordinary love life, with the episodes of dissociation ending when he realizes he is not in bed with her, but in fact simply watching some play of his imagination from a distance), engages Lydia's interest passionately. His plan involves separation from Ardalion, a rival he refuses, through dogged self-deceit, to acknowledge, but whose presence and the necessity for his removal from the scene are interwoven with the formation of the plan (the murder happens on Ardalion's land, Hermann consistently uses Ardalion's name at poste restante addresses, Hermann pays to remove Ardalion from the city at the crucial moment). If there is one clichéd mystery plot device involved (to fake one's death for profit), there is also the shadow of another: the love triangle which leads to murder. Yet here there is a twist, because Hermann kills his imagined double rather than his real rival.

There are a number of similarities between Ronald Oliphant's story, "The Man who Forged Himself," which appeared in the issue of *Excitement* whose spider cover is reproduced in Figure 6.1, and *Despair*. Jim Rosslow is a conterfeiter of genius, who, like Hermann, is being driven mad by the pressures of his work (Oliphant 1930: p. 114). He lives in an isolated hideout in woods about one mile from the nearest road (1930: p. 116) where there is a "drone of myriad grasshoppers" (p. 114) and "the soughing of the wind in the trees" (p. 114) much as Hermann finds himself among "stammering crickets" (Nabokov 2000: p. 40) and pines which "soughed gently" (2000: p. 41) in Ardalion's wood. Like Hermann, Rosslow at least gives "the impression of being a literary man, an author who liked solitude in order to do his work" (p. 115). Both possess guns and kill with them, and in both cases a car is involved, with Rosslow killing his double, Winn, in his car and Hermann doing it beside his car (Oliphant 1930: pp. 115, 121; Nabokov 2000: p. 143). There is a similar apparent motive involved: financial gain. Rosslow is tempted to murder Winn and assume his identity because Winn has a steady and easy stream of income that only requires a periodic appearance at a bank to sign a form and prove identity with fingerprints, while the stress of Rosslow's own work as a counterfeiter for a criminal organization is driving him insane. There is also a similar element of unbelievability in the plot devised by Hermann and that devised by Oliphant. With Hermann, of course, what is implausible to all but himself is the fact of the resemblance. In Oliphant's story the manner in which identification is achieved requires a powerful suspension of disbelief: Rosslow and Winn only vaguely resemble one another, yet Winn becomes Rosslow's true double after a brilliant yet evil plastic surgeon, Dr. Barthol, who has been handsomely paid for his troubles, has performed two operations: one to make Rosslow's face uncannily resemble Winn, and another, performed at the same time, which involves swapping Winn's fingerprints with those of Rosslow using a technique Barthol alone has perfected. Winn, like Hermann, is well dressed, and stumbles onto Rosslow's cabin after having been shot. Rosslow, like Hermann, pretends to help Winn, when he in fact has begun to hatch the plot of stealing his identity right from the beginning. Like Hermann, Rosslow believes he is committing the perfect, undetectable crime:

> When he had finished, there was nothing about either the car or the shack to show that a cowardly and brutal crime had been committed. (Oliphant 1930: p. 121)

Rosslow, then, like Hermann, assumes his victim's identity. Rosslow seeks to use it to gain access to Winn's ongoing monthly remittance. He practices Winn's signature and drives to town to draw upon the money, only to be delayed by an apparently simple-minded bank clerk and arrested as Anthony Winn, who is wanted for murder and bank robbery:

> Jim Rosslow, counterfeiter and murderer, masquerading for the man he had killed, suddenly became aware of the trap into which he had walked. He awoke to the fact that Winn had really been making his get-away from the bank holdup and murder when he came to his shack and had lied to him. He realized, too, that the stupid-looking teller had tricked him, playing him for time until the detective for whom he had sent, should arrive. His identification as the wanted murdered, Anthony Winn, would hold good in any court of law in the land, and it was useless to try and assert his real identity and reveal the part Doctor Barthol had played in the conspiracy. In that case the murder of Winn would be discovered. He was caught either way — trapped by his supposed cleverness. With a resigned gesture, he held out his hands for the manacles.

134   Thinking in Literature

"All right, Mr. Detective. Slip 'em on!"

And Jim Rosslow — his own dastardly crime undiscovered — walked out of the bank to answer to the law for the crime of the man he had killed and robbed of his very personality. (Oliphant 1930: p. 122)

Like Hermann, Rosslow is undone through the identity he has assumed; like Rosslow, he is overcome by others whom he had assumed to be stupid. Yet while there are important similarities between Hermann's plot and Rosslow's, there are major differences between Nabokov's use of Hermann's plot as an element within his greater composition and Oliphant's use of Rosslow's plot (which comprises, in effect, the sum of his composition). Nabokov's composition puts Hermann's plot into relation with many other things: its real effectiveness; its relationship to cliché and hackneyed convention; the disparity between Hermann's intentions and his achievement; the disparity between Hermann's views and the thoughts of others; the crudeness of Hermann's conception in comparison with that of Nabokov himself in *Despair*. In doing this Nabokov sets out to exemplify his own methods of composition: but this is by no means the only element of the composition.

"Hell will never pardon Hermann"

Perhaps the most curious passage from Nabokov's foreword to *Despair* concerns the comparison he makes between *Lolita*'s Humbert and *Despair*'s Hermann:

Both are neurotic scoundrels, yet there is a green lane in Paradise where Humbert is permitted to wander at dusk once a year; but Hell will never pardon Hermann. (Nabokov 2000: p. 11)

This is a puzzling statement as it makes one question both what is so good about Humbert (who, like Hermann, is a murderer, and, unlike Hermann, is also a pedophile) and what is so evil about Hermann. An answer might be that we are being offered the kind of clue Boyd has identified through his reading of *Pale Fire*: that is, perhaps, in some way, we are being encouraged to think about Hermann in relation to Hell. Once we begin to do this a surprising trail opens up, one which leads, indeed, to the very threshold of the kind of solution Boyd hunts down in *Pale Fire*. Perhaps, as he stated in *Strong Opinions* when asked had he been influenced by Joyce (Nabokov 1990: pp. 102–3), Nabokov had indeed already developed a good deal of the aesthetic methods he was to bring to later works by 1932. Perhaps *Despair* is composed to include a puzzle within it, one which might be traced through a web of intertextual references.

The great Western book related to Hell is, of course, Dante's *Inferno*, a book Nabokov knew well. While Dante is never explicitly referred to in *Despair*, it might be suggested that this book is so well known as to need no such specific signposting. Indeed, Dante was one of the great favorites of English language Modernists, and this is something Nabokov would also have been well aware of: he might well have expected an English language audience, then, the same audience he would have expected to have read James Joyce's *A Portrait of the Artist as a Young Man*, a book to which he does specifically allude, to be alert to references from Dante.

Canto I of the Inferno begins the night before Good Friday in 1300 (which fell on April 7 on the Julian calendar, which would be April 18 in the proleptic Georgian calendar): Dante is 35 years old. *Despair* begins with Hermann, at the age of 35, meeting Felix on Friday May 9, 1930. Good Friday that year fell on April 18, some 21 days before:

> Since 1920, I had been living in Berlin. On the ninth of May 1930, having passed the age of thirty-five . . . (Nabokov 2000: p. 14)

Like Dante, Hermann finds himself climbing a hill to gain a prospect; while Dante encounters Virgil, his guide through the underworld, and a kind of spiritual double for the poet, Hermann meets Felix. While Hermann sees a white horse, Dante encounters, before meeting Virgil, a Leopard (symbol of lust) and a Lion (symbol of pride) and a she-wolf (symbol of avarice). In Canto V, Virgil and Dante enter the second circle of Hell, where the souls of those damned for sins of physical passion are constantly buffeted by unremitting winds, just as Hermann finds himself beset by winds in his mountain hideout in the village in Roussillon, winds that enter his narrative from the very first chapter as the present of his narrative interferes with the past he recounts. In Canto XXX Dante and Virgil, in the tenth chasm of the eighth circle of Hell, encounter the "counterfeiters of person" who are punished with madness (Dante 1972: pp. 159–61): this circle would have some claim on Hermann, as would the seventh circle where those guilty of violent crimes against others are punished, and Caina in the ninth circle where those who have done violence to their kin (if Felix is thought of as a kind of half-brother) are punished.

The repetition of the number nine also brings Dante's *Inferno*, with its nine circles of Hell, to mind. Hermann meets Felix first on May 9, 1930; he then writes to Felix suggesting that they meet in Tarnitz, on September 9, 1930, and the two nines of this date are emphasized for the reader: "On the wall a calendar showed a huge black nine, rather like the tongue of a bull: the ninth of September" (Nabokov 2000: p. 56), and a page or two later Hermann points out the date could have no possible meaning: "what does it matter to [a reader] whether a given letter was written on the ninth of September or on September the sixteenth?" (2000: p. 58). Hermann picks up the letters sent to him by Felix after their October 1 meeting, from counter nine of the post office (p. 102). Hermann meets Felix and murders him on the ninth of March 1931 (p. 128), and this is described in chapter 9 of the novel.[9]

If the number nine is taken to refer to Dante's nine circles, a further, interesting possible interpretation comes to light. There are four concentric rings in the ninth circle: Caina, containing those who have killed their kin; Antenora, for those who have betrayed their country; Ptolomea and Giudecca. Giudecca is where the giant figure of Lucifer himself is imprisoned. Ptolomea, however, is revealed as having a particular property in Canto XXXIII: from time to time a soul that has committed a particularly heinous deed is carried down to this region even before the person to whom the soul belongs has died, immediately after having committed their crime, while the apparently living physical being who remains on earth is possessed by a demon (Dante 1972: pp. 180–2). A kind of demon possession is at least alluded to in *Despair*, as Hermann considers the possibility of attempting to possess and inhabit Felix's soul, the rights to which he has now stolen:

> Ah, if I had known him well, from years of intimacy, I might even have found it amusing to take up new quarters in the soul I had inherited. I would have known every cranny in it; all the corridors of its past; I could have enjoyed the use of all its accommodations. But Felix's soul I had studied very cursorily, so that all I knew of it were the bare outlines of his personality, two or three chance traits. (Nabokov 2000: p. 147)

Indeed, in some sense, Hermann considers, Felix's name, at least, now possesses him: "how could I divest myself of a name, which, with such art, I have made my own? For I look like my name, gentlemen, and it fits me as exactly as it used to fit him" (Nabokov 2000: p. 161). Might one go further? Is it possible that Hermann, in some more than metaphorical sense, is already in Hell? What Hermann says of "Felix," the suicidal identical brother he imagines for Lydia's sake, could just as well be said of Hermann himself: "On one hand the abyss of a soul in torment, on the other, business prospects" (2000: p. 119). Chapter 4, where Hermann awaits Felix in Tarnitz is a region of uncanny resemblances. Hermann

---

9 The number nine might also be of interest to Nabokov because of its peculiar "mirror" properties. The 9-times-table up to 10 times the number provides a strange mirroring of figures once these reach 5 × 9: that is the numbers [0]9, 18, 27, 36, 45, are reflected in mirror image by the numbers achieved from 6 to 10 times 9, 54, 63, 72, 81, 90. Thanks to Amanda Uhlmann for pointing this out to me.

sees a picture in a shop, which he believes he recognizes as one painted by Ardarlion. He is told he is mistaken, but cannot quite believe it:

> Well, I'm damned! (thought I). For had I not seen something very similar, if not identical, among Ardalion's pictures? Well, I'm damned! (Nabokov 2000: p. 65)

The uncanny resemblances of chapter 4 also recall the uncanny represented in German Expressionist cinema: a horror aligned with evil. As Balduin pursues his double in *The Student of Prague* he encounters elements of his past life strangely transformed: he knocks at the door of his house and the door is answered by himself, causing him to flee in terror. He returns to the quarters he once haunted as a student and so on. The horror of resemblance in chapter 4 is linked with madness, which, in turn, is linked with a fiercely blowing wind ("the wind had died in the madhouse" [Nabokov 2000: p. 68]) similar to that Hermann encounters in his hotel at the story's end:

> Well do I remember that little town — and feel oddly perplexed: should I go on giving instances of such aspects of it, which in a horribly unpleasant way echoed things I had somewhere seen long ago? It even seems to me now that it was, that town, constructed of certain refuse particles of my past [. . .]. (Nabokov 2000: p. 66)

Opposed to the madness, or hell of resemblances, an image of Pascal's comment that no two grapes are the same occurs in this scene, in the form of an old man in the square eating grapes (Nabokov 2000: p. 66). In short, there is something surreal in these passages, something which suggests the possibility of another reading, of the idea that this is already Hell, reconstructed as Tarnitz to torment Hermann. The feeling occurs again when Hermann's dream-like journey to his rendezvous with Felix at the yellow pole is described. There is the sense of a possible reality beyond or behind the one he describes:

> [T]he feeling grew upon me that there was a great number of people around, all speaking together, and then falling silent and giving one another dim errands and dispersing without a sound. (Nabokov 2000: p. 135)

Nabokov's composition, then, involves processes of doubling and distortion: the mirror both reflects and distorts and the work as a whole is organized in a similar way. The Hermann/Felix double is not the only such pair in *Despair*. Hermann is also doubled by Ardalion: both, through self-deceit, see themselves as great artists and this pride is linked to passion which is named by Ardor-lion (Nabokov 2000: p. 93), with the Lion, as in Dante, symbolizing pride. They are rivals, both as artists (with Hermann believing in an aesthetic of similarity opposed to Ardalion's aesthetic of difference) and as lovers of Lydia, and in both these roles Hermann seems dimly aware that he is being usurped by Ardalion:

> So they went on for a good while, talking now of their cards and now about me, as though I were not in the room or as though I were a shadow, a ghost, a dumb creature; and that joking habit of theirs, which before used to leave me indifferent, now seemed to me loaded with meaning, as if indeed it were merely my reflection that was present, my real body being far away. (Nabokov 2000: p. 62)

Hermann, too, assumes Ardalion's identity just as he later assumes that of Felix. Yet this is not all: Hermann's false double, Felix, himself is doubled by Ardalion's friend, the rather more sophisticated vagabond and would-be artist, Perebrodov, who appears at Hermann's door and whose resemblance to Felix, as conveyed through the distorted reflection of the maid's description as interpreted by Hermann's fevered mind, throws Hermann into a paranoid confusion (Nabokov 2000: p. 97). So too, Perebrodov, unlike Felix who only dreams of getting hold of it, actually does filtch Hermann's thousand-mark note from him (2000: p. 86), via the intermediary of Ardalion who passes it on to him (pp. 114–15). Hermann only meets Perebrodov once as Ardalion is about to depart for Italy, and he makes the following, enigmatic statement:

> "My name's Perebrodov, professional artist," blurted [Ardalion's] grim companion, confidentially thrusting out, as if it held a dirty postcard, an unshakeable hand in my direction. "Had the fortune of meeting you in the gambling hells of Cairo." (Nabokov 2000: p. 116)

In Guidecca, in the ninth circle of Hell, Dante finds Lucifer:

> The Emperor of the kingdom of despair
> From the mid-breast emerged out of the ice . . .
> O what a marvel smote me with amaze
> When I beheld three faces on his head!
> The one in front showed crimson to my gaze;
> Thereunto were the other faces wed . . .
> The right was coloured between yellow and white,
> The left was such to look upon as those
> Who come from where the Nile flows out of the night.
> (Dante 1972: pp. 183–4)

Hermann's face is rendered with a strange ruddy hue by Ardalion in his portrait of Hermann (Nabokov 2000: p. 55); the signpost marking where the murder takes place is yellow and, on the day of the murder shrouded in white snow, and the dark complexion of those from the region of the Nile might remind us of Perebrodov's otherwise inexplicable reference to Cairo.

The links to Hell are strengthened by a number of other references, which might be traced back to James Joyce's *A Portrait of the Artist as a Young Man*, and to the fire sermons of chapter 3 of that book, and the various references to damnation it contains, in particular. As we have seen, Hermann explicitly refers to this novel in searching for a title to his own novel (Nabokov 2000: p. 167). Both novels, too, end with diary entries, but to somewhat opposite effect: whereas Stephen Dedalus's diary recounts with immediacy the manner in which he is at last able to slip his bonds, to set himself free (though perhaps overconfidently, in the manner of Icarus), Hermann is "reduced" to this diary form, which he reviles and which, in turn, recounts his final slide into captivity (2000: pp. 173–5). There is a particular passage from Joyce, however, which I would suggest is also alluded to in *Despair*. In one of the fire sermons delivered in chapter 3 of *A Portrait*, Father Arnall states:

> — A holy saint (one of our own fathers I believe it was) was once vouchsafed a vision of hell. It seemed to him that he stood in the midst of a great hall, dark and silent save for the ticking of a great clock. The ticking went on unceasingly; and it seemed to this saint that the sound of the ticking was the ceaseless repetition of the words: ever, never; ever, never. Ever to be in hell, never to be in heaven; ever to be shut off from the presence of God, never to enjoy the beatific vision; ever to be eaten with flames, gnawed by vermin, goaded with burning spikes, never to be free from those pains; . . . ever, never; ever, never. (Joyce 2003: p. 143)

The meaning of this passage is ironically inverted as Hermann blasphemously seeks to prove the non-existence of God in chapter 6. He proceeds to do this by committing one of the unforgivable sins against the holy ghost: the sin of refusing to recognize the work of God as God's own work, specifically by attributing this work to the work of demons (as the Pharisees did when they attributed Christ's works to the devil). Indeed, the unforgivable sins against the Holy Ghost are referred to more than once in *A Portrait*. There are six such unforgivable sins: "despair, presumption, impenitence or a fixed determination not to repent, obstinacy, resisting the known truth, and envy of another's spiritual welfare" (Forget 2009). In chapter 6, Hermann, also making reference to Descartes' *Discourse on Method*, and Shakespeare, wonders how you could be sure that one was in fact in heaven, how you could be sure it was not some trick being played upon you by demons who were simply deceiving you:

> Now tell me, please, what guarantee do you possess that those beloved ghosts are genuine; that it is really your dear dead mother and not some petty demon mystifying you, masked as your mother and impersonating her with consummate art and naturalness? There is the rub, there is the horror; the more so as the acting will go on and on, endlessly; never, never, never, never, never will your soul in that other world be quite sure that the sweet gentle spirits crowding about it are not fiends in disguise, and forever, and forever, and forever shall your soul remain in doubt, expecting every moment some awful change, some diabolical sneer to disfigure the dear face bending over you. (Nabokov 2000: p. 91)

If Hermann were already damned, this might explain some of the disturbing effects of the tricks of memory: the marble-playing girls who appear twice, first in Tarnitz as Hermann awaits Felix (Nabokov 2000: p. 65), then in Berlin as Hermann, who cannot bring himself to post his final letter of assignation to Felix, calls upon an innocent girl, whom, by implication, he has perverted (2000: pp. 108–9), thereby devising a sophistry that allows him to deceive himself into believing he has a clean conscience because the fatal letter was not posted by himself but another. This second passage again echoes *A Portrait* when Hermann imagines the misfortunes that will accompany the innocent girl because of her role in this matter and how she will fail to understand what she has done to deserve them: "never, never, never will she understand" (p. 109).

In any case, whether he is already in Hell as we read, and the narrative he composes is some kind of figment of his tormented imagination, or whether he will enter Hell in the extra-diegetic world after his narrative, Hell will never pardon Hermann because he has committed an unforgivable sin, a sin against the Holy Ghost: he is in despair.[10] Despair itself, indeed, might even be understood to be a state that offers a foretaste of Hell: Hell is the place of utter despair, where all hope is abandoned, as the gates to Dante's Hell announce. There is a long tradition of understanding despair to be such a state of damnation — a state of damnation that anticipates and so, in effect, brings into being the real state of damnation. An illustration of how damnation is prefigured in the very emotion of despair can be seen in a series of sketches by the seventeenth-century French artist Charles Le Brun (Figure 6.2).

---

10 He is also guilty of presumption, impenitence, obstinacy, resisting truth, and envy of another's spiritual welfare.

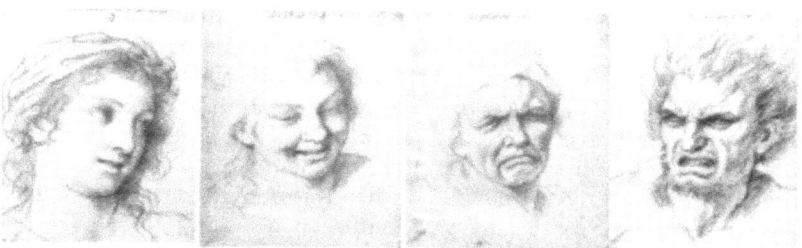

Figure 6.2 Fours faces by Charles Le Brun (1619–1690), Adoration; Smiling; Crying; Despair, (from Morel d'Arleux 1806)

Yet what is the nature of this despair, what causes this despair? One might argue that it is doubt itself, the kind of doubt which Hermann fears might assail one in Heaven: a doubt which is absolute and involves every aspect of the real, but which begins with a sense of uncertainty about one's own self and one's own powers. We begin to see, then, how the various layers of allusion and the distortions involved in the use of some of the sources is drawn together by Nabokov into a univocal whole: a single word "despair" echoes through the various components of the whole, encompassing and adequately naming it.

Intention, Intuition, Influence

That Hermann wishes to be seen as an artist is clear and has been much commented upon, yet a number of things have not been fully drawn to light in relation to this. Hermann wishes to create and to control. When he seeks to prove the non-existence of God at the beginning of chapter 6 he builds an argument based upon an understanding of the nature of the artist, something which Hermann considers inseparable from pride in creation, with creation understood to be a mastery, a control of things and others:

> The non-existence of God is simple to prove. Impossible to concede, for example, that a serious Jah, all wise and almighty, could employ his time in such inane fashion as playing with manikins, and — what is more incongruous — should restrict his game to the dreadfully trite laws of mechanics, chemistry, mathematics, and never — mind you, never! — show his face, but allow himself surreptitious peeps and circumlocutions, and the sneaky whispering (revelations, indeed!) of contentious truths from behind the back of some gentle hysteric. (Nabokov 2000: p. 90)

It would be beneath the dignity of a powerful God, in Hermann's view, to allow the possibility of misinterpretation. As Hermann's own plans as an artist begin to unravel he seeks to defend himself by writing memoirs that will explain the genius of his work, a work which is, in the end, a work of control, of power over others, of creation understood as the manipulation of events. Yet Hermann's work depends, for its effect, on the ability to influence others, to make them see in a given way and therefore act in a given way. Rather than this aligning Hermann with a creative God (who creates the world rather than seeking to influence the world) it aligns him with the devil; the devil whose sole power resides in the ability to manipulate, to influence. In *The Student of Prague*, Scallipini, the devil, is shown influencing events: he causes the hounds to run in a given direction by controlling one of the beasts he is able to command (the deceitful fox), drawing it on with gestures of his hands; he causes a letter which implicates Balduin to fall into the wrong hands, and so on. In each case the devil requires the (ill-)will of others to complete his plans, he only influences them, he only tempts them. Hermann's "work" is a work that seeks to influence and depends for its outcome on the correct reactions of others. A true creation, on the other hand, would be, like the work of God, open to understanding within the limits of comprehensible rules (the laws of nature). Misunderstanding does not undermine this kind of creative composition, which proceeds in accordance with its laws; whereas an incorrect interpretation would completely undo a work which seeks to influence, as it requires the one who is influenced to complete the work.

So the writing of his story involves an intervention that insists upon a strong understanding of intention. Yet the intention Hermann insists upon is, in effect, powerless: he insists that the intention be recognized simply because he has had this intention, simply because his intention came first and directed the actions that were made. Hermann does not understand that a real artist cannot simply stop the game to remind the audience of the intention: what is conveyed must be conveyed *through* the work: that is, it must be felt or sensed through the composition of the whole into a univocal expression. The authorities simply *must* see the uncanny resemblance he believes is there, if they do not, they will not be influenced to act in the way Hermann intends, and the work will unravel. Yet it is not possible to force people to recognize an intention (through another form, for example). The first work fails to act as intended so one writes a book to explain the intentions of the work, yet how can a second work built of words make us see the intention behind a first work built of physical resemblances? Hermann himself is aware of this problem right from the start:

> How I long to convince you! And I will, I will convince you! I will force you all, you rogues, to believe . . . though I am afraid that

words alone, owing to their special nature, are unable to convey visually a likeness of that kind: the two faces should be pictured side by side, by means of real colours, not words, then and only then would the spectator see my point. (Nabokov 2000: p. 23)

I have argued that Nabokov develops a compositional method which involves three elements, thesis, antithesis and synthesis with the reflections and distortions of irony produced in the play between each. In *Despair* this involves our being allowed to compare Hermann as he sees himself, to Hermann as others see him, so as to find Hermann as he really might be.

Besides the fact that no one else perceives the likeness Hermann claims to see, the supposed identity between Hermann and Felix is strongly associated with the word "nonsense" throughout the novel.[11] "Nonsense," in turn, makes us think of the mirrors of *Alice in Wonderland*, which Nabokov translated, but it is also further related here with Nansen, a proper name that refers to the Norwegian Arctic explorer Fridtjof Nansen, who was later a High Commissioner of the League of Nations. In the latter capacity, Nansen organized for the League of Nations to furnish Russian and other émigrés with identification papers to allow them to travel internationally, which were dubbed Nansen passports. So "Nansen" refers both to the explorer and to the inadequate identification papers that émigré Russians were forced to carry, and which Hermann is proud not to possess.[12] The identification of Hermann and Felix, then, is understood to be inadequate if one follows the trail of "nonsense" Nabokov leaves:

> Somebody told me once that I looked like Amundsen, the Polar explorer. Well, Felix, too, looked like Amundsen. But it is not every person that can recall Amundsen's face. I myself recall it but faintly, nor am I sure whether there had not been some mix-up with Nansen. (Nabokov 2000: p. 24)

Hermann, then, perhaps resembles Felix as much as the Norwegian explorer Amundsen resembles the Norwegian explorer Nansen, or as much as a "Nansen-sical" passport resembles accurate identification papers.

Yet Nabokov makes us think very hard about the nature of intention

---

11 When Hermann first sees Felix he thinks he is dead. His immediate response then is "'Nonsense,' I told myself. 'Asleep, merely asleep.'" (Nabokov 2000: p. 16). For other references see pp. 113, 125, 127, 135, 146, 154.
12 Ardalion, on the other hand, has a Nansen passport, for which Hermann chides him: "You have, I suppose, one of those Nansen-sical passports, not a solid German one, as all decent people have" (Nabokov 2000: p. 111).

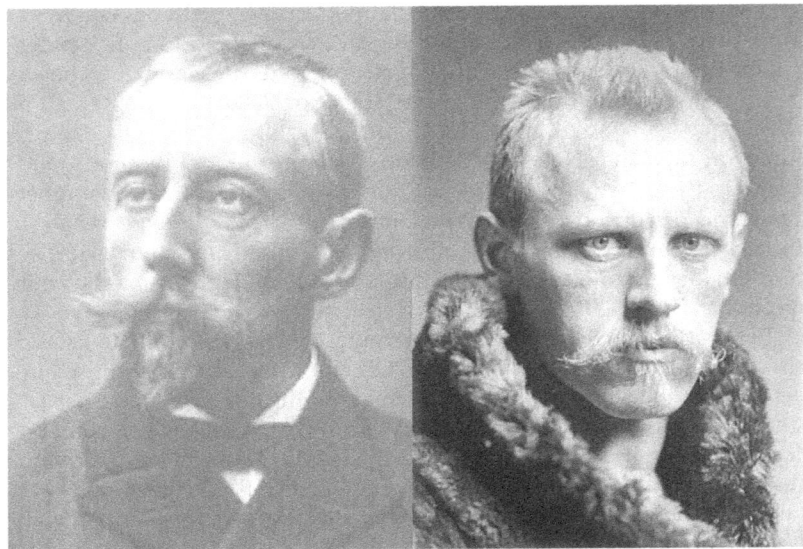

Roald Amundsen   Fridtjof Nansen

Figure 6.3 Amundsen photo by Ludwik Szacinski *c.* 1890; Nansen photo Library of Congress

here. Clearly Hermann is wrong, but how? Does the work of art require an understanding of intention? How are we to interpret without some such guide, without some Virgil to light our way? The paradoxes here are real and not easily unraveled. Intention, indeed, is shown to be at the heart of art, and the methods of composition, which *Despair*, like Sebastian Knight's *The Prismatic Bezel*, illustrates, but it reveals itself to be a problem rather than a solution.

For Hermann, it is the intention, and not small details, which might include insignificant errors, which is important. There is an interesting contrast between how Hermann views his relations with Felix, and the interaction of intention and interpretation that is necessary to any exchange, and his relations to his reader. Hermann pictures Felix as a feeble creature, and is particularly contemptuous of Felix's letters and his attempts to manipulate or control the game being played out between them. The artist is the one who creates through the composition of elements that, rather than generating a specific meaning, generate a powerful sense that the work as a whole is meaningful and that meaning rests within it, waiting to be uncovered. Felix, for Hermann, is like a parody of a bad artist: he is a bumbling fool, who, nevertheless, though in a manner that produces effects quite different to those intended, does manage some hopeless travesty of the creative gesture of control which Hermann equates with art:

> I rocked with laughter as I sat on that bench . . . How did he conceive it — the simpleton? That his letters would, by some sort of telepathy, inform me of their arrival and that after a magical perusal of their contents I would magically believe in the potency of his phantom menaces? How amusing that I *did* somehow feel that the letters awaited me, counter number nine, and that I *did* intend answering them, in other words, what he — in his arrogant stupidity — had conjectured, *had* happened! (Nabokov 2000: p. 105)

Is it that there is another hand, another artist, behind all this, who magically (number nine) makes use of Hermann within the composition of a true work of art? Some Sirin? Yet a work cannot only be built upon an intention, it has to be realized: it must function of its own accord separate from all those forces that brought it into being. That is, it needs itself to become or be something real: an object in the world which functions according to laws which not only allow it to exist (through its intra- and inter-textual relations), but insist upon the necessity of its existence. This, in effect, requires complex processes of composition. An unrealized work of art, in effect, does not exist: it is not a work of art, is nothing but a feeble collection of intentions one might only defend through an appeal to some illusory higher authority, or power (such as the superiority of the artist, or of the world view that supports the artist in the view that he or she is an artist). *Despair*, as a meditation on "methods of composition" (that is, drawing together of possible worlds) allows us to see how insignificant, how pathetic a defense of this kind really is. A page after his sneering attack on Felix's feeble intentions Hermann hysterically defends his own:

> The genius of a perfect crime is not admitted by people and does not make them dream and wonder; instead, they do their best to pick out something that can be pecked at and pulled to bits, something to prod the author with, so as to hurt him as much as possible. And when they think they have discovered the lapse they are after, hear their guffaws and jeers! But it is they who have erred, not the author; they lack his keensightedness and see nothing out of the common there, where the author perceived a marvel. (Nabokov 2000: pp. 106–7)

In the end one can only marvel at the complexity both of the intra- and inter-textual world and the method of composition Nabokov has imagined in *Despair*, a world whose complexity poses problems that multiply as they are identified and pursued.

Insofar as a writer is the kind of writer who is driven to encounter the real, rather than being content to subscribe to conventions built by tradition or genre, it is perhaps necessary to have or develop an analogical reality within works: a structure that is sufficiently malleable to allow for a translation of the real experience of life into something that can be realized as a work of art. That is, an object whose compositional complexity is analogous to the complexities of the real. In a way Nabokov shows us this, in *Despair*, by building a world which *fails* to be real: Hermann's world as he seeks to construct it. In part because he seeks to construct and control that world absolutely, with a paranoid rigidity, we fail to believe in that world, which may not be a real world, which might well be a world imagined by someone haunted by madness or paranoia. Or even by someone who is possessed by demons, or already in Hell, as Hermann himself might dimly perceive near the very end, before again turning to fantasy to escape the real:

> Maybe it is all mock existence, an evil dream: and presently I shall wake up somewhere; on a patch of grass near Prague. A good thing, at least, that they brought me to bay so speedily. (Nabokov 2000: p. 176)

Such an analogue of the real, as we have seen, requires an extraordinary level of organization or composition in drawing together disparate possible worlds within an overview, even within the divided mind of a single individual, into an image of thought. The analogue of the real, then, is experienced in thinking as the composed univocity of the work as a whole, which exists within a real world full of other texts and contexts to which it relates. Composition, then, involves sensations that draw together multiple viewpoints, and processes of relation that situate these sensations in relation to other sensations both "inside" and "outside" the works, and cause them to resonate, generating a sense of meaning.

Conclusion

Throughout this study I have argued that three important components to the concept of thinking in literature are relation, sensation, and composition. Each of these elements is identified with thinking, though I do not claim that they comprise all of thinking in literature (there are, no doubt, other elements that are not included here). Bakhtin has argued that objects have different sides and in conceiving of them we necessarily approach from and illuminate a *particular* side (Bakhtin 1994: p. 277). Deleuze and Guattari have made a similar point with regard to the nature of concepts: they have a number of components, and we need to develop an understanding of the combination of these components (Deleuze and Guattari 1994: pp. 15–34). In this way each of these three elements are understood as parts of a greater idea. So too, all three might be understood to inhere in art in general, not simply as examples specific to the three writers considered here.

Relation, as we have seen in Chapter 1 is one aspect of thinking: it is at the heart of thinking itself. Etymologically the word "ratio" links reason, relation, and proportional relation to ratiocination or thinking. Further, as we have seen, the coincidence of the relation of two things with understanding can be affirmed as *being* the idea itself; that is, as *being* the process of understanding itself.

Sensation, which comprises the drawing together of multiple viewpoints, shows us another aspect of thought. It allows us to understand how the outside and the inside, the external and the internal, the world and the self, the objective and the subjective are implicated with one another, inter-folded and inter-involved. This is outlined in detail in Chapter 2 and Chapter 5 through the discussion of Leibniz's viewpoint and Paul Cézanne's understanding of "sensation." As we have seen, sensation comes to us from outside: it is, or comprises the expression of the world; it is a sign or a multiplicity of signs. It is then registered internally, by the human brain, for example. In the case of art, it is then organized by the mind of the artist before being expressed once more as sensation through the work of art. Sensation, therefore, is the very matter of thought, yet as we have already noticed, it is implicated with relation and composition.

Composition, in turn, is another aspect of thought, and one which is of central importance to the artistic process, or aesthetic method. That is, it involves the *organization* of sensations and relations (i.e. it defines how sensations are related and understood).

As we have seen, then, in Chapters 1, 2, and 3, and throughout this study, all three aspects of thinking require the others to express thinking in a work of art. Yet there is a second aspect of this interrelation that has been brought to light here: all three aspects of thinking are also connected to "the real."

One might question the order of the terms I have outlined here. Why relation, sensation, and composition, and not some other order? That is, while composition clearly comes after the other two, which process might be understood to begin the process of thinking: relation or sensation?

In some ways it is a chicken and egg question. Yet, sensation (as a kind of perception, viewpoint, or viewpoints) presupposes relation — that which senses and that which is sensed are needed for there to be sensation: that is, relation is a prerequisite for sensation and sensation is in part defined as relation. That which senses and that which is sensed are parts in relation that allow, or *are*, thinking in its fundamental state. For this reason I begin with relation. What is related, however, is in the first instance sensation: that is, our first thoughts are perceptions, and thought itself is perception or viewpoint: the first relation, which in turn brings relation into being, is the relation of sensation.

A second question is now begged. How, then, does this begin to connect with the real?

Perception, or the relation to sensation is that which gives rise to the idea of the real; that is, (the idea of) the real is perceived in the relation (of ourselves) to sensation. The great conflicts between materialism and idealism announce themselves here. Yet it is worth not being distracted; it is worth following the line of thought a little further. Would it not be nonsensical to claim that there is a real which is not *in relation to* something (to itself at the very least), that there is a real which *is not sensed* (in that it is not necessarily composed of sensation)? It is, of course, not possible to answer this question in a modest work of literary criticism, yet literature does allow us to see that the sensation of the real *is thinking*.

The process of course does not end there. Thinking (the perception of the real) comes into relation with our natures and with our minds, which in turn organize what we perceive. So too, as philosophers have sometimes argued, our reason answers the reason of the universe as it is expressed through the laws of nature: we are able to understand because the organization of the "external" thought is in sympathy with the organization of the "internal" mind.[1] With regard to literature: sensations

---

[1] For an example of this view, which was known to most of the writers considered in this study, see Bergson's (1998) *Creative Evolution*.

Conclusion 149

and intra- and inter-textual relations are composed in order to create the work of art. For this reason, art can and does have a particular relation to the real.

The external world we sense, of course, is not solely responsible for our understandings. Constructed forms or systems, developed by groups or individuals and influenced by culture, language and other environmental factors, will necessarily be applied to our sensations and inflect or determine the nature of our understanding of the real sensations we perceive. Yet just as sensation comes from outside, impresses itself on us, and is in part responsible for the kinds of organization that ensue within us, so too, in an inverse movement, we tend to see our own understandings as being reflected back to us by the world and we then seek to shape the world in accordance with those understandings.

Some artists, then, attempt to understand the world and the functioning of the world: not all writers or artists attempt to do this, and it is not compulsory. My claim is, however, that any artist who does attempt to understand the world in or through their works will necessarily work through variations on the processes of relation, sensation, and composition outlined in general terms and through specific examples in this study. That is, they reflect this understanding through their art, though not by "representing" it (that is, not by producing something that is simply a reflection of the real) but by producing something that, like the real, enables and involves both reflection and distortion, and the meaningful composition of these disparate elements. They create works that involve similar processes of organization within themselves and between themselves and other texts and contexts to those processes that already exist in the relation of the mind to the real: they create works that in turn create or enable "reflection." It is in this sense that they "mimic" or "imitate" the real: they are both systems that generate the levels of imperfect reflection that express our relation to thought. Such artists, then, use their understanding of what it is that is the real to compose their works and organize the sensations and relations that comprise their works. In doing this they develop a secondary relation or analogue of the real (such as they have conceived it to be) by organizing or composing their works in such a way that the composition produces the kind of reflections they perceive in the real. The organization of the work is analogous to (the conception they have of) the organization of the real.

In short, then, not only does literature think or reflect upon, but also it generates thinking in causing us to reflect even upon the distortion that inheres within the reflective surfaces that are our own minds, as well as the minds of others. My argument in this study is that all writers that consider writing to be a process of thinking develop this process; that they all work with relation, sensation, and composition in developing works that are analogues of the real.

Bibliography

Anker, Elizabeth S. "Where Was Moses When the Candle Went Out? Infinity, Prophecy, and Ethics in Spinoza and 'Ithaca,'" *James Joyce Quarterly*, 44, (4), Summer 2007: 661–77.
Appel, Jr., Alfred. "*Lolita*: The Springboard of Parody," *Wisconsin Studies in Contemporary Literature*, 8, (2), Spring 1967: 201–41.
Ascher, Marcia. *Ethnomathematics: A Multicultural View of Mathematical Ideas*. Belmont, CA: Chapman and Hall, 1991.
——. *Mathematics Elsewhere: An Exploration of Ideas Across Cultures*. Princeton, NJ: Princeton University Press, 2004.
Asmus, Walter D. "Beckett Directs Godot," *Theatre Quarterly*, 5, (19), 1975: 19–26.
Aubert, Jaques. *The Aesthetics of James Joyce*. Baltimore, MD: Johns Hopkins University Press, 1992.
Bakhtin, M. M. *The Dialogic Imagination: Four Essays*, Michael Holquist (ed.), Caryl Emerson and Michael Holquist (trans.). Austin, TX: University of Texas Press, 1994.
Bair, Deirdre. *Samuel Beckett: A Biography*. London: Vintage, 1990.
Banfield, Ann. *The Phantom Table*. Cambridge: Cambridge University Press, 2000.
Baumgarten, Alexander Gottlieb. *Reflections on Poetry*, translated with the original text, an Introduction and Notes by Karl Aschenbrenner and William B. Holtner. Berkeley, CA and Los Angeles, CA: University of California Press, 1954.
Beckett, Samuel. *Molloy*. New York: Grove Press, 1955
——. *Murphy* New York: Grove Press, 1957.
——. *Disjecta: Miscellaneous Writings and a Dramatic Fragment*, Ruby Cohn (ed.). London: John Calder, 1983.
——. *The Complete Dramatic Works*. London: Faber and Faber. 1990.
——. *Dream of Fair to Middling Women*. New York: Arcade, 1993.
——. *The Complete Short Prose*, Stanley Gontarski (ed.). New York: Grove Press, 1995.
——. "Letter to Georges Duthuit, 9–10 March 1949," Walter Redfern (trans.), in S. E. Gontarski and Anthony Uhlmann (eds.), *Beckett after Beckett*. Gainesville, FL: University Press of Florida, 2006.
Bergson, Henri. *Creative Evolution*. London: Dover, 1998.

Boyd, Brian. *Vladimir Nabokov: The Russian Years*. Princeton, NJ: Princeton University Press, 1990.
———. *Vladimir Nabokov: The American Years*. Princeton, NJ: Princeton University Press, 1991.
———. *Nabokov's Pale Fire: The Magic of Artistic Discovery*. Princeton, NJ: Princeton University Press, 1999.
Bowen, Zack. "Ulysses," in Zack Bowen and James F. Carens (eds.), *A Companion to Joyce Studies*. Westport, CT: Greenwood Press, 1984.
Brater, Enoch. *Why Beckett*. London: Thames and Hudson, 1989.
Bréhier, Émile. *La théorie des incorporels dans l'ancien stoïcisme*, J. Vrin (ed.). (1st edn. 1908). Paris: Librairie philosophique, 1997.
Brown, Richard. "Introduction," in Richard Brown (ed.), *Joyce, "Penelope" and the Body*. Amsterdam: Rodopi, 2006.
Campbell, Joseph and Henry Morton Robinson. *A Skeleton Key to Finnegans Wake: Unlocking James Joyce's Masterwork*. Novato, CA: New World Library, 2005.
Cézanne, Paul. *Paul Cézanne, Letters*, John Rewald (ed.). New York: Da Capo Press, 1976.
Chabert, Pierre. "Samuel Beckett as Director," in M. A. Bonney and J. Knowlson (trans.), Knowlson, James (ed.), *Theatre Workbook 1, Samuel Beckett: Krapp's Last Tape. A Theatre Workbook edited by James Knowlson*. London: Brutus Books, 1980.
Clément, Bruno. *Le récit de la method*. Paris: Seuil, 2005.
Coetzee, J. M. "Dostoevsky: The Miraculous Years," in *Stranger Shores*. London: Penguin, 2002.
Colum, Padraic. "Introduction," in James Joyce, *Exiles: A Play in Three Acts*, with the author's own notes and an introduction by Padraic Colum. London: Penguin, 1973.
Connolly, Thomas E. *James Joyce's Books, Portraits, Manuscripts, Notebooks, Typescripts, Page Proofs: Together with Critical Essays about Some of His Works*. Lewiston, NY: Edwin Mellen Press, 1997.
Connor, Steven "What if There Were no Such Thing as the Aesthetic?" Paper presented at the *The Function of Contemporary Aesthetics Conference*, organised by John Armstrong for the Centre for English Studies and the University of London Philosophy Programme on March 3, 1999. For a full text version see: http://www.stevenconnor.com/aes/ (accessed February 7, 2011).
Cordingley, Anthony. "Beckett and 'L'ordre naturel': The Universal Grammar of Comment c'est/How It Is," in *"All Sturm and No Drang," Beckett and Romanticism, Beckett at Reading 2006, Samuel Beckett Today/Aujourd'hui 18*. Amsterdam: Rodopi, 2007: pp. 185–200.
Craig, Edward Gordon. *On the Art of the Theatre*. New York: Theatre Arts Books, 1956.
Damasio, Antonio. *Descartes' Error: Emotion, Reason, and the Human Brain*. New York: Quill, 2000.

Dante Alighieri. "The Inferno," in *The Divine Comedy*, Laurence Binyon (trans.), with notes from C. H. Grandgent, in Paola Milano (ed.) and introduction, *Dante: The Selected Works*. London: Chatto and Windus, 1972.
Deleuze, Gilles. *Nietzsche et la philosophie*. Paris: Presses Universitaires de France, 1962a.
——. *Marcel Proust et les signes*. Paris: Presses Universitaires de France, 1962b.
——. *Différence et Repetition*. Paris: Presses Universitaires de France, 1968.
——. *Nietzsche and Philosophy*, Hugh Tomlinson (trans.). New York: Columbia University Press, 1983.
——. *Cinema 1: The Movement-Image*, Hugh Tomlinson and Barbara Habberjam (trans.). Minneapolis, MN: University of Minnesota Press, 1986.
——. *Spinoza: Practical Philosophy*, Robert Hurley (trans.). San Francisco, CA: City Lights, 1988.
——. *Cinema 2: The Time-Image*, Hugh Tomlinson and Robert Galeta (trans.). Minneapolis, MN: University of Minnesota Press, 1989.
——. *Expressionism in Philosophy: Spinoza*, Martin Joughin (trans.). New York: Zone, 1990.
——. *The Fold: Leibniz and the Baroque*, Tom Conley (trans. and foreword). Minneapolis, MN: University of Minnesota Press, 1993.
——. *Difference and Repetition*, Paul Patton (trans.). New York: Columbia University Press, 1994.
——. *Negotiations, 1972–1990*, Martin Joughin (trans.). New York: Columbia University Press, 1995.
——. *Francis Bacon: logique de la sensation*. Paris: Éditions de la difference, 1996.
——. "The Greatest Irish Film," in Daniel W. Smith and Michael A. Greco (trans.), *Essays Critical and Clinical*. Minneapolis, MN: University of Minnesota Press, 1997: pp. 23–6.
——. *Proust and Signs*, Richard Howard (trans.). London: Athlone Press, 2000.
——. *Desert Islands and Other Texts 1953–1974*, David Lapoujade (ed.), Michael Taormina (trans.). Los Angeles: Semiotext(e), 2004.
——. *The Fold: Leibniz and the Baroque*, Tom Conley (trans. and foreword). London: Continuum, 2006.
Deleuze, Gilles and Félix Guattari. *A Thousand Plateaus*, Brian Massumi (trans.). Minneapolis, MN: University of Minnesota Press, 1987.
——. *What is Philosophy?*, Hugh Tomlinson and Graham Burchell (trans.). New York: Columbia University Press, 1994.
Dobbs, Darrell. "Reckless Rationalism and Heroic Reverence in Homer's *Odyssey*," *American Political Science Review*, 81, (2), June 1987: 491–508.
Driver, Tom. F. "Beckett By The Madeleine," *Columbia University Forum*, 4, Summer 1961: 21–5.

Eagleton, Terry. *The Ideology of the Aesthetic*. London: Blackwell, 1991.
Eliot, T. S. "The Waste Land," in *Collected Poems 1909–1962*. London: Faber, 1963.
Ellmann, Richard. *James Joyce*. Oxford: Oxford University Press, 1983.
———. "The Big Word in 'Ulysses,'" *New York Review of Books*, 31, (16), October 25, 1984. http://www.nybooks.com/articles/5695 (accessed August 3 2009).
———. "Finally, the Last Word on 'Ulysses': The Ideal Text, and Portable Too," *New York Times*, June 15, 1986: Books. http://www.nytimes.com/books/00/01/09/specials/joyce–ideal.html (accessed August 3 2009).
Esslin, Martin. "Review: 'Godot,' the Authorized Version" (Schiller Theater Company at the Royal Court Theatre), *Journal of Beckett Studies*, 1, Winter, 1976: 98–9.
Euclid. *Euclid's Elements*, Sir Thomas Little Heath (trans.). New York: Dover, 1956.
Faulkner, William. *The Sound and the Fury*, David Minter (ed.) New York: Norton, 1994.
Ferrer, Daniel. *Virginia Woolf and the Madness of Language*. London: Routledge, 1990.
Feuer, Lewis S. *Einstein and the Generations of Science*. New York: Transaction, 1982.
Fields, Andrew. *Nabokov: His Life in Art*. London: Hodder and Stoughton, 1967.
Fordham, Finn. "Spinning with 'Penelope,'" in Richard Brown (ed.), *Joyce, "Penelope" and the Body*. Amsterdam: Rodopi, 2006.
Forget, Jacques. "Holy Ghost" *The Catholic Encyclopedia*, 7. New York: Robert Appleton Company, 1910. http://www.newadvent.org/cathen/07409a.htm (accessed April 22, 2009).
Foucault, Michel. *Les mots et les choses: une archéologie des sciences humaines*. Paris: Gallimard, 1990.
Freidman, Melvin J. *Stream of Consciousness: A Study in Literary Method*. New Haven, CT: Yale University Press, 1955.
Fry, Roger. *Cézanne: A Study of his Development*. London: Hogarth Press, 1927.
———. *A Roger Fry Reader*, introductory essays by Christopher Reed (ed.). Chicago: The University of Chicago Press, 1996.
Gagarin, Michael. "Morality in Homer," *Classical Philology*, 82, (4), October 1987: 285–306.
Gasquet, Joaquim. *Cézanne: a memoir with conversations*, preface by John Rewald, introduction by Richard Shiff, Christopher Pemberton (trans.). London: Thames and Hudson, 1991.
Gibson, Andrew. *Joyce's Revenge: History, Politics, and Aesthetics in* Ulysses. Oxford: Oxford University Press, 2002.
Gifford, Don with R. J. Seidman. *Notes for Joyce: An Annotation of James Joyce's* Ulysses. New York: Dutton, 1974.

Gilbert, Stuart. *James Joyce's* Ulysses. New York: Vintage, 1955.
Gillespie, Michael Patrick. *Reading the Book of Himself: Narrative Strategies in the Works of James Joyce.* Columbus, OH: Ohio State University Press, 1989.
Goldman, Jane. *The Feminist Aesthetics of Virginia Woolf: Modernism, Postimpressionism, and the Politics of the Visual.* Cambridge: Cambridge University Press, 1998.
Greenblatt, Stephen. *Will in the World: How Shakespeare became Shakespeare.* London: Jonathan Cape, 2004.
Groden, Michael. *Ulysses in Progress,* Princeton, NJ: Princeton University Press, 1977.
Handler, Philip Leonard. "James Joyce: From Hero to Artist." Master's dissertation. Columbia University, 1956.
Henry, Holly. *Virginia Woolf and the Discourse of Science: The Aesthetics of Astronomy.* Cambridge: Cambridge University Press, 2003.
Homer. *The Odyssey*, E. V. Rieu and D. C. H. Rieu (trans.). London: Penguin, 2003.
Hopper, Vincent Foster. *Medieval Number Symbolism: Its Sources, Meaning, and Influence on Thought and Expression.* London: Dover, 2000.
Humphrey, Robert. *Stream of Consciousness in the Modern Novel.* Berkeley, CA: University of California Press, 1954.
Innes, Christopher. *Edward Gordon Craig.* Cambridge: Cambridge University Press. 1983.
James, William. *Psychology: The Briefer Course.* London: Dover, 2001.
Jones, Peter. "Introduction," in Homer, *The Odyssey*, E. V. Rieu and D. C. H. Rieu (trans.). London: Penguin, 2003.
Joyce, James. *Stephen Hero.* New York: New Directions, 1963.
——. *Exiles: A Play in Three Acts*, with the author's own Notes and an Introduction by Padraic Colum. London: Penguin, 1973.
——. *Dubliners, Text, Criticism and Notes*, Robert Scholes and A. Walton Litz (eds.). London: Penguin, 1976.
——. *Ulysses*, Hans Walter Gabler with Wolfhard Steppe and Claus Melchior (eds.), afterword by Michael Groden. London: The Bodley Head, 1993.
——. *A Portrait of the Artist as a Young Man*, Seamus Deane (ed.). London: Penguin, 2003.
——. *Occasional, Critical and Political Writing*, Kevin Barry (ed.). Oxford: Oxford University Press, 2008.
Kendall, Richard (ed.). *Cézanne by Himself: Drawings, Paintings, Writings.* London: Macdonald Orbis, 1988.
Kernan, Alvin B. "Reading Zemblan: The Audience Disappears in Nabokov's Pale Fire," in Harold Bloom (ed.), *Vladimir Nabokov: Modern Critical Views.* New York: Chelsea House, 1987: pp. 101–25.
Kleist, Heinrich Von. *The Prince of Homburg*, Neil Bartlett (trans.). London: Oberon, 2002.
——. "On the Marionette Theatre," Idris Parry (trans.). *Southern Cross*

Bibliography 155

Review, Argentina, 2003. http://southerncrossreview.org/9/kleist.htm (accessed 7 February 2011).

Knowlson, James. *Damned to Fame: the Life of Samuel Beckett.* London: Bloomsbury, 1996.

Knowlson, James. (ed.) *Happy Days: Samuel Beckett's Production Notebook.* London: Faber and Faber, 1985.

Knowlson, James and Elizabeth Knowlson. *Beckett Remembering: Remembering Beckett: Uncollected Interviews with Samuel Beckett and Memories of Those Who Knew Him.* London: Bloomsbury, 2007.

Kumar, Shiv Kumar. *Bergson and the Stream of Consciousness Novel.* New York: New York University Press, 1963.

Lagrée, Jacqueline. *Juste Lipse: La Restauration du Stoïcisme, Étude et Traductions de divers traités Stoïciens.* Paris: Vrin, 1994.

Lee, Hermione. *Virginia Woolf.* London: Vintage, 1999.

Leibniz, G. W. *Theodicy: Essays on the Goodness of God the Freedom of Man and the Origin of Evil*, introduction by Austin Farrer (ed.), E. M. Huggard (trans.). Chicago, IL: Open Court, 1990.

——. "Monadology. 1714," in G. H. R. Parkinson (ed.), Mary Morris and G. H. R. Parkinson (trans.), *Philosophical Writings*. London: J. M. Dent, 1992a.

——. "Principles of Nature and of Grace. 1714," in G. H. R. Parkinson (ed.), Mary Morris and G. H. R. Parkinson (trans.), *Philosophical Writings*. London: J. M. Dent, 1992b.

——. "Of an Organum or Ars Magna of Thinking," (1679), in G. H. R. Parkinson (ed.), Mary Morris and G. H. R. Parkinson (trans.), *Philosophical Writings*. London: J. M. Dent, 1992c.

Lévi–Strauss, Claude. *The Elementary Structures of Kinship.* Boston, MA: Beacon Press, 1969.

Liu, Pin-hsiung. *Foundations of Kinship Mathematics.* Nan-kang, Taipei: Institute of Ethnology, Academia Sinica, 1986.

Litz, A. Walton. *The Art of James Joyce: Method and Design in* Ulysses *and* Finnegans Wake. London: Oxford University Press, 1961.

Long, A. A. "Morals and Values in Homer," *The Journal of Hellenic Studies*, 90, 1970: 121–39.

Maloon, Terence. "Classic Cézanne: Exhibition Notes," *Classic Cézanne.* Sydney: Art Gallery of NSW, 1998a.

Maloon, Terence (ed.). *Classic Cézanne.* Sydney: Art Gallery of NSW, 1998b.

Mamigonian, M. A. and Turner, J. N. "Annotations for Stephen Hero," *James Joyce Quarterly*, 40, (3), 2003: 347.

Manganiello, Dominic. "Reading the Book of Himself: The Confessional Imagination of St. Augustine and Joyce", in *Biography & Autobiography: Essays on Irish and Canadian History and Literature.* Ottowa, ON: Carleton University Press, 1993.

McIver, Mia. "Joyce with Spinoza: Legal Fiction and Double Truth." Paper delivered at the *XXIst International Joyce Symposium*, June 15–20, 2008 at Tours, France.

Bibliography

McLaren, Stephen. "Framing *A Portrait of the Artist*: Evolution in Design," PhD thesis, University of Western Sydney, 2005.

McLaurin, Allen. *Virginia Woolf: The Echoes Enslaved*. Cambridge: Cambridge University Press, 1973.

McMillan, Dougald and Fehsenfeld, Martha. *Beckett in the Theatre: The Author as Practical Playwright and Director. Volume 1: From "Waiting for Godot" to "Krapp's Last Tape."* London: John Calder, 1988.

Morel d'Arleux, Louis-Jean-Marie. *Dissertation sur un Traité de Charles Lebrun concernant le Rapport de la Physionomie Humaine avec Celle des Animaux*. Paris, Chalcographie du Musée Napoléon, 1806.

Morton, John. "Country, People, Art: The Western Aranda 1870–1990," in Jane Hardy, J. V. S. Megaw and Ruth Megaw (eds.), *The Heritage of Namatjira*. Melbourne: William Heinemann, 1992.

Nadler, Steven. *Spinoza: A Life*. Cambridge: Cambridge University Press, 1999.

Nabokov, Vladimir. *The Real Life of Sebastian Knight*. London: Penguin, 1982.

———. *Speak, Memory*. New York: Vintage, 1989a.

———. *Pale Fire*. New York: Vintage, 1989b.

———. *Lolita*. New York: Vintage, 1989c.

———. *Laughter in the Dark*. New York: Vintage, 1989d.

———. *King, Queen, Knave*. New York: Vintage, 1989e.

———. *Strong Opinions*. New York: Vintage, 1990.

———. *The Gift*. New York: Vintage, 1991.

———. *The Stories of Vladimir Nabokov*. New York: Vintage, 1997.

———. *Despair*. London: Penguin, 2000.

———. *Lectures on Russian Literature*. New York: Harvest, 2002.

Newton, Rick M. "Assembly and Hospitality in the Cyclôpeia," *College Literature*, 35, (4), Fall 2008: 1–44.

Nietzsche, Friedrich. *Beyond Good and Evil*, R. J. Hollingdale (trans.), introduction by Michael Tanner. London: Penguin, 2003.

Nussbaum, Martha. *Upheavals of Thought: The Intelligence of Emotions*. Cambridge: Cambridge University Press, 2001.

Oliphant, Ronald. "The Man Who Forged Himself," *Excitement*, 20, (6), August. New York: Street and Smith, 1930.

Pascal, Blaise. *Pensées*, W. F. Trotter (trans.), introduction by T. S. Eliot. New York: Dutton, 1958.

Plato. *The Collected Dialogues, Including the Letters*, Edith Hamilton and Huntington Cairns (eds.). Princeton, NJ: Princeton University Press, 1996.

Proffer, Carl R. "*Otchaianie* to *Despair*," *Slavic Review*, 27, (2), June 1968: 258–67.

Proust, Marcel. *In Search of Lost Time*, C. K. Scott Moncrieff and Terence Kilmartin (trans.), revised by D. J. Enright, introduction by Harold Bloom. London: Everyman, 2001.

Pushkin, Aleksandr. *Eugene Onegin: A Novel in Verse*, Vladimir Nabokov (trans.), Vol. 3, commentary and index. Princeton, NJ: Princeton University Press, 1975.

Raleigh, John Henry. "Bloom as Modern Epic Hero," *Critical Inquiry*, 3, (3), Spring, 1977: 583–98.

Riquelme, John Paul. *Teller and Tale in Joyce's Fiction*. Baltimore, MD: Johns Hopkins University Press, 1983.

——. "*Stephen Hero* and *A Portrait of the Artist as a Young Man*: transforming the nightmare of history," in Derek Attridge (ed.), *The Cambridge Companion to James Joyce*. Cambridge: Cambridge University Press, 2004.

Saunders, Jason Lewis. *Justus Lipsius. The Philosophy of Renaissance Stoicism*. New York: The Liberal Arts Press, 1955.

Schneider, Alan. "'Any Way You Like, Alan': Working with Beckett," *Theatre Quarterly*, 5, (19), 1975: 27–38.

Scott, Bonnie Kime. "Lyceum: An Early Resource for Joyce," *James Joyce Quarterly*, 22, (1), Fall, 1984: 77–81.

Seiden, Melvin. "Nabokov and Dostoevsky," *Contemporary Literature*, 13, (4), Autumn, 1972: 423–44.

Shakespeare, William. *Othello*, Edward Pechter (ed.). New York: Norton, 2004.

——. *Hamlet*, T. J. B. Spencer (ed.). London: Penguin, 2005.

Shenker, Israel. "Moody Man of Letters," interview with Samuel Beckett, *New York Times*, section 2, May 6, 1956: 1–3.

Shiff, Richard. "Introduction," in Joaquim Gasquet, *Cézanne: A Memoir with Conversations*, Christopher Pemberton (trans.), preface by John Rewald. London: Thames and Hudson, 1991.

——. "Sensation, Movement, Cézanne," in Terence Maloon (ed.), *Classic Cézanne*. Sydney: Art Gallery of NSW, 1998.

Slote, Sam. "The Medieval Irony of Joyce's Portrait," *Medieval Joyce*, Lucia Boldrini (ed.). European Joyce Studies 13. Amsterdam: Rodopi, 2002: pp. 185–98.

Spinoza, Benedictus de. *Opera quotquot reperta sunt Benedicti de Spinoza*; recognoverunt J. van Vloten et J. P. N. Land. Hagae Comitum: M. Nijhoff, 1914.

——. *The Collected Works of Spinoza*, Vol. 1, Edwin Curley (ed. and trans.). Princeton, NJ: Princeton University Press, 1985.

——. *Spinoza: Complete Works*, Samuel Shirley (trans.), Michael L. Morgan (ed.) introduction and notes. Indianapolis, IN/Cambridge: Hackett Publishing Company, 2002.

Strehlow, T. G. H. *Aranda Traditions*. Melbourne: Melbourne University Press, 1947.

The Student of Prague [*Der Student von Prag*], dir. Stellan Rye and Paul Wegener, based on a novel by Hanns Heinze Ewers from a story by Edgar Allan Poe. Perf. Paul Wegener, John Gottowt, Grete Berger, Lyda Salmonova, Lothar Korner and Fritz Weidenmann, Germany, Deutsche Bioscop GmbH, 1913, Film.

The Student of Prague [*Der Student von Prag*], written and directed by Henrik Galeen, based on a novel by Hanns Heinze Ewers from a story by Edgar

Allan Poe. Cinematographers: Günther Krampf and Erich Nitzschmann. Perf. Conrad Veidt, Werner Krauss, Agnes Esterhazy, Elizza La Porta, Fritz Alberti, Ferdinand von Alten, Erich Kober, Max Maximillian, Germany, Sokal–Film GmbH, 1926, Film.
Uhlmann, Anthony. *Beckett and Poststructuralism*. Cambridge: Cambridge University Press, 1999.
———. *Samuel Beckett and the Philosophical Image*. Cambridge: Cambridge University Press, 2006a.
———. "Samuel Beckett and the Occluded Image," in S. E. Gontarski and Anthony Uhlmann (eds.), *Beckett after Beckett*. Gainesville, FL: University Press of Florida, 2006b: pp. 79–97.
Vollard, Ambroise. *Cézanne*. New York: Crown, 1937.
Volosinov, V. N. *Marxism and the Philosophy of Language*, Ladislav Matejka and I. R. Titunik (trans.). Cambridge, MA: Harvard University Press, 1986.
Watson, Helen, with the Yolgnu community at Yirrkala and D. W. Chambers. *Singing the Land, Signing the Land*. Geelong, VIC: Deakin University Press, 1989.
Weil, André. "Appendix to Part One: On the Algebraic Study of Certain Types of Marriage Laws (Murngin System)," in *The Elementary Structures of Kinship*, by Claude Lévi-Strauss. Boston, MA: Beacon Press, 1969.
White, H. C. *An Anatomy of Kinship: Mathematical Models for Structures of Cumulated Roles*. New York: Prentice-Hall, 1963.
Wilde, Oscar. *The Portrait of Mr. W. H. — The greatly enlarged version prepared by the author after the appearance of the story in 1889 but not published*. London: Methuen, 1958.
———. *Complete Short Fiction*. London: Penguin, 2003.
Wimsatt, W. K. and Monroe C. Beardsley. "The Intentional Fallacy," in *The Verbal Icon: Studies in the Meaning of Poetry*. Lexington, KY: The University of Kentucky Press, 1954: pp. 3–20.
Windelband, Wilhelm. *A History of Western Philosophy*, James H. Tufts (trans.). London: Macmillan, 1901.
Wittgenstein, Ludwig. *Tractatus Logico-Philosophicus*, D. F. Pears and B. F. McGuinness (trans.), with an introduction by Bertrand Russell. London: Routledge, 1995.
Woolf, Virginia. *Walter Sickert: A Conversation*. London: Hogarth Press, 1934.
———. *Roger Fry: A Biography*. New York: Harcourt Brace Jovanovich, 1976.
———. *The Diary of Virginia Woolf*, Vol. 2, Anne Olivier Bell and Andrew McNeillie (eds.). New York: Harvest, 1980a.
———. *The Letters of Virginia Woolf*, Vol. 3, Nigel Nicolson and Joanne Trautmann (eds.). London: Hogarth Press, 1980b.
———. *To the Lighthouse. The Original Holography Draft*, transcribed by Susan Dick (ed). London: The Hogarth Press, 1983.
———. *To the Lighthouse*, Stella McNichol (ed.), with an introduction by Hermione Lee. London: Penguin, 2000a.

———. *The Waves*. London: Penguin, 2000b.
———. *Moments of Being*. London: Pimlico, 2002.

Index

absolute meaning 114, 116, 122
actualisation 26
aesthetic 1–5, 14, 35, 51–2, 64, 68, 73, 83–6, 108, 138
  method 2, 4–5, 29, 52–3, 59, 63, 67, 83, 85, 89, 91, 115–16, 121–4, 134, 147
Akalaitis, J. 37
Alice in Wonderland 143
allusion 15, 71, 124–8, 141
Amundsen, R. 143–4
analytical philosophy 86–8
Appel, A. 5, 123
archetype 53, 67, 69
Aristotle 61, 76
Arrente people 68, 82
attributes 9, 18, 35–6, 40, 42

Bair, D. 37
Bakhtin, M. 28, 39, 147
Banfield, Ann 83, 86–8, 98
Barry, K. 61
Baumgarten, A. 1–2, 84, 87
Beckett, S. 9–10, 14–15, 36–40, 44, 51–2
  Breath 37
  Dream of Fair to Middling Women 14, 51
  Endgame 37
  Film 14
  Ghost Trio 38
  Happy Days 37–8
Bell, C. 110

Bell, V. 85, 110
Bergson, H. 4, 64
Berkeley, G. 64
Bernard, E. 91–4, 105
Bloomsbury group 37, 85, 104–5
Boyd, B. 5, 114–17, 119, 122, 124–5, 134
Brater, E. 37

Cambridge Apostles 86, 88
Campbell, J. 75
causation 14, 18, 21–3, 27, 30, 32, 40, 42, 81, 102
  affective 64
  logical 73
  spiritual 81
Cézanne, P. 5, 16–17, 85–100, 105–9, 111–13, 147
Clément, B. 17
Coleridge, S. 10, 107–8
complication 31, 39
composition 4–5, 7, 27, 29, 33, 41, 47, 92, 100, 104, 113–15, 117–26, 129, 134, 137, 142–9
  artistic 86, 105
  methods of 49, 115, 123–4, 134, 144–5
Conan Doyle, A. 125
Connolly, T. 66–7
consciousness 19, 27, 30, 45–7, 56, 101
  objective 16, 94, 105
  subjective 16, 94
constructionism 33

Craig, E. 37–8, 108
Curley, E. 9–10

Damasio, A. 2, 96
Dante A. 75, 135–6, 138, 140
Deleuze, G. 2–4, 7, 9–10, 14–15, 18, 21–2, 24–33, 35, 39, 41, 43–4, 66, 73, 83, 96, 105, 112, 121, 147
  Cinema 2 20
  Difference and Repetition 33
  Expressionism in Philosophy: Spinoza 35–6
  The Fold: Leibniz and the Baroque 20, 27–8, 43
  Negotiations 33
  Proust and Signs 27, 31–3
  Spinoza: Practical Philosophy 46–7
Descartes, R. 1, 20, 35, 139
determinism 23, 25
Dick, S. 100
Dostoevsky, F. 125, 129
Duthuit, G. 14, 51

Einstein, A. 4
Eliot, G. 10
Ellmann, R. 66
essence 9–10, 18, 22–5, 28, 31–2, 36, 40–1, 52, 55–9, 61, 68, 80
Euclid 13–14, 73
Ewers, H. 127
Excitement 130–2
exhaustion 14
Exiles 5, 29, 52, 54, 59, 62–3, 65–6, 83
expression 7, 11n2, 33–6, 39–42, 44, 46–7, 114–15, 118, 121
  univocal 39–41, 47, 120, 124, 141–2
Extension 9, 23, 35–6

Farrer, Austin 25, 30
Faulkner, W. 2, 17
  The Sound and the Fury 17

fragmentation 29
freedom 25, 59, 63
Fry, R. 5, 85–92, 94–8, 100, 105–11, 113

Gasquet, B. 94
Gasquet, J. 16, 37, 94, 98–9, 105–6, 109, 112
Gauguin, P. 93
Gilbert, S. 71
God 4, 9, 18, 20–5, 27–8, 36, 39, 41, 58–9, 69, 81–5, 96, 139, 141–2
Goldman, J. 86
Grant, D. 110
Greenblatt, S. 15
Guattari, F. 10, 24–5, 27, 29, 32, 35, 41, 44, 105, 147

harmony 18, 25, 28, 39, 45, 47, 89, 92, 97, 103, 105
Hegel, G. 77, 119
Heine, H. 10
heteroglossia 28, 39–40, 47
Homer 53, 69–70
  Odyssey 53, 69–72, 75
Hopper, V. 75
Hume, D. 64

idea, the 9–12, 147
imagination 3, 10, 12–13, 16–17, 80, 107, 109, 117, 132, 140
Impressionists 16, 91, 96–7
incompossible 20, 22, 26, 28, 83
individualistic subjectivism 34, 41
Innes, C. 38, 108
intellect 14, 16, 18, 58, 86, 93, 97
  emotional 100
interior monologue 3
intuition 3, 12, 14, 18, 24, 39, 88, 94, 114
irony 52, 72–3, 119–20, 125, 143

James, W. 2
jealousy 29, 52, 54, 62–7, 76–7, 79, 81, 131
Joyce, J. 2–5, 10, 29, 47, 49, 51–82
and aesthetic method 52–3, 59
and Beckett 51–2
and comedy 61
Dubliners 59–61, 63
Exiles 5, 29, 52, 54, 59, 62–3, 65–6, 83
A Portrait of the Artist as a Young Man 5, 52, 61, 63, 67, 125, 135, 139–40
and Shakespeare 63–4, 72
and Spinoza 53–9, 63–5
Stephen Hero 5, 52, 65, 67, 82
Ulysses 5, 29, 47, 52–4, 62, 64, 66–7, 69, 71–2, 80, 83

Kleist, H. Von 37–40, 43–7, 107–8
'On the Marionette Theatre' 37–8, 44–5
The Prince of Homburg 38, 44
knowledge 3, 9–18, 23–5, 32, 35–6, 41–2, 45–7, 59, 69, 78, 94, 117, 120
sacred 68
secular 68
in Spinoza 9, 12–13, 15–16, 18, 24
Knowlson, J. 38

Le Brun, C. 140
Leblanc, M. 125
Lee, H. 108, 110–11
Leibniz, G. W. 1, 4, 7, 18, 20–3, 25–33, 35–6, 39, 43, 66, 73, 78, 82–3, 85–6, 96–8, 100, 104, 112, 147
Theodicy 20–2, 25, 27–8
Lipsius, J. 11
'literary painting' 109–10
logic 1–4, 12, 14, 17, 45–6, 53, 55, 57, 68, 70–2, 74, 82, 85–8, 100, 109

of relationships 71–2, 78, 80, 82
of sensations 2, 17, 85–9, 92, 98, 100, 103
love 13, 29, 44, 51–2, 55, 57, 59–67, 76–9, 81

Macheray, P. 9
McLaurin, A. 86, 90, 95–6
Matharan, M. 67
mathematics 11, 68, 84–8, 141
memory 18, 30, 54, 140
metempsychosis 71–2, 80
moments of being 102, 113
monad 20–2, 25–30, 39, 43, 82–3, 94, 96–7, 100
Moore, G. 86

Nabokov, V. 2, 4–5, 29, 47, 49, 102, 114–46
Despair 5, 47, 49, 114, 120, 123–9, 131–46
The Gift (Dar) 121, 123
Invitation to a Beheading 123
and James Joyce 134–5, 139
King, Queen, Knave 124
Laughter in the Dark 124
Lolita 47, 120, 123, 134
Pale Fire 47, 115–16, 119–20, 125, 134
and patterns 29, 116–18, 125
The Real Life of Sebastian Knight 29, 114, 116, 120–1, 123, 125
Speak, Memory 117, 119
Strong Opinions 115, 123, 134
'The Vane Sisters' 115
Nadeau, M. 51
Nansen, F. 143–4
Nature 9, 21, 24, 36, 39, 57–9, 82, 122
Nietzsche, F. 63
nonrelation 14, 51–2

Novalis 10
Nussbaum, M. 2, 96

Oliphant, R. 132–4

parallax 53, 71–2, 80
Pascal, B. 128, 137
perception 1–3, 7–8, 18, 20–1,
 28–30, 32, 42–3, 83–5, 94, 100,
 107–8, 116, 122, 124, 129, 148
Pickup, R. 38
Pierce, C. 88
Pissaro, C. 92
Plato 67, 76, 110
 and 'forms' 67
Platonic love 77
Popper, K. 115, 122
possible worlds 21–3, 25–31, 47, 83,
 86, 88, 104, 113, 124, 145–6
Proust, M. 15, 22, 27–33
Pythagoras 12

Raleigh, J. 53–4
ratio 7, 9, 12–13, 40, 44–5, 53–5, 58,
 80, 97, 147
ratiocination 12, 147
realism 38, 76, 118
reality 27, 30, 37, 81, 84–5, 88, 92,
 98, 112, 116, 118, 120–3, 137
 analogical 118, 146
realization 23–4, 105
relation 4–5, 7, 9, 12–18, 21, 47, 49,
 51–82, 146–9
 between literature and
  painting 109–12
 proportional 12–13, 85, 147
relational identity 67, 69
Rewald, J. 94
rhythm 44, 85, 88–91, 96, 98–9, 101,
 104–5, 107, 110–11
Robinson, H. 75
Russell, B. 4, 83–8, 98

Ruyer, Raymond 27

Sackville-West, V. 89–90
Schroeder, E. 40
self-consciousness 39, 45–7, 85–6,
 105, 108
sensation 1–5, 7, 10–12, 16–18, 21,
 28, 32–3, 35, 39, 41–2, 47, 49, 57, 63,
 67, 82–113, 115, 117, 119, 146–9
Shakespeare, W. 15, 54, 63–4, 72,
 75–81, 139
 Hamlet 15, 38, 64, 72–4, 78–80
 Othello 54, 63–4, 81
Shelley, P. 10, 80
Shiff, R. 94
Sickert, W. 87, 109–11, 113
Spinoza, B. 3–5, 7, 9–15, 17–18, 20,
 22–4, 27, 30, 32–3, 35–6, 39, 42,
 45–6, 52–9, 61–5, 68, 73, 80, 82, 94,
 120–1
 Ethics 10–11, 12–13, 23–4, 41–2,
  54, 56–9, 62–5, 73
Stanislavski, K. 37–8
Stoics 11, 25, 63
stream of consciousness 2–3, 30,
 46–7
The Student of Prague 127–8, 137,
 142
Substance 35–6, 39–41
Synge, J. 53–4, 61, 63

Thought 9, 22–4, 35–6, 51, 55
translation 5, 31, 40, 49, 85–6, 96,
 104, 146
truth 22, 29–30, 66, 70–1, 73, 98,
 107, 110, 112, 120, 139–40
 value 52, 75
Tynan, K. 37
types 88–9

Van Gogh, V. 89, 94, 96
Vasari, G. 105

Velasquez, D. 112–13
viewpoint 7, 17, 21, 23, 26–32, 39, 83–4, 88, 99–102, 104, 112–13, 115, 118, 146–8
visual arts 5, 86, 88
Volosinov, V. 34–5

Wallace, E. 125
White, K. 115
Wilde, O. 72–3, 75, 77
Windelband, W. 9
Wittgenstein, L. 4, 11, 86

Woolf, Virginia 2–5, 16, 21, 30, 37, 46–7, 49, 83–113
  Between the Acts 109
  Reading at Random 109
  Roger Fry: A Biography 91
  To the Lighthouse 29, 47, 83, 85, 89–90, 93, 96, 98, 100, 104–5, 113
  Walter Sickert: A Conversation 85, 88, 109–10
  The Waves 88, 93, 96, 101, 104–5
Wordsworth, W. 10, 107
  Lyrical Ballads 108

www.ingramcontent.com/pod-product-compliance
Lightning Source LLC
Chambersburg PA
CBHW061838300426
44115CB00013B/2439